Discovering Ph
and Phonol

CW00542399

DISCOVERING PHONETICS AND PHONOLOGY

LYNNE CAHILL

First published 2019 by
RED GLOBE PRESS

Red Globe Press in the UK is an imprint of Springer Nature Limited, registered in England, company number 785998, of 4 Crinan Street, London, N1 9XW.

Red Globe Press® is a registered trademark in the United States, the United Kingdom, Europe and other countries.

ISBN 978–1–137–54571–8 paperback

A catalogue record for this book is available from the British Library.

A catalog record for this book is available from the Library of Congress.

This book is dedicated to the memory of my mum,
Valerie Sheppard, 1940–2017

THE INTERNATIONAL PHONETIC ALPHABET (revised to 2005)

CONSONANTS (PULMONIC)

	Bilabial	Labiodental	Dental	Alveolar	Postalveolar	Retroflex	Palatal	Velar	Uvular	Pharyngeal	Glottal
Plosive	p b			t d		ʈ ɖ	c ɟ	k g	q ɢ		ʔ
Nasal	m	ɱ		n		ɳ	ɲ	ŋ	N		
Trill	B			r					R		
Tap or Flap		ⱱ		ɾ		ɽ					
Fricative	ɸ β	f v	θ ð	s z	ʃ ʒ	ʂ ʐ	ç ʝ	x ɣ	χ ʁ	ħ ʕ	h ɦ
Lateral fricative				ɬ ɮ							
Approximant		ʋ		ɹ		ɻ	j	ɰ			
Lateral approximant				l		ɭ	ʎ	L			

Where symbols appear in pairs, the one to the right represents a voiced consonant. Shaded areas denote articulations judged impossible.

CONSONANTS (NON-PULMONIC)

Clicks		Voiced implosives		Ejectives	
ʘ	Bilabial	ɓ	Bilabial	ʼ	Examples:
ǀ	Dental	ɗ	Dental/alveolar	pʼ	Bilabial
ǃ	(Postalveolar	ʄ	Palatal	tʼ	Dental/alveolar
ǂ	Palatoalveolar	ɠ	Velar	kʼ	Velar
ǁ	Alveolar lateral	ʛ	Uvular	sʼ	Alveolar fricative

OTHER SYMBOLS

ʍ Voiceless labial-velar fricative	ɕ ʑ Alveolo-palatal fricatives
w Voiced labial-velar approximant	ɺ Voiced alveolar lateral flap
ɥ Voiced labial-palatal approximant	ɧ Simultaneous ʃ and x
ʜ Voiceless epiglottal fricative	
ʢ Voiced epiglottal fricative	Affricates and double articulations can be represented by two symbols joined by a tie bar if necessary.
ʡ Epiglottal plosive	k͡p t͡s

VOWELS

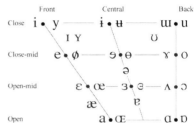

Where symbols appear in pairs, the one to the right represents a rounded vowel.

DIACRITICS   Diacritics may be placed above a symbol with a descender, e.g. ŋ̊

̥	Voiceless	n̥ d̥	̤	Breathy voiced	b̤ a̤	̪	Dental	t̪ d̪
̬	Voiced	s̬ t̬	̰	Creaky voiced	b̰ a̰	̺	Apical	t̺ d̺
ʰ	Aspirated	tʰ dʰ	̼	Linguolabial	t̼ d̼	̻	Laminal	t̻ d̻
̹	More rounded	ɔ̹	ʷ	Labialized	tʷ dʷ	̃	Nasalized	ẽ
̜	Less rounded	ɔ̜	ʲ	Palatalized	tʲ dʲ	ⁿ	Nasal release	dⁿ
̟	Advanced	u̟	ˠ	Velarized	tˠ dˠ	ˡ	Lateral release	dˡ
̠	Retracted	e̠	ˤ	Pharyngealized	tˤ dˤ	̚	No audible release	d̚
̈	Centralized	ë	̴	Velarized or pharyngealized	ɫ			
̽	Mid-centralized	e̽	̝	Raised	e̝	(ɹ̝ = voiced alveolar fricative)		
̩	Syllabic	n̩	̞	Lowered	e̞	(β̞ = voiced bilabial approximant)		
̯	Non-syllabic	e̯	̘	Advanced Tongue Root	e̘			
˞	Rhoticity	ɚ a˞	̙	Retracted Tongue Root	e̙			

SUPRASEGMENTALS

ˈ	Primary stress
ˌ	Secondary stress ˌfoʊnəˈtɪʃən
ː	Long eː
ˑ	Half-long eˑ
̆	Extra-short ĕ
ǀ	Minor (foot) group
‖	Major (intonation) group
.	Syllable break ɹi.ækt
‿	Linking (absence of a break)

TONES AND WORD ACCENTS

LEVEL			CONTOUR		
e̋ or	˥	Extra high	ě or	˩˥	Rising
é	˦	High	ê	˥˩	Falling
ē	˧	Mid	e᷄	˦˥	High rising
è	˨	Low	e᷅	˩˨	Low rising
ȅ	˩	Extra low	e᷈	˧˦˨	Rising-falling
ꜜ	Downstep		↗	Global rise	
ꜛ	Upstep		↘	Global fall	

Contents

List of tables

List of figures

Preface for teachers

This book is intended to give a basic, and non-threatening, introduction to the study of phonetics and phonology. It is aimed primarily at first-year undergraduates, and the main focus is on English. It is my experience that, unlike when I started university, students coming to university to study for linguistics and English-language degrees often have no experience of languages other than English and often don't expect the level of technical analysis involved in linguistics. They sometimes find being thrown into subjects like phonetics and syntax quite daunting, and this can put them off going on to other areas of linguistics. My intention in this book is to make their first exposure to phonetics (and a bit of phonology) a bit less threatening than traditional approaches.

The book is based on the first-year module that I teach, with broadly the content that I deliver in a 12-week semester. There are 14 chapters, which is more than one for each week in a typical introductory course. Some of the topics might be ones that don't have their own week (e.g. in my course I don't have separate weeks on features or on tone and length). What makes this book different from most introductory textbooks on phonetics and phonology is the emphasis on the relationship to spelling. This partly reflects my own interests, but also the approach I take in teaching, relating some of the technical aspects of phonetics and phonology to concepts that most students are more familiar with. We have all learned to read and write, and for most of us that's the time when we have had to really think about pronunciation and the sounds of language. I have therefore tried to tap into that knowledge in order to make some of the ideas more accessible, especially to students who are not familiar with other languages. I have also included 'brief asides', which give some additional information which is not essential for understanding the rest of the material, but which should be interesting to students of linguistics.

This is not a book about the accents of English, so I have chosen to focus most discussion on the accent that I call Standard Southern British English (SSBE). I have avoided using the term *Received Pronunciation* because of its many and varied associations. In several places I have talked about other accents of English, both regional British accents and international accents, where it was particularly relevant to the aspects of pronunciation under discussion. I have not assumed that readers will necessarily be SSBE speakers, although I have assumed that they have some familiarity with SSBE.

There are sets of exercises at the end of each chapter. The answers to those can be found at the back of the book, but they can also be used as they are, or with variation (e.g. substituting different examples) for class exercises. In addition I have provided an appendix with some ideas for classroom activities that I use in my own teaching.

Preface for students

This is a book about phonetics and phonology. That is, it's about studying the sounds of language. Like a lot of linguistic study, it means thinking about how we use language in a way that we don't normally do. Language is something most of us use every day without really thinking about it. There are several different areas of linguistic study. How words have meanings, how words combine into phrases and sentences and how sentences are combined into stories, speeches or conversations all have their own fields of study. What this book looks at is the sounds of language.

Before you start reading this book, a couple of warnings. First, you may have to try to unlearn a lot of what you learnt in school about spelling. I know it may have been hard-won knowledge and you may be reluctant to let it go, but, trust me, it will help you to understand the sounds of English in a much deeper way, and once you get through the book, you'll also have a much better understanding of the whys and wherefores of English spelling. Secondly, it's probably not a good idea to read it in a library or on public transport, unless you don't mind people staring at you while you make strange faces and noises. To really get what I'm talking about, at least in places, you're going to need to make those noises.

In each chapter there is at least one quick quiz. These are to get you to think about what I'm about to talk about. You don't have to spend a lot of time on these, but do try to pause and have a think before you read on. I'm counting on you having some ideas about these before you actually read the chapters. Some of your ideas might be right and some might be wrong, but exploring the answers you've come up with and what that tells us about how we think about language are all part of the approach I've taken in this book. There are also sets of exercises at the end of each chapter. The answers to those can be found at the back of the book.

This is not a book about the accents of English, so I have chosen to focus most discussion on the accent that I call Standard Southern British English (SSBE). I have avoided using the term *Received Pronunciation* because of its many and varied associations. In several places I have talked about other accents of English, both regional British accents and international accents, where it was particularly relevant to the aspects of pronunciation under discussion. You do not have to be an SSBE speaker to understand the book, although I have assumed you have some familiarity with it.

Acknowledgements

I have been teaching phonetics and phonology at the Universities of Sussex and Brighton for over 20 years, and this book is the result of my experiences. The exercises, in particular, are ones that I have tried out on many students over many years, but I can't take the credit for all of them. As with most university teaching, I have had the benefit of being able to make use of the teaching materials of those who taught the courses before me, and many of these exercises and the examples used to illustrate the points I'm explaining are the result of sometimes minimal adaptation and development of the materials passed down to me. I therefore want to express my thanks to all of those who may have inadvertently contributed. In particular, I must thank Christian Uffmann, Max Wheeler, Judy Delin and the person who taught me phonetics and phonology in my first year as an undergraduate, Richard Coates. I would also like to thank Des Ryan, whose PhD gave me lots of ideas for the aspects of pronunciation that relate to the spelling.

I must thank many people who have contributed in more ephemeral ways to the writing of this book. My writing partners, Lynne Murphy, Sandra Jansen and Phil Viner have helped to keep me focused and Sarah Carroll and Sophie Niles were a wonderful late-night virtual writing group during the final push. Evan Hazenberg helped with getting the Praat images right. My publishers have given support, encouragement and advice at various stages. In particular, I must thank Paul Stevens, who conceived the project in the first place and whose enthusiasm for the book inspired me, and Helen Caunce, who has supported me during the later stages of writing the book. Last, but very definitely not least, my daughters, Alice and Hannah, are my best friends, my supporters and my inspiration.

Part I

What is phonetics and why do I need it?

Phonetics is the study of speech sounds. For many people the pronunciation is bound up with the spelling, but phonetics requires thinking about the sounds themselves. In the first chapter of this part, I explain why thinking about spelling is not always helpful for thinking about pronunciation and explain the complex relationship between speaking and writing, especially in English. In the second chapter I give some examples of why studying phonetics is not only interesting but useful.

1 Sound and spelling

When you first went to school, you probably had a pretty good grasp of your native language. You may even have already started to learn the basics of writing, but for many children their first experience of the world of reading and writing will have come at that point. Suddenly it wasn't enough to be able to listen and speak; you had to work out how to break down the words you had learned into their individual sounds and then work out which of those funny symbols you were being taught was the right one for the sound. Luckily, most people manage to pick that up over the course of their schooling without too much pain. Now you find you have to learn about phonetics (I'm not even going into phonology just yet), and you have to 'unlearn' much of what your literacy teachers taught you. Your phonetics instructor (if you have one) will try to convince you that the 'sounds' you think you hear in words of your language are not all what they seem. Some of them may be pronounced very differently from how you think they are, and some may not be pronounced at all. If you are a native speaker of English, you are probably already aware that there are some issues with the relationship between spelling and pronunciation, but you may not be aware just quite how serious those issues are. By the way, if you're a native speaker of a language that uses a non-alphabetic writing system, I come to those a bit later in this chapter.

So what is the point of phonetics? In this first part of the book, I try to answer that question in a number of ways. First, I look at the issues of pronunciation and spelling in English and other languages. In chapter 2, I go on to look at the kinds of thing you need to know about to do phonetics and what kinds of phonetic information are useful, and look at three case studies, showing you how understanding phonetics can be useful for different kinds of work in linguistics. Phonetics is a thing of beauty in its own right, but learning about glottal stops and secondary stress will also help you to study other interesting areas of linguistics like sociolinguistics and discourse analysis.

1.1 What's wrong with English spelling?

Quick quiz

1. How many sounds are there in *gnaw, exit, vision, use, thick*?
2. Can you think of other ways of spelling the sound often represented by *ee*?
3. How many different ways can you think of to pronounce *ough*?

English, like many other languages, has an **alphabetic** writing system. That means words are written by using strings of letters, each of which represents, in some sense, a sound. As a young schoolchild a large part of the process of learning to read and write is learning which sounds are represented by which letters. At various times in various education systems, the attitudes and approaches to teaching this process vary, but many use something like the **phonics** system currently being used in the UK state education system. This involves teaching children to sound out words and associate letters with the individual sounds. So, when teaching children how to spell the word *pig*, they might be asked to sound it out as P-I-G, then to write the letters that match those sounds. For simple words that may work okay, but think about another, apparently equally simple, word: *cat*. If children sound out the word into its three sounds, they then have to decide which letter represents the first sound. Is it *c* or is it *k*?

This really simple example shows that English spelling does not reliably match the pronunciation. In particular there is not a **one-to-one mapping** between the sounds and the letters. In English this is true more than in some other languages, but it is generally true in all languages. The most simple situation in which the one-to-one relationship falls down is when more than one letter is used to represent one sound in a particular word, or vice versa. The first quiz question above shows this. For example, *th* in *thick* represents a single sound (it's actually a dental fricative, and it's written in phonetics with the symbol [θ], but don't worry about that for now!) as does *ck* at the end. On the other hand, the *x* in *exit* represents two sounds, written as [ks]. Check that you can hear the two different sounds represented by that one letter. The *x* example is actually relatively rare – the other situation happens much more frequently. This is because there are fewer letters in the alphabet than different sounds in the language. I call this the **strict one-to-one problem**.

The other way that the one-to-one system is upset is by having different ways of representing the same sounds in different words, or different ways of pronouncing the same letters or letter combinations. I call this the **variation problem**. These are the kinds of problem shown in the other two quiz questions. The sound that is written *ee*, as in words like *see, meet, feel*, can also be written in a number of different ways (you might not agree that all of these have the same sound – there are variations):

- *ea* in s**ea**
- *ie* in th**ie**f
- *ei* in rec**ei**ve
- *y* in happ**y**
- *ey* in k**ey**

- *e* in *me*

- *i* in *multi-storey*

- *ee_e* in *squeeze*

- *i_e* in *suite*

- *oe* in *foetus*

You may have learned some guidelines for how to spell sounds, like '*i* before *e* except after *c*', and you may also have realised that they rarely work for all examples.

The letter combination *ough* in English is notorious for having different pronunciations, as in the words *though, through, cough, bough, enough, thorough, bought, hiccough*. There are lots of reasons why the English spelling system is quite complex and unpredictable. The most obvious one is that the way words are pronounced has changed over time, and the spellings haven't kept up. In the case of English in particular, there are also various historical reasons why the spelling is not regular. This is not the place to go into detail, but when the Normans invaded in 1066, they brought their language (French) with them, which became mixed up with the Anglo-Saxon that was here before. Many of the spellings found in English today are a direct result of French spellings, and in some cases there's influence from Latin, too. For example, have you ever wondered why *choir* isn't spelled *quire*? The simple answer is that it's from the Latin *chorus*, but it's more complex than that. Old French took the word and respelled it as *quer*, and Middle English borrowed that as it was. Then, in the seventeenth century someone decided that it should revert to something closer to the Latin spelling, so it became *choir*. This was actually a compromise, which used the *-oir* because the pronunciation didn't match the pure Latin version. You might think it strange that we would change the way words are spelled, but I wonder how many of you would write *gaol* instead of *jail*? The main difference between pronunciation and spelling is that more conscious decisions are made about how to spell words than about how to pronounce them, and though children learn to speak simply by being surrounded by other people speaking, they only learn to read and write by being explicitly taught. That means that people in positions of power can choose how everyone should spell words, and they rarely make those decisions in a purely logical way.

The number of words in English that came from French and/or Latin is huge – some estimates put it at 60 per cent, although that is in a dictionary and not representative of the words in everyday use. One of the problems with English spelling is that it has borrowed words from lots of different languages. It has *veranda* from Hindi, *alcohol* from Arabic, *kangaroo* from Guugu Yimidhirr (an Aboriginal language), *schadenfreude* from German and *spaghetti* from Italian, to name just a few examples. Having these words, which often come into English with their own idiosyncratic spellings (or rather, spellings based on their own language conventions) makes the spelling system more irregular.

A brief aside on the history of English spelling . . .

The English language as we know it today has developed as a result of a long history of movements of people and political and social changes. After the Romans left, Britain was invaded by a succession of Germanic people: Vikings, Angles, Saxons and Jutes, who all spoke variants of Germanic, the ancestors of German, Dutch and the Scandinavian languages. The Celts largely fled to the parts we now know as Scotland, Wales and Ireland, so the inhabitants of England were mostly speakers of these Germanic languages; hence the term *Anglo-Saxon* to refer to the mix of languages spoken by the Angles and the Saxons. For several hundred years the language developed and became what we now call Old English. In 1066 the Normans invaded, bringing their Romance language, descended from Latin. There was a big divide at that time between written and spoken language. Very few people could write, and those who did would often write in Latin, so there is very little written evidence for what Old English was really like (and they didn't, unfortunately, have recording equipment then, so we have to guess at how they pronounced it). The few writings of Old English that exist suggest a fairly standardised system of spelling, although that might just be because they were all written by a pretty small group of people. After the Norman invasion, into the period we call Middle English, the spelling gets much more varied, with some spellings clearly influenced by French spelling. For example, French did not have the thorn (þ) character, so during this period the thorn was replaced with *th*. The crucial point for English spelling came when the first dictionaries were written, the most influential of these being Samuel Johnson's in 1755. This gave a reference point for everyone and helped in the process of standardisation, which was then taken further by the spread of education. Johnson's dictionary was a wonderful exercise in descriptive rather than prescriptive linguistics – that is, he wrote down what people actually used rather than what he thought they should use – and so it crystallised the already rather irregular spelling system. Unlike some languages, such as German and Dutch, English has never undergone a spelling reform to make the spelling more regular. And so, folks, that's why English has the wonderfully enigmatic spelling system it has today.

So this shows that the relationship between spelling and pronunciation in a language like English is messy and complex. It gets even more tricky when thinking about other languages.

Just imagine you want to explain the differences between English and French pronunciation. How far would you get if you just used their respective spelling systems? If you are familiar with French, you will know that the way that the letter *r* is pronounced in French is very different from how it is pronounced in English (actually, it's pronounced pretty differently in different accents of English, but very few of them are similar to the French one). The French *r* is actually a uvular fricative – don't worry about exactly what that means for now, but it's pronounced right at the back of the mouth. Some letters tend to have very similar pronunciations across the languages that use the same alphabets. For example, *p* is quite predictable. Others are much less so, including *r*. Sounds can also be more or less predictable. The sound represented by the letter *p* is generally straightforward, but the sound represented by *sh* in English is represented in other languages as follows:

Language	Letter(s)	E.g. Word
French	*ch*	chou
German	*sch*	Schuh
Italian	*sci*	sciarpa
Polish	*sz*	szafa
Hungarian	*s*	egesegedere
Norwegian	*sj*	sjø
Czech	*š*	škoda
Basque	*x*	kaixo

So it isn't possible to just use the spelling to represent the sounds without first trying to get speakers of all languages to agree on which letter(s) represent which sound(s). Of course that is never going to happen. Even if the will were there (and, let's be honest, it would definitely result in diplomatic incidents, if not war), different languages have different sets of sounds. I talk about that a lot more later in the book. I call this the **cross-linguistic problem**. Now I'm going to have a quick look at the other side of the problem – languages which have other ways of writing.

1.2   Other writing systems

Quick quiz

Can you read these?

1. Ολυμπιακός
2. Россия
3. h s v th
4. c u l8r 2night

Many languages use an alphabetic writing system like English. They all fall into the one-to-one mapping trap to some degree. Some languages, like Spanish, behave much better than English in terms of the variation problem. To a very large degree, knowing how a word is spelled in Spanish will tell you how it is pronounced, and vice versa. However, even in Spanish there are some cases of variation. The letters *b* and *v* are both pronounced the same, as are *y* and *ll* (at least in some parts of Spain). This last example is also a case of the strict one-to-one problem, with one sound represented by two letters.

You are probably familiar with some other languages which use either slightly different letters or letters with accents. French, for example, has the acute accent (é), the grave accent (è) and the cedilla (ç). German has the umlaut (ä) and the eszett (ß). The Scandinavian languages have other variants on the Roman alphabet (å, ø) as do the Slavic languages (š). These all help with the strict one-to-one problem by providing some more characters to map to sounds, but they still leave some examples of both the strict one-to-one problem and the variation problem.

Other languages have completely different alphabets, like Greek and Russian. These languages look very different from English, French or German, but that's just because the letters they use are unfamiliar. Once you learn that a π in Greek is just like *p* in English, it's very simple – you're just learning a different set of mappings. The first two quiz questions above are examples of this. If I tell you that the letters map to Roman alphabet characters, as in the table below, can you work out what they say?

Greek	Roman	Cyrillic	Roman
λ	l	P	R
υ	y	c	s
μ	m	и	i
π	p	я	a
ι	i		
α	a		
κ	k		
ζ	z		

The first one is *Olympiakos* and the second is *Russia*.

Not all languages do use an alphabetic system, however. Arabic has a writing system which only (usually) writes the consonants. If you want to put the vowels in, you can as 'diacritics' (like accents) on the consonant letters, but for most purposes the language is written without vowels. Think about what that would look like in English. The third quiz question above shows what this would look like for the English sentence 'he is over there'. Can you work out what this says?

Th Grnd ld Dk f Yk h hd tn thsnd mn.

H mchd thm p t th tp f th hll.

nd h mchd thm dn gn.

Whn th w p, th w p,

nd whn th w dn, th w dn,

nd whn th w nl hlfw p

Th w nth p n dn.

If you are familiar with British nursery rhymes, you probably recognised it as 'The Grand Old Duke of York' without too much trouble, thanks in part to the capitals in the first line, but the fourth to the seventh lines look rather tricky, don't they? Children learning Arabic generally do learn to read and write with the vowels, but adults get used to reading and writing without. The technical term for a writing system of this kind is an **abjad**. One thing that is important to note there is that I have left out the bits that are vowels in the spoken word, not necessarily letter vowels. This means that the word *there* becomes just *th* because the *ere* part is all pronounced as a single vowel sound. In the UK, there is a quiz programme called *Only Connect*, which has a 'missing vowels round'. Familiar names or phrases have their vowels removed, and the teams have to work out what it says. It's worth noting that it wouldn't work using only vowels instead of consonants. Compare the two representations of 'The cat sat on the mat' below. One has had the vowels removed, and the other has had the consonants removed.

- Th ct st n th mt

- e a a o e a

You would probably be able to work out what the first one says, but the second one is unrecognisable. That's why there are no writing systems where only the vowels are written.

Another way in which some languages choose to write the sounds is by using **syllabaries**. That is, instead of a mapping between individual sounds and letters, the mapping is between syllables and characters. Japanese has a complex writing system which uses logograms (based on Chinese characters), alphabetic characters (based on the Roman alphabet) and two

マ	ミ	ム	メ	モ
ma	mi	mu	me	mo

FIGURE 1.1   JAPANESE KATAKANA CHARACTERS

different syllabaries, katakana and hirigana. For example, figure 1.1 shows the katakana characters for the syllables beginning with *m*. As you'll see when I talk about syllables in chapter 5, this kind of system wouldn't work well for all languages.

Finally, some languages use writing systems that bear no relation to the pronunciation at all. These are called **ideographic** or **logographic** scripts and use characters that represent ideas or meanings rather than pronunciation. There is some debate about whether there is any genuinely ideographic script (representing meanings) rather than logographic (representing words) and whether logographic scripts represent words or morphemes. I come back to this in chapter 6. The Chinese languages, Mandarin and Cantonese, as well as Japanese Kanji use this type of system.

So I've shown that the way different languages are written can have a different relationship to the pronunciation. This is one of the reasons linguists need a **standardised** way of representing sounds from different languages.

There's actually another reason why something other than spelling is needed, and I hinted at it above. When I mentioned the pronunciation of *r* in French, I said that it's pronounced differently in various accents of English. It's not only *r* that behaves like that. If you come from the South of England, you probably pronounce the sound in the middle of *bath* differently from people who come from the North of England. If you come from Scotland, you might pronounce the *r* at the end of words like *star*, but if you come from (most parts of) England, you probably don't. Most speakers of English pronounce *do* and *dew* differently, but people with some accents, for example from Suffolk, pronounce them the same. This is what I call the **accent problem**.

One of the main purposes of spelling, and the reason that there are standardised spelling systems across countries which have different accents, is so that everyone can read the same books, newspapers and magazines, even though they might read them aloud rather differently. If someone from Newcastle wrote exactly how they spoke, then someone from Ipswich would probably struggle to read it. The Chinese writing system is an extreme version of this. There are two major 'dialects' of Chinese – Mandarin and

A brief aside on how writing systems developed …

Interestingly, the alphabetic writing systems we see today developed ultimately from ideographic systems. The first move towards writing was found in the earliest cave paintings, which had pictures of important objects such as animals, the sun and so on. The earliest writing involved **pictograms** which were small, stylised pictures of objects. Gradually these developed into **ideograms**, pictures of objects used to represent connected ideas. For example, a picture of the sun might be used to represent the idea of 'heat' or 'daytime'. Once these usages become conventionalised, each word has a written form, and these are then known as **logograms**. This is when the 'writing' first really represents something linguistic, that is, words rather than ideas (which might have more than one spoken word associated with them). Once the written symbol stands for a linguistic word, links can be made not just with the word meaning but also with the pronunciation. The first phase of this is rebus writing, which uses logograms to represent the sound of the original meaning. For example, suppose there is a symbol for the word eye: ⊙, and a symbol for boat: ⌣. They can then be combined to make a new word which has no connection to those two meanings, but just combines the sounds of the two, that is, 'bow tie': ⌣ ⊙. You probably do something like this if you use text-speak: *m8*, for example, combines the pronunciation of the letter *m* with the pronunciation of the digit *8* to make *mate*, and the final quiz question above has several examples of this, with *c* being used for *see* and so on. One of the big advantages of this kind of system is that the symbols can be reused, so there aren't as many characters to learn as for a logographic script. Modern Chinese, for example, has around 50,000 different symbols, although they are not all in everyday use. Once characters are reused by combining them to make different meanings, there are a lot fewer symbols to learn. The next step is syllabic writing where each syllable has a character. At this stage there has been a shift from links between writing and meaning to links between writing and sound and it's a few short steps via abjads with no vowels and on to full alphabetic systems with vowels and consonants represented separately.

Cantonese. If you can speak Mandarin, you will not necessarily be able to understand spoken Cantonese, and vice versa, but you'll be able to understand the written language because the two languages are written essentially the same. This is one of the advantages of having a writing system that is not related to the pronunciation at all. Can you think of any disadvantages? One problem is that, unlike alphabets, abjads and syllabaries, it is not as easy to combine the characters to spell new words, or to recognise a character you haven't seen before.

1.3 Intonation, stress and syllables

Quick quiz

1. What is the difference between the sentence 'You like phonetics' when it is meant as a statement or as a question?
2. Is this difference represented in any way when it's written down?
3. What is the difference between the noun *record* (as in the sentence 'Keep a record of it') and the verb *record* (as in the sentence 'Make sure you record it')?
4. How do you know which one it is when you see them written down?

Most of the discussion earlier related to individual sounds, which can, in some sense at least, be represented as letters in an alphabetic writing system. This is clearly very important – if it weren't then we wouldn't find many of the world's languages written with spelling systems that essentially only represent this information. Several reasons were given for why spelling systems aren't enough to represent the actual pronunciation of the strings of sounds in speech, such as the fact that there tend to be more sounds than letters, and words may be pronounced differently on different occasions (in different contexts, in different accents) but in ways that don't need to be represented in the written language. Another kind of problem is that pronunciation isn't just about individual sounds. This section briefly mentions some other aspects that need to be considered.

1.3.1 Intonation

What the quiz questions show is that there are other aspects of spoken language, in addition to those to do with the individual sounds and letters, that are really important in terms of how we use language. If I say 'You like phonetics' as a statement, the tune or pitch of the utterance tends to go down towards the end. If, on the other hand, I say 'You like phonetics?' as a question, the tune tends to go up at the end. This use of different tunes is called **intonation**. Did you work out how these differences are represented in English? The intonation isn't directly represented, but punctuation is used to show whether it is a statement or a question, so the examples here either have a full stop (period) or a question mark.

1.3.2 Stress

The third question relates to something rather different (although, as chapters 7 and 8 show, they are not unrelated). How would you describe the difference between the two words? There is actually quite a lot that you could say. For example, the first vowels in the noun and the verb are different. Listen carefully to how you say the two words in a sentence like 'I'm going to record a record.' Can you hear that the way you say the first *record* sounds a bit like you're saying 'ricord', but the second one sounds like 'record'? But is that the only difference? In fact, the reason that the vowels sound different is because the two syllables are stressed differently in the noun and the verb. In the noun, the **stress** is on the first syllable, and in the verb it is on the second. I mentioned that these things are not unrelated, and you may also have realised that you probably pronounce the two words with a different tune, or intonation, as well. Stressed syllables tend to have higher pitch, as I explain later in the book.

What did you answer to question 4? If you said that there is no way of telling them apart, then you are technically correct, and you have begun to really focus in on the aspects of linguistics with which this book is concerned. If you answered that you would usually be able to tell which one was intended because of its position in a sentence, then you are already thinking about the broader issues in linguistics, like grammar (syntax) and meaning (semantics). What this really shows is that a normal writing system doesn't usually need to be detailed enough to give all of the stress and intonation information, because readers can use either punctuation or the context in which a word appears to know what is intended. However, it is important to know how these differences are represented in spoken language. Speakers need to know the difference between the noun and the verb in order to speak correctly and, similarly, need to know how to indicate a question by using appropriate intonation.

1.3.3 Syllables

I've been talking about intonation and stress here, and mentioned syllables. I would guess that you didn't stop and ask yourself 'What's a **syllable**?' because native speakers mostly seem to understand what they are. But what do you really know about syllables in English?

Quick quiz

1. How many syllables are there in *record*?
2. What about *fascism*?
3. What about *fire*?
4. In *record* does the second syllable begin before or after the *c*?
5. Where does the second syllable begin in *simple*?

Question 1 should be easy. You probably (hopefully!) said two. That one's pretty straightforward. Question 2 is a bit more tricky. Did you say two or three? Similarly for question 3. Did you say one or two? Can you see why there might be different answers to those questions? And even in a word like *record*, there are some interesting questions about the syllables, as in questions 4 and 5. If you were thinking of the verb in question 4, you most probably said before. If you were thinking of the noun, you may have been less certain. Chapter 5 explains why that is, but for now, just have a quick think about the word *simple* from question 5. I hope you all agree that it has two syllables, but does the second syllable start after the *i*, the *m*, *p* or *l*? You probably went for either *m* or *p*, but which one, and why? And why not either of the others? There are answers to these questions that apply to all languages and some that only apply to English, but chapter 5 covers those in detail.

Syllable boundaries tend not to be explicitly represented in written language, but syllable structures are very important in spelling. For example, the different spellings of the words *matting* and *mating* tells us that the vowel is pronounced differently, but the reason there is a double *t* is because of the fact that the *a* in *matting* is a short vowel and needs a consonant to complete that syllable. Chapter 5 explains this in more detail.

1.4   Why phonetic transcription?

Quick quiz

1. If you have access to a dictionary, look up how it says you should pronounce *bit, beat, bet* and *bite*.
2. What do you think are the differences between them?

This chapter has given lots of reasons why it isn't possible to just use normal spelling to represent the pronunciation of languages. The next question is, what should be used instead? The simple answer is 'phonetic transcription', but there are several options here, so as linguists we have to make some decisions about exactly what kind of transcription system we want.

You may have come across some version of phonetic transcription. At the very least, you have probably seen the pronunciations in dictionaries like the *Oxford English Dictionary*, which use a mixture of Roman letters and other symbols to indicate the pronunciation of words. You may also have come across the IPA (International Phonetic Alphabet). This is the alphabet I'll be using in this book. But what are the other options, and why choose this one?

Dictionary publishers tend to devise their own system which suits their own purposes. For the examples in the quiz, you may have found representations like *bahyt* for *bite*. In some areas of academic linguistics, the same thing happens. For example, linguists researching different language families often devise their own systems to represent the sounds in the languages they are working on. There are good reasons for doing this. If the languages you are interested in don't have certain sounds, then you can limit the number of different symbols you need to use, and that can mean avoiding using symbols that are hard to find in your word-processing package (or which might not display or print the same when other people look at your document).

That brings us to another type of phonetic transcription system – the family of computer-readable alphabets. Many widely available word-processing packages allow you to enter IPA characters relatively easily now, and some have add-ons that allow you to do it via a specialised set of keyboard mappings. However, if you want to do more complex things with your phonetic transcription than just view or print it, then you might need something that is more universally computable. (If you don't want to know about computer-internal representations of characters, ignore the rest of this paragraph!) The Unicode character system allows many newer applications to process IPA characters, but if your computer application really needs simple ASCII, then there are systems that allow this. The most widely used is SAMPA (Speech Assessment Methods Phonetic Alphabet, available at https://www.phon.ucl. ac.uk/home/sampa/). Slightly different subsets of characters are suggested for different languages, and the website gives these. Appendix A gives the SAMPA characters for Standard British and American English.

The IPA, though, is the international standard. It was originally developed by the International Phonetic Association, which was founded in 1886, and the first version of the alphabet was published in 1888. Since then there have been regular revisions, for two reasons: linguists change their understanding of how sounds relate to one another in different languages, and new languages are discovered which may have different sounds. There are a few sounds for which American linguists standardly use different symbols from those in the IPA, and I point those out as I go along. The aim of the IPA is to give a standard representation for the sounds of every language in the world. This means that it's possible to compare the exact pronunciation of different languages and document the ways in which different speech sounds are used in different languages. The IPA gives us different symbols for the different sounds, like the example of [θ] for *th*. But it also gives ways of indicating very precise and quite subtle differences between very similar sounds.

The IPA is based on the Roman alphabet, which makes it convenient for those of us whose language already uses this alphabet, but that does mean that it is sometimes easy to slip into using the character you'd use for spelling, by mistake, when the correct IPA character is different. For example, going back to one of our examples of why spelling and pronunciation don't always match up, remember the example of *cat*? In the IPA the sound at the beginning is written as *k*, not *c*. The use of the Roman alphabet therefore means that if that's the alphabet your language is written in, you'll have to concentrate to avoid making careless mistakes, and will have to learn the more complex aspects of phonetic transcription.

Although quite a lot of the symbols in the IPA are Roman alphabet characters, there are also many that are variants on these, such as ŋ; some that are Greek letters, such as β; and some that are from punctuation or mathematical symbols, such as ! and ⊙. The IPA also makes use of **diacritics** – marks that are added like accents, usually either above or below the symbol – and sub- and superscript letters or symbols. I explain how and why these are used as I go along. For quite a lot of phonetic transcription, you won't really need to use many of these, but they can be very important.

When you want to transcribe speech, the IPA symbols can be used to represent each of the sounds in a word. To use a simple example, the word *cat*, as it is normally pronounced, would be represented in the IPA as kæt. The [k] represents the *c*, the [æ] represents the *a* and the [t] represents the *t*. Of course, you can represent more than just single words. The sentence 'I like eating chocolate,' for example, can be transcribed as [aɪ laɪk iːtɪŋ tʃɒklət]. I explain how to decide which IPA characters to use and how much detail is needed as I go along.

Hopefully I've convinced you that there is a point to using phonetic transcription to represent the pronunciation of language, but you may still be wondering why this is a useful thing to do. In the next chapter, I explain why it's a useful enterprise. What I also show is that just learning the IPA characters for individual sounds is not going to be enough for a lot of what you might want to do in studying speech.

Additional reading

Sampson (2015) gives a thorough exploration of the development of writing throughout history and explains why he believes that English spelling, rather than being an irregular anomaly, is actually ideally suited to its use. Crystal (2009) is an excellent introduction to how language is used in computer-mediated communication (CMC), and presents arguments to support his claim that the use of 'text language', especially by young people, is not going to destroy the English (or any other) language or lead to a generation of illiterate people. Other books that discuss writing systems in detail are Coulmas (2002) and Daniels and Bright (1996). Knight (2012), chapter 1, also compares sounds and spelling, and Tench (2011) is a thorough introduction to phonetic transcription.

Exercises

1. How many ways are there of spelling the sound that is spelled *ay* in a word like *say*?

2. How many ways are there of pronouncing the letter *o*?

3. George Bernard Shaw famously claimed that *fish* could be written *ghoti* (*gh*, from *laugh*, *o* from *women* and *ti* from *nation*). Can you come up with some alternative spellings of your name based on actual sound/spelling combinations in English? The weirder, the better!

4. Can you think of any reasons why Bernard Shaw's claim was not correct?

5. Below are some examples of 'textspeak'.

    (a) Identify all of the places where this 'text language' differs from standard written English.

    (b) What kinds of differences are there?

    (c) Which are influenced directly by pronunciation?

    c u l8r
    wud u eva meet each uvva?
    im plsd u r cumin
    th@ is def gd
    u gonna go?

2 Doing phonetics

Chapter 1 showed that something other than spelling is needed to represent spoken language. This chapter looks at how to do phonetic analysis and also what it can be used for. In this chapter I look at some of the practical questions and some of the practical solutions, and then tell you about some of the interesting ways you can use phonetic analysis.

2.1 Collecting data

Quick quiz

1. How do you pronounce the word *garage*?
2. How do you know?
3. Do you always pronounce it the same?
4. If not, how and why?

So far in this book I've talked in general terms about how you pronounce words and suggested that you should listen to how you say them. So is that all there is to studying spoken language? Well, no, not really. To be honest, you, especially if you are a native speaker of English, can probably get quite a long way by doing just that. I'll continue to ask you to say words and phrases and work out how you're saying them by listening, feeling and maybe looking in a mirror, because I understand that while you're reading this book, you might not have easy access to recording and playback equipment. In this section I explain that for some of this analysis, and certainly if you are planning to get seriously interested in phonetics, just listening to yourself speaking is not enough.

Why is this? Well, in the first place, you may not be a native speaker of English. Even if you are, you may not be a native speaker of a standard variety of English. I am not, in any way, suggesting that speakers of non-standard varieties are less valid/important than speakers of the standard (linguists like to be **descriptive**, describing how people actually speak, not **prescriptive**, telling people how they should speak), but I don't have the space in this book to document all possible varieties, even of British English. This means that, when I refer to how you, the reader, might pronounce words and phrases, I generally assume that you speak, or are at least familiar with, Standard

Southern British English, although at points I refer explicitly to other varieties, including other national varieties and other regional British varieties. If your own accent is very different from this, then you may well want to listen to how a native speaker of Standard Southern British English (SSBE) would pronounce these words. You can do this either by finding a helpful person with the appropriate accent and asking them to pronounce the words or by seeking out recordings. I recommend using the BBC radio iPlayer or archive as most (although by no means all) of the speakers on there do have SSBE accents.

Another reason why just listening to yourself saying something is not enough, though, also applies to native speakers. If you are consciously aware of how you pronounce something, there's a very good chance that you won't be pronouncing it in the way you normally would in natural conversation. What did you respond to question 1 in the quiz? This is a word that different people pronounce differently, so there are going to be differences depending on your normal accent. But it's also a word that carries connotations of other social factors in the way you pronounce it. If you pronounce the second part to rhyme with *fridge* then you might be considered a bit less posh than if you say it to rhyme with *large*. On the other hand, if the last sound for you is the same as the sound in the middle of *measure* then you may be considered the poshest. The reason I picked that word is that I can never decide how I actually say it. When I just say it naturally in conversation, I genuinely don't notice what I say, and as soon as I start thinking about how I say it, I'm stymied by my awareness of the potential implications. Another example that illustrates the problem, although it isn't to do with pronunciation, is the story I like to tell my students about a radio game I heard. The game involved a celebrity being asked questions and contestants guessing what the celebrity's answer would be. In this case, the celebrity was asked whether he would use *bloke*, *guy* or something else to refer to an unnamed male friend. The celebrity answered that he would always use *bloke*, and that *guy* was too American. In the subsequent conversation, though, the celebrity used the word *guy* several times, and never once used *bloke*. This is a classic example of why you should never rely on people's conscious views on what they say or how they speak. The way people think they speak is very often not actually the way they do speak. The third question also gets at another problem with this kind of thinking about speech. The way someone pronounces a word when just saying that word on its own is usually very different from the way it is said when used in a sentence. People will pronounce words differently if they are the first or last words in a sentence, if they are relatively important or unimportant and so on. They're also likely to pronounce words differently depending on other factors including who they're speaking to, how happy/

sad/bored/excited they are and where they are (if they're having to speak particularly loudly or quietly, for instance).

When sociolinguists want to collect spoken data, they use a variety of different techniques in order to avoid these problems. For the purposes of most of the exercises in this book, a good way to avoid the problems is to find a passage which contains the sounds that you're interested in and ask a friend to read it aloud. Record them reading it, and then you can play it back. This has several advantages. If you simply say a sound or word yourself, you will pronounce it ever so slightly differently every time. If you have recorded it, you can listen to it repeatedly and know that it is the same every time. If you have asked someone who doesn't know which sounds you are interested in to read the passage, then they will be pronouncing it just as they would in a natural situation.

Of course, when you get into doing serious phonetic analysis, it's not just to work out how you (or some idealised SSBE speaker) normally pronounces something. Phonetic analysis is used to investigate how real people actually speak, and that can mean all sorts of differences in the kind of data that need to be collected. In the early decades of sociolinguistic research, most studies were carried out by ear. That is, sociolinguists would listen and make notes of what they heard. One of the most famous of these is the New York department store study carried out by William Labov back in 1962. He went into three different department stores and asked people who worked there where he could find a department that he knew was on the fourth floor. He then asked them to repeat their answer. This was a very clever technique. He was interested in whether they pronounced the *r* in these words, because that was believed to be a characteristic of 'lower-class' speech in New York. The method he used allowed him to hear whether they pronounced the *r* at the end of a word, as in *floor* and also before another consonant, as in *fourth*. By asking them to repeat their answer, he could also distinguish between relatively casual speech, as in their first response, and more careful speech in their repeated answer. In sociolinguistic terms, his was a landmark study (especially impressive as it was actually his master's project and he was still a student!). It led the way for many such studies which elicited specific responses from people in relatively natural situations. In phonetic terms, however, it would not be considered good data collection today, because his actual phonetic data was based solely on his own impressions of whether people pronounced the *r* or not, and so the data could not be analysed by anyone else to check whether he'd actually got it right.

So how would a linguist do a similar study today? The simple answer is that they record people's responses so that they can analyse and reanalyse them as much as they want. That simple answer does come with two types of problem, though: ethics and the observer's paradox.

Unlike when Labov did his study, there are now strict rules on the ethics of different types of data collection. It is not acceptable to record people without their express permission. That means that subjects have to consent to being recorded, preferably before the recording. That might not seem to be too bad – just ask them nicely and tell them that it will be anonymous, and surely most people will not mind? But it's not as simple as that either.

Another of William Labov's gifts to the field of sociolinguistics was the idea of the **observer's paradox**. What this means is that as soon as people know that they are being recorded or observed, they will behave in unnatural ways. If they are told exactly why they are being recorded and what is being studied, then it becomes even more likely that they will behave unnaturally, being conscious of that specific bit of their language. There are a number of ways to get round the observer's paradox. One way is to not be too specific about what you're studying, at least until after you've done the recording. Another is to spend a good deal of time and effort creating a situation in which your subjects are comfortable and relax into relatively natural behaviour. Some sociolinguists have indeed spent long periods getting to know their subjects well and effectively being accepted as part of the group in order to avoid the observer's paradox.

There is another way to avoid these problems. In recent years there have been a lot of studies of famous people whose voices have been recorded over a long time (and I tell you about a study that one of my students did in more detail shortly). The Queen is probably the most famous of these, with studies by Jonathan Harrington and his colleagues showing that the Queen's accent has gradually become less like what is called (ironically) 'the Queen's English'. So how did they do these studies? They certainly didn't go to Buckingham Palace and ask Her Majesty to pronounce a few well-chosen vowels. Even if they had, they wouldn't have been able to do a comparison from 50 years ago. No, they studied existing recordings of her speech, in this case, her annual Christmas messages. For someone like the Queen, there are good-quality recordings spanning well over 50 years, so there was no need to do any special recording for those studies. With the existence of the internet and the ever expanding availability of audio (and video) recordings of all kinds of people speaking, it is now possible for anyone to get access to recorded speech that they can analyse. That means linguists can analyse different speakers of different ages, genders, nationalities, regional identities and in different contexts very easily. There are just a few warnings about doing this, though. First, the audio quality does need to be good. Recordings done with a lot of background noise are difficult to analyse whether you're using software or trying to do it by ear. One area that students often get interested in (and for which there have been some excellent studies) is singing accent (e.g. British singers who sing with a more or less 'Americanised' accent), but analysing the accent when there's background music can cause difficulties, so you need to use software that can separate the vocal track from the music. Second, although it may be easy to find out all the information you need for famous people, it is not always easy, or even possible, to find out about less famous people whose voices are on the internet. You can't, for example, compare the accents of two people from different regions unless you know that they definitely do come from those regions, and you need to know information like their ages, their educational backgrounds and so on to do a genuine comparison.

2.2   Doing linguistic analysis

Quick quiz

1. Say the sentence *The cat sat on the mat.* Are the vowels in the words *cat, sat* and *mat* all the same?
2. If you think they are, say the sentence again, several times, quite quickly. What do you think now?
3. If you can, record yourself saying the sentence, and listen back to it.
4. If you think they are not all the same, what do you think is different?
5. How easy is it to describe the difference?

I've already said that people tend to pronounce words differently in different situations and also that they probably pronounce them differently from how they think they pronounce them. Hopefully you thought about this while answering questions 1 and 2. Your own impressions of how you speak might be reasonably accurate, but they might not. If you managed to record yourself saying the sentence and play it back, did you notice anything that surprised you? Whether you noticed it from just thinking about how you said it or from listening to a recording of how you said it, I would have expected that the sound in *sat* is different from the other two. This is because, when that sentence is said in a neutral way, *sat* will usually be less stressed than the other words, so the vowel sound in it is likely to be different. If you managed to hear that, then you might be thinking that there's no need for any more detailed analysis of speech, but what did you say for question 4? It's a bit unfair, because I haven't yet explained the ways in which vowels can be different or how to describe them, but even when you do have that knowledge, it's quite difficult to pin down exactly what's different. That's where linguists benefit from specialist software packages that do the analysis for them.

There is software which will analyse the sound waves and which can be used to give you much more detail than you could ever pick up by just listening. I talk about the **acoustic analysis** of consonants and vowels as I go along. In Appendix B, you can find out how to use one of the freely available software packages to do phonetic analysis.

If you're using recordings, you may find that they have already been transcribed, maybe not phonetically, but into standard spelling. This can be very helpful for identifying specific sounds you want to analyse or sounds in specific contexts (words, syllables etc.). Video often has subtitling, which can be a useful shortcut, although you shouldn't rely on it being accurate. There are lots of funny subtitling errors, including the example from the BBC where viewers were welcomed to the Chinese Year of the Whores (instead of horse)! Incidentally, even though they don't always work perfectly, automatic subtitling is actually an excellent example of a practical application of phonetic analysis. The systems could only be trained to recognise the spoken language and translate it into written language because expert phoneticians spent many years developing detailed models of how spoken language works. Obviously, they're still working on perfecting it!

When linguists do a transcription, they can choose what level of detail they want to include. That decision might be dictated by your teacher if it's an exercise they've set, but if you're doing it for a different reason, then it's a choice you'll have to make. There are three main types of transcription, but even within those, there's a lot of possible variation.

The first type of transcription you might want to do is called a **phonemic transcription**. This has the least detail. It's based around the idea of **phonemes**, which I talk about in chapter 11. For now, all you need to know is that it's the kind of transcription you see in dictionaries where it tells you how to pronounce a word. That tells you how most people usually pronounce the word in slow careful speech. It's handy if you want to know how a word you've never heard should be pronounced, and it's also handy if you want to look at how the spelling of a word matches the pronunciation (not very well in English, as Chapter 1 showed). It's also used for describing differences between different accents. So it's possible to talk about the way British English people pronounce a word compared to Americans or Australians, or to talk about how people from Liverpool pronounce a word compared to people from London. In fact, if I'm going to be picky, it's not really a transcription at all. The word *transcription* means a written version of a piece of spoken language, but a phonemic transcription is a written version of a hypothetical piece of spoken language, or a generalisation over lots of different pieces of spoken language. I explain this more with examples when I talk about phonemes in Chapter 11.

The second type of transcription is called a **broad phonetic transcription**. This has the word *phonetic* in it, and that says that it's a real transcription. That is, at least in theory, it's a written representation of a real piece of spoken language. A phonetic transcription does not make assumptions about how words should be pronounced in an ideal situation; it records how they are actually pronounced in real spoken language. That means it includes what speakers do when they speak naturally, including running sounds together or leaving them out completely. I talk about what happens to sounds in normal speech in chapters 5, 11 and 12. Exactly what is transcribed will depend on what it's for. For some studies, you might be interested in just a small number of different sounds, so you might want more detail about them and less about the other sounds. You might want to mark things like syllable boundaries and/or stress, or you might not really be interested in them. I look at examples of how to transcribe all of these as I go along.

The third type of transcription is a **narrow phonetic transcription**. This is another phonetic one, so it's representing a real piece of speech. For a narrow phonetic transcription, there's a lot more detail about the actual pronunciation. Again, exactly what will depend on what you're interested in, but it usually includes details of the random variation that happens in natural situations. A narrow phonetic transcription is useful when you really want to look at the details of the pronunciation on a single occasion, for example if you want to compare a person's speech when they are relaxed and when they are stressed. I say more about what this looks like as I go through the book.

2.3 Some examples of phonetic analysis

This section focuses on different ways that studying phonetics can lead to a variety of interesting and useful applications of phonetic analysis. I also tell you a bit about some projects that students of mine have done.

2.3.1 Accent studies

One of the aspects of language that nearly everyone notices, and many have strong views on, is the range of different accents speakers have. What accent do you have? If you answered 'I don't have an accent,' I'm sorry, but you are mistaken. Everybody has an accent. Your accent is just your pronunciation. If you said that you don't have an accent, what you probably meant is that you don't have a **non-standard** accent. If you speak the way most BBC newsreaders speak, for example, then your accent is probably what we'd call **Standard Southern British English** (SSBE, sometimes called **received pronunciation**, or RP). Whether people are linguists or not, everyone is aware of different accents, and many people can imitate other accents with varying degrees of success. I imagine if I ask you to do an American accent or a Scottish, Welsh or Irish accent, most of you would be able to give it a good go. But what exactly is meant by 'an American accent' and how do you know what to do to imitate it?

Quick quiz

1. When you think of an American accent, what do you think of?
2. What sounds are different?
3. When you think of a 'Northern English accent', what do you think of?

For most people it's enough to identify a few specific features of an accent to do a passable imitation. For an American accent, for example, people usually make their accent **rhotic**. What that means is that they pronounce the *r* in words like *fourth* and *floor*. Assuming you have (something like) a SSBE accent yourself, try saying those words in your normal accent and then in an American accent. Can you hear the difference? Did you say any other sounds in answer to question 2? You may have thought of different vowels, for example in words like *lot* and *caught*. Or what about the sound in the middle of a word like *writer*? Now think about some British accents. If I ask you to do a Northern English accent, you will probably pick a couple of key features to imitate, like the vowels in *bath* and *but*. If you have an SSBE accent, the vowel in *bath* is a long vowel, the same as the sound in *palm*. If you have a Northern accent, the vowel is shorter, the same as the vowel in *trap*. Another vowel that is different in Northern and Southern English accents is the vowel in words like *but*. Now, if you come from the Northern part of England you're probably shouting at the book right now that there's no such thing as a single Northern accent and, of course, you're right. The accents across the north of England vary enormously, even within quite small geographical distances. Very few people would confuse a Liverpool accent with a Newcastle one. However, linguists have done lots of studies of the various accents, and it is true to say that there is a large group of accents, spread across a wide area of the north of England that do share certain features, and those two vowels are two of the features they share.

What is important here is that, whatever you (or your friends or family) think about your accent and the accents of others, with phonetic analysis it is possible to actually test to see if you're right. If you tell me that your accent is the same as the Queen's, I can record your voice and do a proper analysis comparing it with the Queen's. If you tell me that your accent is the same as David Beckham's, I can do the same. It's then not a question of opinion. I can provide scientific evidence that says that, for example, your vowels are the same as the Queen's, but you drop your aitches as much as David Beckham.

I've so far just talked about studying accents in order to imitate them, but most linguists who study accents are interested in them for much broader reasons. Sociolinguistics is the study of the interaction between language and society. It looks at things like how the words people choose to use reflect the social group they most closely associate with, or how they adapt the words they use according to the company they're in. Do older people use language differently from younger people? Do males and females use language differently? How much of the language people use is determined by where they were born and grew up? Sociolinguists study all aspects of language – grammar, choice of words and accent or pronunciation. Sociolinguists who study accent specifically are called **sociophoneticians**. They study the variation and change in accents. Variation includes the different accents used in different parts of the country (or world); different accents used by different social groups (traditionally that meant class, but these days there are much more sophisticated ways of talking about social groups); and different accents used by individuals in different social contexts. Change includes change within a group (either a geographical or social group) and change in individuals.

Sometimes people identify specific aspects that vary or change. You might hear people (or see letters of complaint from traditionalists) saying things like 'He's started dropping his aitches' or 'Why do young people all sound like they're Australian?', referring to specific accent features. For some of these, you don't need much specialist knowledge. If someone is 'dropping their aitches' you can usually hear that quite easily, and it's not too difficult to simply listen and count how many aitches are dropped. Other features are much harder to spot, though. If you want to know exactly how someone's accent is changing, you need to do a proper phonetic analysis.

When people talk about young people sounding Australian, they usually mean the use of HRT (no, not hormone replacement therapy, but high rising terminals). When you listen to Australians talk, you may notice that their intonation pattern, the pitch or tune of their speech, goes up at the end of a sentence, even when they're stating something. That's different from what happens in SSBE, where that intonation pattern is used for questions. It gives the impression that Australians are always asking questions. But there are other features of the Australian accent that seem to be appearing in British speech, especially some of the vowel sounds. If you listen to how an Australian says the word *said* you might think it sounds more like *Sid*. Proper phonetic accent studies allow linguists first to document the differences in accent in different places (whether north and south England, Newcastle and Sunderland or Britain and Australia) and then compare the speech of individuals or groups to see whether they are closer to or moving closer to other accents.

2.3.2   Case study: Mick Jagger

I'm now going to describe a study done by one of my students, analysing the accent of Sir Mick Jagger in interviews spanning 50 years. Jagger is, like the Queen, someone who has been in the public eye (or ear) for a long time, and good-quality audio recordings of interviews with him are available from the 1960s to the present day. My student chose him as an interesting subject because his accent has been commented on by various people, from journalists to fellow members of the Rolling Stones. He is claimed to have a 'Mockney' or 'faux-Cockney' accent, with many people claiming that he deliberately tries to adapt his natural middle-class RP accent to make himself sound more lower class. In order to test this, she focused on three vowel sounds that have been reported as being significantly different in RP and Cockney. These are the sounds in the words *goat*, *face* and *price*. In chapter 4, I explain how to refer to the vowels of English even though they are pronounced differently in different accents.

To do the comparison she needed to have samples of Jagger's speech, as well as samples of RP and Cockney. She collected recordings of interviews from roughly 10-year intervals from 1967 to 2013 and samples of RP speakers from the 1960s and 2010s. She got hold of data for Cockney for the two early and late periods from another study done by Paul Kerswill.

As chapter 4 and appendix B show, it is possible to do accurate acoustic analyses of vowel sounds and work out exactly how they have been pronounced. It's a little bit more tricky with the vowels she looked at, because they have two different sounds. Try saying *face* and see if you can hear that the first part of the vowel sounds like the vowel in *bet* but the end of the vowel sounds like the vowel in *beat*. It's still possible to measure these and work out the two vowel sounds that they're made up of.

So how do linguists go about doing a study like this? First of all they choose recordings that are good for what they want to do. These need to be representative of the kind of speech they want to analyse. That might mean quite formal speech, like the Queen's Christmas broadcast, or it might mean more informal speech, like a conversation between friends. The really important thing is that all of the recordings are of similar situations. If you record a person in a friendly conversation at one point and then in a formal speech setting at another point, then you're not comparing like with like, so you can't be sure that any differences you find are actually changes. They might just be the way the person speaks in different situations.

Once you've decided on your recordings, you have to identify where the sounds you want to analyse are. There are lots of ways of doing that. Some recordings come with subtitles or a transcription so you can just look out for words that have the sounds in them. If your recording doesn't have a transcription, then you might need to do one. This doesn't have to be very detailed or precise – you just need to spot which words are where so that you can pick out the sounds when you go to analyse them. If you've got quite a long recording, then you will want to link the transcription to the audio, or at least keep a note of the times of certain points. For the Jagger project, Kate identified all words that had one of the three sounds she was looking at; then she chose ones that were clearly pronounced, ensuring that she had a selection of different words, with different sounds around the vowels she was looking at.

Appendix B explains in a bit more detail how you can use software packages that are freely available to do this kind of analysis. For now, I'll just tell you that the next step is to look at the sound waves, identify the vowel sounds you're examining and ask the software to do the measurements for you. I give you more of the detail of what she found after I've said a bit more about how vowels work, but her main findings were as follows:

- Mick Jagger's vowels are mostly closer to Cockney than to RP.

- These three vowels start more like Cockney but end more like RP.

- In the 1980s his accent went off in a different direction (possibly more American, as he was with Jerry Hall at the time and they had two children, born in 1984 and 1985).

- The pronunciation of these three vowels has changed in both RP and Cockney in this period.

So what's the point of all of this? Well, it's interesting to see how an individual's accent has changed over time. It is also interesting to compare what's happened to his accent with the changes in other people. The Queen, for example, has apparently become more 'common' – that is, her accent is less like what we might call 'the Queen's English' and more like the way 'normal people' speak. Jagger doesn't seem to have changed in the same way – his accent doesn't move closer to either Cockney or RP during the period, and he's not just in between the two accents, either. The important thing here is that you can only find these things out accurately if you do proper phonetic analysis. In order to do the project Kate did, she needed to understand which vowels are pronounced differently in the different accents. She had to be able to identify the words that had those vowel sounds and understand what the numbers the software gave her meant in terms of the actual pronunciation of the vowels.

2.3.3   Second language acquisition

Quick quiz

1. If you are a native speaker of English, how would you imitate someone who is French, trying to speak English? (If you're not, or you're not sure, think about people who have used comedy French accents, like Steve Martin in the *Pink Panther* film).
2. Can you identify which sounds you (or they) pronounce differently?
3. Why do you think you (they) do this?
4. If you have learned a second language, were there particular sounds you had trouble pronouncing?
5. Why do you think speakers of some Asian languages have trouble pronouncing *l* and *r* in English?

When you learn your first language you do it automatically and very easily. You don't have to be taught what words are or how to pronounce them; you just pick it up by hearing it spoken around you. I'm not going to go into all the debates and theories about what that says about language and the human brain here, but it's pretty universally accepted that everyone (provided they don't have any special circumstances like hearing impairment) learn their first language in this way. Another fact that is generally accepted is that the pronunciation or accent is fixed very early on, so it is harder to learn the correct pronunciation of a language you learn later.

That brings us to second language learning. For many people the first experience they have of learning a second language comes when they go to secondary or high school at around age 11. They have to learn a whole new set of words, new ways of putting those words together and how to pronounce that language. For most people learning their second language at this age, these are very different tasks. Learning lists of vocabulary is tedious, but not very complicated. (Learning exactly how those words are used and the subtly different meanings they might have compared to the translations in our own language is another matter, but not one that is important here.) Learning different grammatical rules is more complex and something that some people are just better at than others. It's a bit like maths, learning how to manipulate symbols, but there are people who are very good at learning languages who don't get on with maths at all. Those people who find it easy to learn a second language will, after a few years of study and practice, reach a level of fluency that comes close to being a native speaker. They may well be able to read, write and understand their second language just as well as their first language. However, they will very rarely be able to *speak* the language like a native speaker. Even the best second-language learners will often have a 'foreign accent' when they speak their second language.

Have you ever tried to learn another language? If you have, you probably found that there are some sounds in that language that you don't have in your first language. Some may be completely new to you. Others might just be a bit different from some of the sounds in your language. If your first language is English and you are learning to speak German, you'll need to be able to make the sound that is written with *ch*, which is the same as the sound at the end of *loch*, if you say it with a proper Scottish accent. You'll probably also notice that some of the vowels are different. If you say the German word *Katze* (*cat*) with the same vowel sound as in *cat* in English, you'll sound like an English person trying to speak German (which you are!). If you want to sound more genuinely German, you'll need to work out that the vowel in *Katze* is actually pronounced with the tongue lower in the mouth. In fact, language teachers don't often talk in these terms. They usually just get you to imitate and try to match the sound, but wouldn't it be easier to pick up those foreign sounds if you really understood what the differences were between your first and second languages?

There are all different kinds of differences. If you want to learn Polish, for example, you'll need to learn how to pronounce strange combinations of sounds at the beginning of a word. It's perfectly okay for a word in Polish to begin with *zd*, for example, which would never be allowed in English. German and Dutch (and lots of other languages, actually) don't allow sounds like *b, d, g* at the ends of words. If you see one of those letters at the end of a word in German, you have to remember to pronounce it as *p, t, k* instead. If you want to learn Mandarin (China) or Yoruba (Nigeria), then you'll have to learn how to use different tones (kind of like the tune – chapter 8 looks at this).

There are at least two ways that phonetics and phonology can help in second language learning. For a start, as I just mentioned, giving learners themselves at least a basic understanding of phonetics – how to make different sounds – would make it much easier to explain the differences between the sounds of their native language and the sounds of the language they're trying to learn. On another level, teachers and educationalists can make use of much more complex ideas within phonetics and phonology to analyse the errors in pronunciation made by learners. There is a lot of research about the typical kinds of errors made by learners of a particular language and/or by speakers of a particular language. This involves looking at the sounds of the two languages and identifying where there are differences and how difficult those particular differences are to recognise and reproduce. A whole different level of use of phonetics comes in the form of teaching apps which users can speak into and have their pronunciation analysed automatically. The app asks you to say a word or phrase, you say it into the microphone and the app tells you how close you got to the proper pronunciation and what was not right. For this the user doesn't need to know about the inner workings of the app, but the app developer needs to have expert knowledge of phonetics and the phonology of the languages in question.

In the first question in the quick quiz earlier, I asked you about French accents. Most English people, if they were imitating a French person speaking English, would drop their *h*'s, pronounce *th* as either *s* or *z* and probably use different vowel sounds, for example, pronouncing the vowel in *sit* as if it was *seat*. They're not usually basing this on any serious analysis of the difference between English or French, but on what they (imagine they) have heard when they hear French people speak English. I say *imagine*, because I had another student who did a project on the difference between what she termed 'comedy French accents' and actual French speakers speaking English. She found that real French people very rarely use *s* or *z* for *th*, although they do often drop *h*'s. First of all, why do you think they drop *h*'s? If you know any French, you probably know that French has the letter *h* in lots of words that look like their English counterparts, like *hôtel* and *herbe*, but they never pronounce the *h*. French doesn't have the sound *h*, so French speakers of English tend to drop it. The fact that there are some English accents that also drop *h* means that this is rarely problematic in terms of understanding. Why do you think that people believe that French people don't pronounce the *th* the same as English speakers? It's a similar thing to the *h*. French doesn't have those sounds (the two sounds at the beginning of *this* and *thing*). French speakers know that they can't just leave those sounds out, though, so they have to substitute them with the most similar sounds in their language. How do you know which sounds are most similar? You do a phonetic analysis of the sounds in each language. But I said that my student found that French people don't actually pronounce the *th* sounds as *s* or *z*, so what's happening here? It is certainly true that French doesn't have those sounds, and French learners of English will probably tell you that they have had to learn to say those sounds. However, they are not actually very difficult sounds to pronounce, so after learning English for a little while, most French speakers are able to manage those sounds. This does beg the question of why so many comedy imitators still use that feature. It's basically a case of cartoonish exaggeration. Some French people, especially when they're first learning English, do have trouble with those sounds, and it's the kind of thing people will pick up on as something noticeable to clearly identify that they're doing a 'foreign accent'.

Another student project, but this time a PhD one, looked at how speakers of Urban Hijazi Arabic (a variety of Arabic spoken in the Hijaz region of Saudi Arabia) pronounce words that have been borrowed from English. This is a rather different question, because the people in this study were not trying to copy an accent, but the study involved a detailed analysis of how much different people adapted English words to make them sound more like words in their native language. It's like asking whether English people pronounce a word like *contretemps* as it would have been pronounced in French (where the word comes from) or as the spelling in English suggests. There are a few differences, including the pronunciation of the vowels, but the biggest difference is that in French the *mps* would not be pronounced, but in English it usually would.

2.3.4   Other applications

Discourse analysts, a bit like sociolinguists, look at the language people use in particular situations to achieve particular effects. In some cases that can be studied using the written word just as easily as the spoken word, but there are some kinds of investigation that require looking at speech rather than writing. If you're interested in the different words people use and what they mean by them, then you are not usually very concerned with exactly how they pronounce them. If you're interested in whether someone is really trying to sound more like (they think) their audience sounds, then you might need to look at that in more detail.

There are two kinds of discourse study that need some understanding of phonetics and phonology. The first is quite similar to an accent study, comparing how someone speaks in different contexts and to different audiences. That's why I said that if you want to compare someone's accent at different times, you need to make sure that the recordings you're working with are of similar situations. A discourse analysis might take the same person addressing different audiences and see if their speech changes. Or it might take two or more different people with different political outlooks and see if the way they speak correlates with their political outlook. The second kind of discourse study, rather than doing any kind of comparison, examines a single speech in great detail, looking at where there are errors or hesitations, where there are unusual patterns of stress or intonation (more on those in chapters 7 and 8), for example. Another type of discourse study involves looking at conversations or dialogues and measuring who speaks most often and for longest, who interrupts whom and where or whether the people involved adjust their speech to match the other person, for example.

This last thing is something everyone tends to do in conversation with another person. It is called **accommodation**. This means that people adapt their speech to be more similar to (or more different from) the speech of the person they are talking to. This includes all sorts of aspects, including the speed and pitch as well as the accent. If two people in a conversation have very different accents, they will tend to 'tone down' those accents and speak in accents that are closer to a standard accent in order to make sure that they are understood. If you want to really study this phenomenon properly, you need to do detailed phonetic analysis.

Another application everyone will have come across in some form or another is the development of various kinds of software to process speech. You have probably all come across dictation software which you can speak into and it will transcribe your speech as written language. These systems work basically like the subtitling systems I mentioned earlier. There are also a lot of voice recognition systems which don't convert the speech to writing, but just follow instructions. And there are a lot of systems that use automatically generated speech, either spoken responses to spoken input or reading aloud. These systems are potentially very useful when you want, for example, to send and receive messages while driving, but for some people with disabilities, they can be genuinely life changing. It's important to have an understanding of the precise physical properties of speech for speech analysis and synthesis. If you have a dictation app on your phone (such as Siri, e.g.), you're making use of decades of research by linguists and speech scientists into analysing the speech signal. For the purposes of this book, you don't need to know all that much detail, but you'll see, as you go along, why it's such a difficult thing to do and why apps like Siri don't always get it right.

One really important application of phonetics is speech and language therapy. Many linguistics students go on to train as speech and language therapists, and a good understanding of how speech sounds are produced is essential in order to understand the problems that people with speech impairments have and how to address those problems. The pronunciation of some consonants is particularly hard if you suffer from a physical condition such as a cleft palate, for example, because the pronunciation of those sounds requires very fine control of how the tongue meets the roof of the mouth. A knowledge of phonetics is required to understand what exactly is happening when sounds are not being pronounced as they should be. It is also needed to help people to achieve better pronunciation, either through practice and exercises to get closer to the correct pronunciation or by working out how the person can get around their own particular impediment.

The final application I mention here is the field of forensic linguistics. There are many aspects of forensic linguistics in addition to phonetic areas, but one relevant application is the forensic analysis of speech samples. For example, if the police have a recording of a telephone call from someone known to have committed a crime, forensic phonetic analysis can help them to determine how likely it is that a suspect is that person. An unusual case where forensic phonetics helped to establish the truth was that of a man claiming to be Lord Buckingham, an English lord. A routine passport check revealed that the name he was using was that of a boy who had died as a baby. The man refused to say what his actual identity was, but after various investigations he was revealed to be Charles Stopford from Florida. One of the pieces of evidence was a study of his accent, which showed that he could not be who he said he was. Although his accent was very convincingly British to a casual observer, there were some key features and pronunciations that were not. One of these was the way he pronounced his name: Buckingham. British speakers will not usually pronounce the *h* in this name, but he did.

As you can see, there are lots of reasons why doing detailed phonetic analyses can be useful, whether it's as a way of studying other aspects of language or for developing practical tools that help us in all areas of our lives.

Additional reading

If you are interested in finding out more about speech science and applications, Ryalls and Behrens (1999) is a good introductory text. Coleman (2005) is also a good introduction, with an emphasis on the speech aspects. Katz (2013) has several chapters (especially 12–14) which talk about using spectrograms and speech perception studies. Collins and Mees (2013) has two whole parts (parts C and D) which cover various kinds of applications, and Zsiga (2013) also talks about practical applications in chapters 8 and 9.

If you want to read about some interesting issues in pronunciation, Wells (2014) and Wells (2016) are collections of musings from a blog about some of the oddities of pronunciation.

Exercises

1. (a) Work out how you pronounce the word *sat* by thinking about how you say it.
   (b) Now work out how you say it in a sentence like *the cat sat on the mat*.
   (c) Now record yourself saying the sentence.
   (d) Finally, record yourself reading the following passage:

   I have lots of animals, including two dogs, a cat, a hamster and four fish. The dogs always sit by the door, waiting to be taken out for a walk, but the cat is more interested in watching the hamster and the fish. When I came back from work yesterday one dog was by the front door, the other was by the back door and the cat sat on the mat.

   Can you hear that your pronunciation of *sat* is different each time? Can you describe the differences? Why do you think they are different?

2. The following are examples of incorrect subtitles. For each one, work out what you think they were supposed to say and exactly what the error was. For example, in the subtitle I mentioned, the word *horse* has been misheard as *whores*, which has a different sound at the end – [z] instead of [s].

   (a) Heinz is rubbing against governor Pat Quinn.

   (b) Will come. This is BBC news.

   (c) When I filo, when I feel blue.

   (d) Police tell me if there was a cat fight.

3. Find someone who is a non-native speaker of English (this could be yourself, a friend or just someone on TV, radio or on the internet).

   (a) Which sounds in English do you/they have difficulty with?

   (b) Are those sounds completely missing from their native language?

   (c) What do they do for those sounds? (Do they drop them, replace them with a different sound, and if so, which one?)

   (d) If they use a different sound, can you work out how different it is and in what way?

Part II

How to describe and classify sounds

Humans can make all sorts of different sounds. People can sing (well, some can), hum, whistle, cough and sneeze, to name just a few. Speech is rather special, though. It's special in that humans are the only species that can do it. Other animals can use sounds to communicate, but even the most sophisticated of them don't have anything even remotely as complex as human language. Making speech sounds can happen in a number of ways, but the general process involves air coming from the lungs (usually), up through the trachea, or windpipe, and out through either the mouth or nose. Of course, that's what happens during breathing, and it doesn't always involve speech. This entire route is called the **vocal tract**, starting with the lungs and ending at the nostrils and lips, where the air meets the outside world. Changing the shape of the vocal tract is what makes different sounds. This part of the book explains how the different sounds are produced (**articulatory phonetics**) and what the properties of the sounds are (**acoustic phonetics**). The two chapters cover first the consonants and then the vowels. Different speech sounds are made by constricting different bits of the vocal tract in different ways and to different degrees. In chapters 3 and 4, I explain how this happens, known as the **articulation** of sounds, how it can be described and how it is transcribed using the IPA.

3 Consonants

Sounds are usually divided into **consonants** and **vowels**. This is the first point when you need to try to forget some of the things you learned when learning to spell. In the Roman alphabet, there are five vowels: *a, e, i, o, u*. All of the other letters are consonants. Unfortunately, the distinction in spoken sounds is not the same.

Quick quiz

1. Which of the following words begin with consonants: *bit, yodel, usual, other, hour?*
2. Which of the following words end with vowels: *other, bit, bite, happy?*

Words that begin with a written vowel don't necessarily start with a vowel in their pronunciation. You should be able to hear that the words *yodel* and *usual* both begin with the same sound, even though only one of them begins with a written consonant. Similarly, words that end with a written vowel don't necessarily end with a spoken vowel. So *bit* and *bite* both end in the same (consonant) sound, even though *bite* has a written vowel at the end. Depending on your accent you might or might not have a consonant at the end of *other*. For speakers of Standard Southern British English (SSBE), there is no vowel (the *r* is not pronounced), but speakers of Scottish or Irish accents or some American accents do pronounce the *r*. Notice also that the *y* at the beginning of *yodel* represents a spoken consonant, but the *y* in *happy* represents a spoken vowel (the same vowel that is represented by *ee* in section 1.1). Some letters are not pronounced at all, like the *h* in *hour*, which means that word begins with a vowel, not a consonant, in the pronunciation. All English words need to have at least one spoken vowel, but they don't necessarily have a written vowel. Think of words like *rhythm* and *sky*. This chapter looks in more detail at how to describe those sounds that are classified as consonants in their pronunciation. The next chapter looks at vowels.

3.1 Articulation

The main difference between consonants and vowels is that for consonants there is a more significant interruption to the airflow through the mouth. Where and how the flow is interrupted are the first two ways in which consonants are classified. It might help here to think about a trombone or a trumpet. If you pick up a trombone and just blow through it, it won't make much of a noise at all. To make a proper noise out of it, you need to place your lips in such a way that there's a vibration which produces the sound. What your lips are actually doing here is forcing the air through a small opening which makes the air vibrate. In order to make speech sounds, the air must be forced through small openings, and this is done by constricting different parts of the route from the lungs upwards. Changing the shape of the vocal tract is what makes different sounds. This is like the difference between a trombone and a trumpet – they are basically just bent into differ- ent shapes to produce different sounds. Another way that the trombone can make different sounds is by sliding the telescopic bit to make the tube longer or shorter. This changes the pitch. The same effect is achieved in a trumpet by closing and opening the valves. In the human vocal tract, the effects are achieved by closing, or nearly closing, different bits of the vocal tract so that the air comes out of the mouth in different ways or out of the nose.

The way different sounds are pronounced is described by reference to the different parts of the vocal tract. Figure 3.1 shows the vocal tract and the specific parts that are referred to for the pronunciation of consonants.

It's no coincidence that the word for *language* in many languages is the same as the word for *tongue* and even in English the word *tongue* is used to mean a language. The **tongue** is used in the production of most sounds. Humans have much greater control over their tongues than other animals.

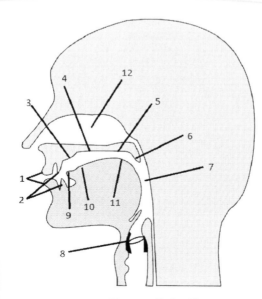

1. Lips
2. Teeth
3. Alveolar ridge
4. (Hard) palate
5. Soft palate (velum)
6. Uvula
7. Pharynx
8. Larynx
9. Tongue tip
10. Tongue blade
11. Tongue back
12. Nasal cavity

FIGURE 3.1   THE PARTS OF THE VOCAL TRACT

We use our tongues to move food around as we eat, but we could manage with much less control than we need to produce all the different speech sounds. The degree of control needed to produce all the various consonants and vowels is enormous. We need to be able to manipulate the tongue to within millimetres of the target in order to distinguish between different consonants, in particular. For example, the sound you make when you say *s* is called a fricative. To make a fricative sound, you need to position your tongue at precisely the right distance from the roof of your mouth so that it allows just the right amount of air to pass through and make the hissing sound.

The other parts of the mouth that are controlled to make speech sounds are also used for other purposes. The **lips** are also quite controllable, but that's not something that's unique to humans. Have a look at most of the great apes and you'll see them using their lips to make facial expressions that are an important part of their communication. Lips are used by humans as part of the eating and drinking process as well as for facial expressions such as smiling and pouting. Sounds that involve the lips are among the first sounds most babies make, possibly because they can see how they are used by the adults around them.

The **teeth** are used in making speech sounds, but only by moving softer movable parts against them (the lips and the tongue). In fact the teeth themselves are not used in many sounds, which may be a reflection of the fact that teeth may be lost, and so it's not ideal if they are absolutely critical for speaking.

The **velum**, or **soft palate**, is also used for a lot of speech sounds. The velum has the little blobby bit that hangs down at the back of your mouth attached to it, called the **uvula**. The velum can be lowered to allow air to go in and out though the nose (this is the normal position for breathing through the nose), or it can be raised to block the nose and only allow air to go in and out through the mouth. This is another thing which is probably useful for situations like swimming, where control of our breathing is important.

3.1.1 Place

The first main difference between different consonant sounds is where in the mouth the main **constriction** is, that is, where the airflow from the lungs is interrupted. The different parts of the mouth can be moved around in different ways to make different sounds. Say *p*, then say *t* then *k*. You should be able to feel that when you say *p* that your lips are pressed together, then opened. When you say *t*, the front part of your tongue is pressed against the front part of the roof of your mouth, whereas when you say *k*, the back part of your tongue is pressed against the back part of the roof of your mouth. Can you feel those positions? Can you see on figure 3.1 where this is happening? For *t* the tongue touches the alveolar ridge, and for *k* it touches the velum. The different places where consonants are produced are described by referring to these parts of the mouth, mostly using Latin terms for the parts of the mouth. Table 3.1 gives the main terms you need for this. There are more that I introduce later, but I focus on those for now. Hopefully, you all know where your lips and teeth are. The alveolar ridge is very important for speech sounds in all languages, but you may not have come across it before. Run your tongue back from your teeth. You should feel the hard ridge just behind them. That's the alveolar ridge. Now keep running your tongue back from there. You should be able to feel that behind the alveolar ridge, the roof of your mouth curves upwards into a kind of dome shape. That bit is the hard palate. Now keep running your tongue back (you'll need to let it go kind of upside down) and you should feel that the hard part ends and there's a softer part. The soft part is the velum (sometimes called the soft palate). Most English consonants can be described in terms of those places.

The bits of the mouth used to pronounce a sound are called the **articulators**. Articulators are just bits that come together to make the vocal tract a different shape and they can be **active** or **passive**. Active articulators are ones that move, and include lips, tongue and velum. Passive articulators are ones that don't move, and include teeth, alveolar ridge and palate. The consonant sounds are described by referring to the articulators. In most cases, the tongue is one of the articulators, which isn't usually mentioned, but when the tongue is not involved, the names of both articulators are used. For example, a **velar** sound involves the tongue moving towards or touching the velum, for example when saying *k* or *g*. A **labiodental** sound involves the lips (active articulator) moving towards the teeth (passive articulator). Try making that movement. Move your bottom lip to touch your top front teeth and breath out. Can you hear what sound that makes? You should hopefully

Part of the Mouth	Technical Term	Adjective Form
Lips	labia	labial
Teeth	dens	dental
Ridge just behind the teeth	alveolar ridge	alveolar
Central part of the roof of the mouth	(hard) palate	palatal
Soft part of the roof of the mouth	velum (soft palate)	velar

TABLE 3.1   PLACES OF ARTICULATION

hear that it's either a *f* or a *v* (I talk about the difference between those in section 3.1.3).

There is one exception to that: the sounds that involve both lips. They are called **bilabial** but they sometimes just get called **labial**. What sounds in English are made by using both lips? There are four consonant sounds that use the lips in English: *p*, *b*, *m* and *w*. (Actually, *w* is a bit odd, so I come back to that later.)

The main places of articulation for consonants in English are:

- **bilabial** sounds use both lips: *pit*, *bit*, *mit*

- **labiodental** sounds use the bottom lip and top teeth: *fat*, *vat*

- **dental** sounds use the teeth (and tongue): *think*, *this*

- **alveolar** sounds use the alvealor ridge (and tongue): *tip*, *dip*, *sip*, *nip*, *lip*, *rip*

- **post-alveolar** (or **palato-alveolar**) sounds are produced just behind the alveolar ridge (with the tongue): *choke*, *joke*, *ship*, *genre*

- **palatal** sounds use the (hard) palate (and tongue): *yellow*

- **velar** sounds use the soft palate (velum) (and tongue): *kit*, *git*, *sing*

There are two more consonants in English that don't use these parts of the mouth, but I address them in section 3.1.3. There is one more place of articulation that I should mention here and that is **retroflex**. In some ways it seems more accurate to think of retroflex as a manner of articulation rather than a place. Retroflex sounds involve folding the tongue back so that the underside of the tip of the tongue goes near to the roof of the mouth. It's classified as a place of articulation because it's possible to put the tongue in that position and still make sounds with the different manners I talk about in the next section. SSBE doesn't have retroflex sounds, but some American accents have a retroflex *r*.

3.1.2   Manner

The second main way that consonants differ is in how much and exactly how the airflow is interrupted. This is called the **manner** of articulation. In a sound like the *p* in *pit*, the airflow is completely stopped (briefly) and then released. Sounds like this are called **plosives** because it is the explosive release of the air that makes the noise. They are also sometimes called **stops** because they involve a complete blockage in the mouth, but that's not strictly the accurate term as it also refers to sounds called **nasals** (see below).

Fricatives are produced when the articulators come close enough to cause friction, but without a complete closure. Fricatives make a constant hissing or shushing sound. There are a lot of different fricatives in the languages of the world, and in English there is a particularly large set of them. Because of the frequency they create, it is possible to distinguish between fricatives produced very close together in the mouth. For example, try saying *said* followed by *shed*. They sound very different, don't they? But the tongue in both cases is actually in very similar positions.

Those two kinds of sound can also be combined to make what we call **affricates**. Affricates are produced with a complete closure, like a plosive, followed by a slow release, causing friction like a fricative. In English there are two affricates, at the beginnings (and ends) of the words *church* and *judge*. Can you feel the complete closure followed by the friction part of the sound?

The other main type of consonant is made with less of a closure than for a fricative, so that there is no friction. These sounds are called **approximants**. Approximant consonants are actually very similar to vowels, and in some cases it's quite difficult to tell the difference. Approximants in English include the sounds at the beginning of *rip*, *whip* and *yell*.

Nasals (or nasal stops) have a complete closure in the mouth, but the air comes out of the nose. Most of the world's languages have at least one nasal sound, and in English there are three of them (well, actually, there are more than that when you start to really think about how sounds are pronounced in specific contexts, but I'm going to stick with those three for now). The sounds at the end of the words *some*, *sun* and *sung* are those three. Say *mmmmmmmm, nnnnnnnnn*. Can you feel the air coming out of your nose when you say them? And can you feel the closure in your mouth? You should be able to feel the different places in the mouth where the closure is for each of those sounds, at the lips and at the alveolar ridge, and that closure position is how they are classified. So, when the tongue is touching the alveolar ridge, but the air is escaping through the nose, it's called an alveolar nasal.

Lateral sounds have a complete closure in the middle of the mouth but allow air to pass down the sides of the tongue. English only has one of these, the sound at the beginning of the word *lateral*. In fact, this is strictly speaking a **lateral approximant**, because there is no friction as the air escapes down the sides of the mouth. In Welsh (and in many Welsh names) the sound represented in the spelling with *ll* is a **lateral fricative**. This has the same closure in the middle of the mouth, but there is friction as the air escapes down the sides of the mouth.

I said that the *r* sound in English is an approximant. This is true for SSBE, but many accents of English actually have different ways of pronouncing this letter. In some Scottish accents, the sound is a **trill**, where the tongue touches the roof of the mouth several times very quickly. A sound that is found in

American accents is the **tap** or **flap**. This is a bit like the trill, but there's only one very quick tap of the tongue on the roof of the mouth. Imagine someone with an American accent saying the word *water*, and the sound in the middle is probably a tap.

Let's sum up those manners of articulation:

- **Plosive** sounds involve a complete closure: *pit, bit, tit, did, kit, git.*

- **Fricative** sounds involve friction: *fat, vat, sat, zip, ship, genre, thin, this.*

- **Affricate** sounds involve friction after a complete closure is released: *church, judge.*

- **Nasal** sounds involve a complete closure in the mouth, but air escapes through the nose: *map, nap, sing.*

- **Approximant** sounds have only an approximate closure: *rope, yoke, woke.*

- **Lateral approximant** sounds have a complete closure in the centre of the mouth, but air escapes down the sides: *lid.*

- **Lateral fricative** sounds have a complete closure in the centre of the mouth, but air escapes down the sides with friction: *Llanelli.*

- **Trill** sounds have a repeated very quick total closure: *rope* in some Scottish accents.

- **Tap or flap** sounds have a single very quick total closure: *write*r in American accents.

3.1.3   Voicing and the larynx

The third main way in which consonant sounds can differ is in their **voicing**. This is all to do with what happens in the **larynx**, or **voicebox**. It's called the voicebox for a good reason, as it often plays the role of the lips at the mouthpiece of a trombone, causing the vibrations that make the resonant sounds. Put your hand on your Adam's apple (that's the bit on the front of your neck that's a bit knobbly). Now say *fffff* followed by *vvvvv*. Can you feel the vibration when you say *vvvvv*? That vibration is voicing. The *f* sound is **voiceless**, or **unvoiced**, while the *v* sound is **voiced**. Consonants can be either voiced or voiceless, although for quite a lot of them there is rarely, if ever, a distinction. If you think back to the section on manner of articulation, basically the plosives, fricatives and affricates can all be either voiced or voiceless, but the others are always voiced. (This is actually a bit of a simplification, but it works for the sounds of English.) Vowels are also always voiced.

So what's actually happening when voiced and voiceless sounds are produced? The larynx is actually a box of cartilage which houses two little strips of mucous membrane called the **vocal chords** (also spelled vocal cords or called the vocal folds). These chords can be stretched tight so that they are forced together, or they can be relaxed so that there's a gap between them. This gap between them is called the **glottis**. During normal breathing, the chords are apart, so air can go through them. When speaking, they can be moved around to make the sounds that are needed. If the chords are close together, but not completely blocking the air, it can be forced through in such a way that they vibrate. That's what makes the voicing sound and what causes the vibrations you can feel when you put your hand on your Adam's apple while saying *vvvv*. This control over the larynx isn't only helpful for speaking. It's helpful for breathing when swimming, so there may be more than one reason why it was helpful in evolutionary terms. The human larynx is lower than in other animals (and in human babies), and there is an evolutionary disadvantage to this, as it means that humans can choke, something which simply can't happen to other animals.

Table 3.2 shows which of the consonants are voiceless or voiced. The groups that aren't in that table are all voiced.

As well as sounds being voiced and voiceless, there are some other differences in the way the vocal chords are used. **Aspiration** is when a little puff of air is released. Exactly what happens with voicing and aspiration is quite complex and to do with the exact point that voicing begins when pronouncing a sound. This is called **voice onset time** (**VOT**).

There are also other sounds the larynx is used for. If the chords are completely closed together and then released, a consonant called a **glottal stop** is produced. This is a kind of plosive, because the sound is produced by the release of air, just like a *p*, but the closure is not in the main part of the vocal tract. The glottal stop is the sound you hear in the middle of words like *Gatwick* in casual speech of a lot of SSBE speakers. It is sometimes written as an apostrophe to indicate that the *t* isn't pronounced like a 'proper' *t*: *Ga'wick*. The other key sound that is pronounced by the larynx is the *h* sound in English. This is a **glottal fricative** and it is produced by holding the chords close enough together to cause friction, but not to make the chords vibrate.

Type of Consonant	Voiceless	Voiced
Plosives	*p*it, *t*it, *k*it	*b*it, *d*id, *g*it
Fricatives	*f*at, *s*at, *sh*ip, *th*in	*v*at, *z*ip, genre, *th*is
Affricates	*ch*urch	*j*udge

TABLE 3.2 VOICED AND VOICELESS CONSONANTS

These are the three main parts of the description of consonants. They are called the **parameters of description**.

3.1.4   Airstream mechanisms

Another aspect of speech sound production that involves the larynx is the use of different **airstream mechanisms**. Earlier I said that speech sounds are produced by air coming out of our lungs, and that's true for most speech sounds and all sounds in normal English speech. But there are other ways sounds can be produced and some of them are used in other languages as genuine speech sounds. When you make the clicking sound to 'tut', or to 'gee-up' a horse, you produce sounds using different airstream mechanisms. This means that there are different ways in which the air can flow in order to produce the sounds. Going back to the musical instrument metaphor, when you blow through a harmonica, you make a sound, but you can also make sounds by sucking the air in instead. It is possible to do that by speaking while breathing in. It's not easy because we don't have as much control over our inward breath as we do our outward breath. It's also possible to make sounds by only pushing the air out from different points. One way is by blocking the larynx by pushing together the vocal chords and trapping the air between that and another blockage, say at the alveolar ridge. That second blockage can then be released, producing a sound like a plosive. The sound is slightly different from one where the air is coming from the lungs, though, and those sounds are called **ejectives**. Some languages use them as different sounds from plosives. Because the air comes the glottis upwards, there is no distinction between voiced and voiceless ejectives. An **implosive** is a sound produced by blocking the mouth at both the glottis and somewhere else in the mouth. The larynx is lowered, producing a vacuum in the mouth, and when the other stoppage is released, the air rushes in (or implodes). There are also sounds that happen all in the mouth, with the tongue blocking the mouth at the velum. These are called **clicks**. They are only found in languages in Southern Africa, although they are used for non-speech sounds, like the *tutting* sound as mentioned above. If you want to hear what they sound like when they're used in speech, listen to Miriam Makeba singing the *Click Song*.

3.1.5   Other features

What I've covered so far is the way in which consonant sounds can be described and classified according to the three main parameters of place, manner and voicing. There are some other features that are important, as well as some ways in which some of those classes can be grouped together that are important in what I cover later in the book, so I just briefly cover those now.

In section 3.1.3, I told you that some sounds are always voiced, whereas others can be either voiced or voiceless. These two different groups are important for a lot that I talk about later in the book, so there are special names for them. The ones that can be voiceless are called **obstruents** and the ones that can't are called **sonorants**. Obstruents include the plosives, fricatives and affricates, and the name comes from the fact that they involve a significant obstruction in the mouth. The sonorants are everything else, and the name reflects the fact that they are more sonorous sounds. Vowels are also sonorants. Some of the sounds I have talked about are a bit confusing in terms of their grouping into obstruents and sonorants, so table 3.3 lists all of the sounds I have talked about and whether they are obstruents or sonorants.

Another group of sounds that is relevant is the **rhotics**. These are all the *r-type* sounds, including the alveolar approximant, the alveolar trill, the alveolar tap or flap, the uvular trill and possibly others. It's a strange group, really, because they're not all very similar in the way they're articulated, but they're grouped together because they kind of seem to be similar. English uses different ones to represent the letter *r* depending on the accent. The **liquids** include the rhotics and the lateral approximants.

There is one other subgroup of approximants known as the **glides**. These are also called the **semi-vowels** because (surprise, surprise!) they are the most vowel-like of the consonants. They are the palatal and labial-velar approximants. I say more about these shortly.

Finally, I just want to mention another slightly odd group called the **sibilants**. They're odd because they are defined not by how they are produced, but by acoustic properties, or how they sound. They are all either fricatives

Obstruents	Sonorants
Plosives	Approximants
Fricatives	Nasals
Affricates	Trills
Lateral fricatives	Lateral approximants
Clicks	Taps/flaps
Ejectives	
Implosives	

TABLE 3.3 OBSTRUENT AND SONORANT SOUNDS

or affricates, but not all fricatives or affricates are sibilants. The sibilants are the fricatives that make a particularly hissing sound. That includes the alveolar and post-alveolar, but not the labio-dental or dental ones in English. There are other articulatory similarities (they all use the front of the tongue, e.g.), but their defining characteristic is the acoustic property of a loud hissing sound.

3.2 Spelling

The spelling of consonants is not as complex as that of vowels. There are some consonant sounds that need two letters (a digraph) in English, such as *th*, *ch*, *sh*. Some sounds have alternate spellings, like *c*, *k*, *ck*. There are also often consonant letters that are not pronounced, as in words like *knee*, *debt* and *lamb*. One of the more interesting aspects of the spelling of consonants is the doubling of consonants in some words. For example, compare *mat* and *matting*. This is to do with the pronunciation of the vowel sound and the syllable structure, which I say more about later in the book.

3.3 Transcription

Now that you know how to describe and classify consonant sounds, next I explain how to represent these sounds in phonetic transcription. In Chapter 1, I explained why using the normal alphabet is not going to work when we're really interested in representing sounds accurately. I told you that there are special alphabets for this, and the one I use in this book is the IPA. This section explains which IPA characters are used for the consonant sounds described earlier.

3.3.1   IPA

Quick quiz

Have a look at the first table of sounds in the IPA chart for pulmonic consonants (shown in table 3.4), and answer the following questions.

1. What do the different rows represent?
2. What do the different columns represent?
3. Which row has the greatest number of different symbols?
4. Which column has the greatest number of different symbols?
5. What does that tell you about the speech sounds of different languages?

CONSONANTS (PULMONIC)   © 2005 IPA

	Bilabial	Labiodental	Dental	Alveolar	Postalveolar	Retroflex	Palatal	Velar	Uvular	Pharyngeal	Glottal
Plosive	p b			t d		ʈ ɖ	c ɟ	k g	q ɢ		ʔ
Nasal	m	ɱ		n		ɳ	ɲ	ŋ	N		
Trill	ʙ			r					R		
Tap or Flap		ⱱ		ɾ		ɽ					
Fricative	ɸ β	f v	θ ð	s z	ʃ ʒ	ʂ ʐ	ç ʝ	x ɣ	χ ʁ	ħ ʕ	h ɦ
Lateral fricative				ɬ ɮ							
Approximant		ʋ		ɹ		ɻ	j	ɰ			
Lateral approximant				l		ɭ	ʎ	ʟ			

Where symbols appear in pairs, the one to the right represents a voiced consonant. Shaded areas denote articulations judged impossible.

TABLE 3.4   THE PULMONIC CONSONANTS IN THE IPA

The IPA chart at the beginning of this book has several different sections. The first section, the table at the top, has most of these consonants, and we'll start with that. The table is reproduced in table 3.4. The table has the different manners of articulation down the left-hand side and the different places of articulation across the top. So, the answers to questions 1 and 2 of the quick quiz are that the rows represent the different manners of articulation and the columns represent the different places of articulation. Where there are two different symbols in a cell of the table, these are the voiceless and voiced sounds for that place and manner, voiceless on the left and voiced on the right. Just looking at the table actually reveals quite a lot about the speech sounds that are available to the languages of the world. For example, did you spot that it's the fricative row that has the greatest number of symbols? That shows that there are a lot more distinct fricative sounds than there are other manners of articulation. Going back to the discussion of obstruents and sonorants, can you see that the rows that have pairs of voiced and voiceless sounds are only the plosive and fricative rows? Don't worry about affricates for now; I come to them later. So, just by looking at the chart, you can see which sounds are obstruents and which are sonorants. Did you spot that it's the alveolar column that has the greatest number of symbols? That says that there are more different alveolar sounds than other places of articulation. What else do you notice about the alveolar coloumn? In the fricative row it is divided into three different sections. For all the other manners, there is just one sound or pair of sounds in that column, but in the fricative row, there is a distinction among dental, alveolar and postalveolar (or palato-alveolar). This doesn't actually mean that you can't produce a dental sound (with the tongue touching the teeth) for any of the other manners of articulation. What it does say is that there are no languages (that linguists know of) where there is a distinction among dental, alveolar and post-alveolar for those manners of articulation. The differences in fricative sounds are more easily distinguished than for the other manners.

There are some cells in the table that have no symbols, and some which are shaded. The shaded ones are where it has been decided that those sounds are not physically possible. For example, it is not possible to produce a lateral bilabial sound, because you can't close your lips just in the middle and let air escape down the sides. Try it! You may find that you can physically do it, but does the sound that comes out sound like a possible speech sound? Some really are impossible, like the velar trill. That would involve rapidly and repeatedly touching the back of the tongue against the velum, or soft palate. Try that! You may be able to say *k k k k* or *g g g g* fairly rapidly, but compare it to the genuine trill that you hear in, for example, some Scots accents for the *r* sound. The unshaded ones are sounds that are believed to be physically possible but which have not (yet) been found in any language.

Can you think of any sounds I have discussed that are not in this main IPA consonant table? The main omission is the affricates, which I said I'd look at later. Affricates are a bit strange. In many ways they behave like individual sounds, and so they are classified as single sounds for most purposes. However, they are transcribed as though they are two sounds combined, representing the closure part of the sound by the appropriate plosive symbol and the friction part by the appropriate fricative symbol. The two affricates in English are represented as having alveolar plosives followed by post-alveolar fricatives: [tʃ] and [dʒ]. Sometimes they are written overlapping (or as a ligature, [ʧ]), and sometimes thay have a linking arc either above ([t͡ʃ]) or below ([t͜ʃ]). The affricates aren't represented as separate sounds in the IPA, so you won't find them on the chart, which can be a bit confusing. In English there are the two affricates described here, but other combinations of a plosive and a fricative are found in other languages. German, for example, has [pf] and [ts].

Another set of consonants that don't appear in the main table are the 'non-pulmonic consonants'. I talked about these – they're the ones that don't use the usual air coming from the lungs (pulmonic) airstream mechanism. English doesn't have these, but have a quick look at them. You can see that the clicks, the rarest of the consonants in the world's languages, use a range of different symbols that don't look like the letters of the alphabet. The others, on the other hand, do look quite like alphabetic characters, albeit with some alterations, like hooks at the top or bottom. That's because those sounds are quite similar to the plosives. Note that the implosives are all voiced, while the ejectives are all voiceless. The symbol for an ejective is just whatever the symbol is for the pulmonic consonant with an apostrophe after, for example [p']. In fact, although most implosives are voiced, voiceless ones can be represented with an extra symbol under the voiced symbol. That's a diacritic, a small circle under the letter, that means 'voiceless' or 'less voiced' and can be

Sound	IPA	American
Voiceless post-alveolar fricative	ʃ	š
Voiced post-alveolar fricative	ʒ	ž
Voiceless post-alveolar affricate	tʃ	č
Voiced post-alveolar affricate	ʤ	ǰ (or ǧ)

TABLE 3.5   AMERICAN ALTERNATIVES TO IPA

used with any voiced sound symbol. These implosive sounds aren't found in English, or any European languages, but they are estimated to be found in around 13 per cent of the world's languages, mainly in Africa, so they're not exactly rare.

I said earlier that American linguists have a few different symbols that they use. They are the symbols for the two post-alveolar fricatives and the two affricates that we have in English. These alternatives are shown in table 3.5.

3.3.2   IPA for English

The IPA chart represents all of the known sounds of the world's languages, but in this book I'm mostly focusing on English. There are three consonants that English has that aren't in the table of pulmonic consonants in the IPA, though. Two of those are the affricates, which I just talked about. The other one is also a little bit odd. Can you think what it is? It's the sound that's usually spelled *w*. Think about what I've said about place and manner of articulation and try to work out what you think it is. First, what's the place of articulation? Say the sound a few times. You should be able to feel that the lips are the main place of articulation, so it's a bilabial. Do they completely close? No, they don't, so it can't be a plosive, an affricate or a nasal. Is there any friction? Again, the answer is no, so it can't be a fricative. You may remember that the IPA doesn't allow for lateral bilabial sounds, and hopefully you can feel that the sound is produced by closing the lips slightly, but not enough to cause friction, so it's an approximant. So why is it not in the cell on the chart for a bilabial approximant? The answer is that although the lips are where the main articulation takes place, there is also a **secondary articulation**, that is, there is another point of near closure. Can you work out where that is? What happens to your tongue when you say the sound? Try saying a *w* with your tongue raised near the front of your mouth. Does that feel natural? And does it sound the same? When you make the *w* sound, you raise the back of your tongue towards the velum, and that movement is an important part of what makes it sound the way it does. Because of this, this sound is called a

labial-velar approximant. Note that it's not **labio-velar** – that would involve placing your lip close to your velum, which is pretty tricky! If you look at the full IPA chart you can find this sound in the table of 'other symbols' below the 'non-pulmonic consonants'. The sound below it is the labial-velar fricative, which SSBE doesn't have, but it is used in some accents of English where there's still a distinction between words like *witch* and *which*. Note that the difference is indicated in the spelling. That's because in Old English, words with *wh* were pronounced with the [ʍ], whereas words with just *w* were pronounced with the [w]. Table 3.6 has just the consonants that are found in English, together with a word that has that sound.

IPA	Description			Example
p	voiceless	bilabial	plosive	as in *pie*
b	voiced	bilabial	plosive	as in *buy*
t	voiceless	alveolar	plosive	as in *tie*
d	voiced	alveolar	plosive	as in *die*
k	voiceless	velar	plosive	as in *kite*
g	voiced	velar	plosive	as in *guy*
tʃ	voiceless	post-alveolar	affricate	as in *chide*
dʒ	voiced	post-alveolar	affricate	as in *jive*
f	voiceless	labiodental	fricative	as in *fine*
v	voiced	labiodental	fricative	as in *vine*
θ	voiceless	dental	fricative	as in *thigh*
ð	voiced	dental	fricative	as in *thy*
s	voiceless	alveolar	fricative	as in *sigh*
z	voiced	alveolar	fricative	as in *Zion*
ʃ	voiceless	post-alveolar	fricative	as in *shy*
ʒ	voiced	post-alveolar	fricative	as in *measure*
h	voiceless	glottal	fricative	as in *high*
m	voiced	bilabial	nasal	as in *my*
n	voiced	alveolar	nasal	as in *nigh*
ŋ	voiced	velar	nasal	as in *sing*
l	voiced	alveolar	lateral	as in *lie*
ɹ	voiced	alveolar	approximant	as in *rye*
j	voiced	palatal	approximant	as in *yikes*
w	voiced	labial-velar	approximant	as in *wine*

TABLE 3.6 THE CONSONANTS OF STANDARD BRITISH ENGLISH

3.4 Acoustics

Sound is actually made up of real physical waves in the air. When you speak, you change the way the air moves, and when you hear, your ears detect these differences in the air. All sounds are made up of **sound waves**, and they can be measured and visualised. Sound can be measured in **frequencies**. Every sound typically has different **intensity**, or volume, at different frequencies, and they all combine to give the sounds we hear. To analyse speech sounds, a **spectrograph** is used. Originally spectrographs were machines that drew lines to indicate the frequencies of sounds, but now it's all done with computers. The image a spectrograph produces is called a **spectrogram**. The next section shows how to spot consonants in a spectrogram.

So far I've only talked about how consonants are produced, or articulated. This section shows how to analyse the sound waves for different kinds of sounds. The acoustics of vowels are a bit more obvious to spot when you look at the actual sound waves produced, but there are characteristics of consonant sounds as well.

3.4.1   Spectrogram characteristics of consonant classes

When you look at a spectrogram of speech, you can identify certain kinds of consonants. Plosives are characterised by a period of silence, when the complete closure is happening, followed by a burst of sound, when the air is released. If you look at the spectrogram in figure 3.2, you should be able to spot the places where there is no sound – the light bits. This is immediately followed by a burst of sound – the dark bits. Can you see this pattern above the plosives [d], [b] and [k] in this spectrogram?

Fricatives are characterised by 'messy' noise, which doesn't have any pattern to it. This is because there is sound at a range of different frequencies across the spectrum, but without any regular patterns. This is what 'white

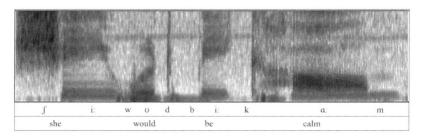

FIGURE 3.2   A SPECTROGRAM FOR 'SHE WOULD BE CALM'

noise' looks like. In the spectrogram here, there is one fricative, the [ʃ] at the beginning. Different fricatives have different amounts of noise at different levels. That's how they can be distinguished.

Approximants, nasals and other sonorant sounds have patterns that look like vowel patterns. I look at vowel acoustics and formant patterns in the next chapter, so I won't go into any detail here.

The other thing that can be identified on the spectrogram for consonants is voicing. Voicing is shown by a narrow band of more regular stripes at the bottom of the spectrogram. Have a look at the bit where the [ʃ] is. Can you see that this doesn't have a band at the bottom that the nasal [m] has at the end? You can also see the band at the bottom for the [d] and [b] (the voiced plosives), compared to the [k], which is voiceless. When I talk about how sounds combine, you'll see that the actual phonetic, or acoustic, realisation of voicing is not as simple as this to identify in normal connected speech, but it's a handy indicator.

Additional reading

The articulation of consonants is covered in Carr (1999), chapters 1 and 2; Davenport and Hannahs (2010), chapter 3; Katamba (1999), chapter 2; and Roca and Johnson (1999), chapters 1 and 3. Ladefoged and Johnson (2015) goes into more detail, especially in chapter 7, and Ladefoged (2001) looks at the consonants in chapters 6 and 11. The consonants of English are covered in Roach (2000), chapters 4, 6 and 7; and in Giegerich (1992), chapter 1. Knight (2012) has several chapters, 2–5, giving much more detail about consonants. For specific detail about voicing and voicing mechanisms, Ashby and Maidment (2011) chapters 2 and 6; and Ogden (2009), chapter 4, are particularly good sources. Katz (2013), chapter 2, gives a good introduction to articulation of speech sounds, and Clark and Yallop (2006) covers articulation in particular detail in chapters 2 and 6–8. Zsiga (2013) is also a good source for articulatory detail, especially chapters 5 and 6.

Exercises

1. In each of the groups of sounds below, there is one that is not produced at the same place of articulation as the others. Identify this odd one out. You may need to look at the IPA chart to help you.

   (a) [t d s ʃ l]
   (b) [ɸ p b f m]
   (c) [k ɢ g ŋ x]

2. For which of the following English words is the place of articulation the same for all the consonant sounds in the word? (Hint: watch out for 'silent' letters.)

   (a) kind
   (b) sent
   (c) palm
   (d) align
   (e) lazy

3. In the sentence 'Suzie saw five of the shows, she says,' all of the consonants have the same manner of articulation. Which? What about 'We were away all year'? And 'Peter kicked a dead toad'?

4. Give an English word that starts with these sounds, and provide the IPA symbol for the sound:

   (a) A voiced bilabial plosive
   (b) A voiceless labiodental fricative
   (c) A voiced alveolar lateral
   (d) A voiceless alveolar fricative

5. Write an English word that contains:

   (a) three different bilabial consonants
   (b) three different voiceless consonants
   (c) three different nasal consonants
   (d) three different alveolar sounds

6. Give the place of articulation for the first sound in these words:

   (a) though
   (b) shift
   (c) yes
   (d) civic
   (e) knee
   (f) phone

7. In the pairs of words below, state the difference between the sounds in bold. For example, *pop* and *bop* differ in voicing: *pop* begins with a voiceless sound, *bop* begins with a voiced sound.

(a)	**t**oe	**d**oe
(b)	**s**in	**sh**in
(c)	li**p**	li**ck**
(d)	bu**s**	but
(e)	lu**ck**	lu**g**
(f)	ri**ft**	wrist
(g)	bi**d**	bi**n**
(h)	**f**ree	**th**ree
(i)	**f**ace	**ph**ase
(j)	be**rr**y	be**ll**y

4   Vowels

The last chapter covered consonants. This chapter looks at the other main group of sounds: the vowels. As you'll see later, the distinction isn't clear-cut, but don't worry about that for now. In the discussion below, I have given the IPA symbols for the vowels I'm talking about as well as a representation from the spelling. I explain the IPA in section 4.4.

4.1   Articulation

Vowels are harder to describe than consonants because they don't involve a significant blockage or articulation. Try saying the sounds *ah* ([aː]), *ee* ([iː]), *oo* ([uː]), as in the words *hard, heed, who'd*. Can you work out what the differences are? Which parts of the mouth move to make the different sounds? It's basically all in the tongue and the lips. The tongue moves around in the mouth. It can be higher or lower, and the highest point can be further forward or further back. You might have thought about the jaw being important, and in a way it is, because usually your jaw opens and closes in order to move the tongue up and down. But it's not really the jaw that is important here. It is possible to make the tongue go high up in the mouth with the jaw quite far open; it's just not very natural. The lips can be more or less **rounded**, that is, making a kind of circle. These are the three main parts of the description of vowels or their **parameters of description**.

Quick quiz

1. Which of the three sounds ([aː], [iː], [uː]) has the tongue in a lower position than the other two?
2. Which of the three sounds has the most rounded lips?
3. Which has the least rounded?
4. Which has the highest part of the tongue furthest forward in the mouth?
5. Why do you think doctors ask you to say *aaah* when they want to look at your throat?

4.1.1   Height

Tongue height refers to how close to the roof of the mouth the tongue is. The terms used to describe tongue height either refer to the height, that is high and low, or to how open the mouth is, that is close and open. (Note, it's 'close', not 'closed', as in, 'The tongue is close to the roof of the mouth,' but it doesn't really quite match 'open'. Don't ask me why, but the terms *open* and *closed* are used for syllables, as you'll see in chapter 5.) Of the three vowels I asked you about in the quiz, you hopefully worked out that in terms of height, *ah* ([ɑː]) is the odd one out. The tongue is low (or the mouth is open) for this sound, but for the other two, the tongue is quite close to the roof of the mouth. It doesn't actually touch the roof of the mouth, although you may feel that it touches the teeth, especially for *ee* ([iː]). Question 5 is getting to the fact that the *ah* ([ɑː]) sound is the sound with the mouth most open, and the tongue lowest. For doctors to be able to see down your throat, they need your tongue to be out of the way, so if you said *ee* ([iː]) they wouldn't be able to see much other than the front of your tongue.

So far I've just talked about vowels being either high or low. Try saying *ee, e, a* ([iː, ɛ, æ]) as in the words *heed, head, had*. Say it in front of a mirror, or if you don't have a mirror but you do have another person handy, ask them to say them. Bearing in mind what I said earlier about the jaw generally opening to lower the tongue, can you see that there are three different heights, with *ee* ([iː]) the highest, *e* ([ɛ]) in the middle and *a* ([æ]) the lowest? Some languages, like Arabic, only have three different vowel positions, basically the three sounds I asked you about in the quiz questions, so they only have two heights. Some languages have more than three, but four seems to be the limit (with the exception of the very special vowel called schwa, which I introduce to you shortly).

The two additional heights are called *high-mid* and *low-mid* (or, of course, *close-mid* and *open-mid*). It's important to note that it's 'mid' and not 'central' for the middle height as you'll see when I talk about backness.

4.1.2   Front/backness

Backness refers to the position of the highest point of the tongue. How did you answer question 4? It's a bit harder to feel than the height question, partly because the tongue tends to have rather different shapes, so it's not quite as simple as just feeling whether it's forward or back. Ignore *ah* ([ɑː]) for now. If you're getting good at this, you should have spotted that the *ee* ([iː]) sound has its highest point further forward and the *oo* ([uː]) sound has its highest point further back. Now what about *ah* ([ɑː])? It's harder to work out, because no part of the tongue is very high. In fact, the lower (or more open) a vowel is, the less possibility of variation in the backness. What this means for linguists is that there are likely to be lots of languages that have more than one, and sometimes three, different vowels that are high or close, but not many languages that have two (and none that have three) different low (or open) vowels.

There's no double terminology here to confuse you, as with the high/close and low/open – they're always front and back – but linguists tend to talk about backness rather than frontness. Again, don't ask me why. It's easy to understand why they use *height* and not *lowness*, but *frontness* and *backness* seem equally acceptable. I've said that there are front and back vowels, but I've also said that there are sometimes high vowels with three different degrees of backness. This is where it's important to distinguish *mid*, which refers to height, and *central*, which refers to backness. The vowels that fall in between front and back are called *central* vowels. There are central vowels at different heights, from *high* down to *mid-low* at least, but not fully low ones.

So now you know a bit about height and backness, you can put them together and imagine a space where all the vowels appear with imaginary lines representing the different degrees of height and backness. Imagine the diagram of the head in figure 3.1, so the left-hand side is the front of the mouth. This shape is used to represent the height and backness of vowels, as in figure 4.1. In this diagram the [i] vowel is, therefore, a high front vowel.

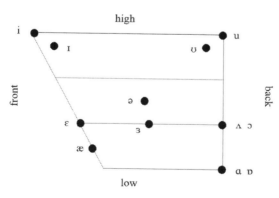

FIGURE 4.1   THE POSITIONS OF THE MAIN VOWELS OF ENGLISH

4.1.3   Rounding

In figure 4.1, there are two pairs of symbols. These pairs are vowels that have the same height and backness, but they are different vowels. That's because they have different **rounding**. Rounding (or lip rounding) refers to the shape of the lips. Look in a mirror (or get a friend to help you with this one). Watch what happens to your lips when you say the following words: *heed, hid, head, had, hard, hod, hoard, hood, who'd*. You should see the shape of your lips going from a smile to a kiss (a nice progression, I'm sure you'll agree). The shape of the lips for *heed* is **unrounded**, or **spread**, whereas the shape of the lips for *who'd* is **rounded**. You should hopefully have seen that these two words are extreme ends of a scale, and the ones in between change fairly gradually. For most purposes, however, linguists make a simple two-way distinction. Can you work out where there is a bigger leap between the unrounded and rounded vowels? It's between *hard* and *hod*. We say that the vowel in *hard* is unrounded and the vowel in *hod* is rounded. When the vowels are placed on the diagram, the unrounded vowel is always on the left and the rounded on the right in the pairs. For the English vowels, there are only two pairs. Of the other vowels, some are rounded and some unrounded. In English, the front vowels are all unrounded. The back vowels, apart from the pairs, are all rounded. The other two vowels, in the middle, are both unrounded.

4.1.4   Other features

Those three parameters define the main differences between vowels. However, there are other ways that vowels can differ. Think back to two of the words in the list. Say *heed* and *hid*. Now just say the vowel sounds in the middle and say them several times. What is different? In fact, there are four differences here. The first is that *ee* ([iː]) in *heed* is slightly higher than *i* ([ɪ]) in *hid*. The second is that *ee* ([iː]) is slightly more front than *i* ([ɪ]). They are small differences, and I say more about this when I talk about transcription. The third is that *ee* ([iː]) is **longer** than *i* ([ɪ]). The fourth is that *ee* ([iː]) is more **tense** than *i* ([ɪ]). I've already talked about height and backness, so let's now think about these last two.

Vowels can have different lengths, that is, they can be short or long. In the words *heed* and *hid*, hopefully you can hear that the vowel in *heed* lasts longer than the vowel in *hid*. In fact, length is much more complex than just being a two-way distinction, and it applies to consonants as well as vowels. For the purposes of this chapter, I'm going to simplify things and just assume that there are short and long vowels, but chapter 9 shows you that length is much more interesting than that!

A brief aside on Scottish vowel length ...

A nice example of how different accents of English have different vowels in particular comes from a number of Scottish (and some Northern Irish) accents. They have what is known as the **Scottish Vowel Length Rule**. In these accents there are no length distinctions between different vowels, but all vowels are longer when they come at the end of a word or before certain consonants. Those consonants are the voiced fricatives, [v], [ð], [z] and [ʒ] as well as [r]. Everywhere else vowels are short. That means that *leave* is pronounced [liːv], but *lead* is pronounced [lid].

The final difference between those two vowels is a bit more tricky to define. Vowels can be described as being either tense or lax. So *ee* is a tense vowel and *i* is a lax vowel. It's not easy to define, and for English it is usually sufficient to talk about the length distinction. The idea of tenseness relates to the muscular effort involved in the tongue position, and it is also related to something known as **advanced tongue root**, or **ATR**, with lax sounds having an advanced tongue root, but these ideas are controversial.

4.2 Monophthongs, diphthongs and triphthongs

So far I've been talking about vowels as single sounds with a single tongue position. That accounts for a lot of the vowel sounds of English, but not all. Those vowels are called **monophthongs**. This is from the Greek, meaning 'single sound'. There are also cases of vowel sounds where the tongue position changes. Say the sound *ee* ([iː]) in *heed*. Can you feel that your tongue stays in the same position for the duration? Now try saying *ay* ([eɪ]), as in the word *hay*. Can you feel that the position of your tongue moves from lower to higher? That kind of sound, one that has two different positions, is called a **diphthong** (hopefully you can spot why – the Greek for 'two sounds'). Diphthongs are quite common in the world's languages, and there are a lot of them in English, so they're important. They're also interesting because they aren't simply two different vowels next to each other. They're more like affricates. A diphthong is treated as a single vowel (even though it's written as two). When I talk about syllables in chapter 5, I give some reasons for this. For the moment, just trust me that as long as the vowel is only in a single syllable, it is considered a diphthong, not two separate vowels.

You might think that it's not an important distinction, but actually it is. There are cases where there are two vowels next to each other, but they're not in the same syllable. In that case it's not considered a diphthong. It's also important when considering the final possibility here—that is, **triphthongs**.

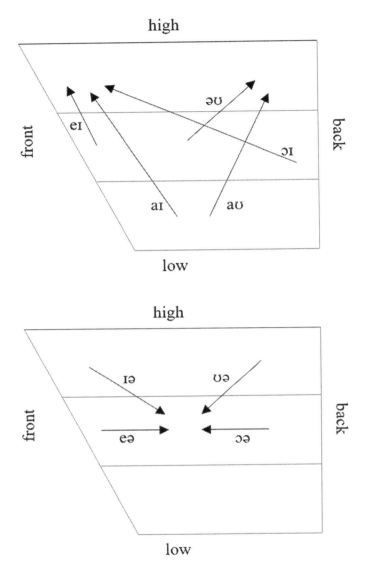

FIGURE 4.2   THE DIPHTHONGS OF ENGLISH, CENTRING DIPHTHONGS ON THE RIGHT

Not surprisingly, this refers to three vowel sounds all together, or, more accurately, a single vowel sound that has two movements between three different positions. Triphthongs are much rarer than diphthongs, but some people with some accents seem to have them in English words like *fire* and *hour*. When you say those words, do you think they have one syllable or two? If you think two syllables, then you probably don't have triphthongs in your accent but if you said one, then you probably do.

Diphthongs can be indicated on the diagram with an arrow from the start point to the end point. Figure 4.2 shows the main diphthongs found in SSBE.

4.3 Spelling vowels

In chapter 1, I showed that in English, especially, the spelling doesn't always match the pronunciation. For vowels that is particularly the case. There are a number of reasons why the spelling of vowels is generally trickier than the spelling of consonants. The first is a simple number problem. There are five alphabetic vowels, but English has over 20 different vowel sounds. This is a very extreme example of the strict one-to-one problem. If there are so many vowels to represent and so few characters to represent them with, then there will have to be character combinations (digraphs) and/or one character representing several different sounds. In English both happen.

The second problem with vowels is that they tend to change over time much more than consonants. English has undergone several shifts in the pronunciation of its vowels throughout its history, which has led to a lot of changes in the patterns of vowels. That is, words which at one point had the same pronunciation now have a different pronunciation, and words which once had different pronunciations now have the same pronunciation. This is why words like *meat* and *meet* have the same pronunciation but are spelled differently, and *meat* and *break* have the same written vowels but are pronounced differently.

The third problem with vowels (which is related to the second) is that vowels are the most common sounds to be different in different accents. So in many parts of the North of England the words *look* and *luck* have the same vowel, but in the South of England they have different vowels. This means that the spelling might reflect one pronunciation, but not all different accents. So these words have different written vowels for English speakers, even though some pronounce them the same. English spelling of vowels is therefore quite complicated, and there are a lot of irregularities. But don't be too disheartened – the spelling is actually a lot more regular than you might think.

Some of the spelling principles for English vowels are interesting. For example, think about the words *mat*, *mate*, *mating* and *matting*. These four words use two different vowels in their pronunciation: *a* ([æ]) and *ay* ([eɪ]). But all four have the same written vowel: *a*. In the case of *mat*, the vowel is [æ] because that's the default pronunciation of *a*. For *mate*, the added *e* after the consonant says that the vowel is pronounced as [eɪ] (sometimes called 'long a'). When the *ing* is added, the *i* plays the same kind of role as the *e* in *mate*, so *mating* has the [eɪ], and that means that the consonant has to be

A brief aside on English vowels . . .

English vowels have gone through several changes since the days of Old English. Some changes have happened gradually and affected just one or two sounds, but there have also been some big shifts that affected the whole vowel system. In Old English there were seven short vowels, [i, y, e, æ, ɑ, o, u] and long vowels that were simply longer versions of the short ones. There were two diphthongs: [eo] and [ea]. Some time between the Old English and Middle English periods the two diphthongs and [æ] and [ɑ] all merged, as did [i] and [y], leaving a system of just five vowels. In the Middle English period, a set of diphthongs emerged, coming from combinations of a vowel with one of the glides, [j, w]. So [aw] became the diphthong [aʊ] and so on. Later on, as Middle English became Early Modern English, there was a big shift, known as the Great Vowel Shift. That involved the front vowels all shifting up a height and the highest front vowel becoming a diphthong. As well as these big changes, there were smaller ones, such as the so-called 'foot-strut split'. That is when the vowels in those two words, which used to be pronounced the same, started to have different vowels. As I said earlier, for many speakers of accents in the North of England, for example, that split didn't happen. These are some of the reasons why the spelling of English vowels is a bit irregular.

doubled in *matting* to get the correct vowel pronunciation of [æ]. It might seem strange that the pronunciation of the vowel is indicated by doubling a consonant rather than doing something to the vowel, but this is actually quite common in other languages, too.

Another thing that can be a bit confusing is the question of diphthongs and monophthongs. You might reasonably expect that a diphthong is more likely to be written with two vowels and a monophthong with a single vowel, but that's not how it works in English. Although many diphthongs are written with two vowels (e.g. *ou* in *house* or *oi* in *noise*), many are not, because they were originally pronounced as monophthongs. So the vowel in *mate*, for example, is not written in a way that suggests a diphthong at all.

4.4 Transcription

So how are vowels transcribed? For the consonants there is a nice neat table, and you can look up the place of articulation across the top and the manner of articulation down the side to find the correct symbol. For vowels you need to refer to that space with the imaginary lines that I talked about earlier. The physical space in the mouth that the tongue occupies is viewed as a trapezium, with a narrower bottom than top, as you can see in figure 4.3. The front of the mouth is on the left and the back on the right. So a high

VOWELS

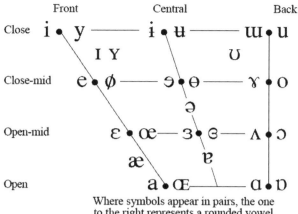

Where symbols appear in pairs, the one
to the right represents a rounded vowel.

FIGURE 4.3   THE VOWELS IN THE IPA

front vowel is considered to be in the top left hand corner of the trapezium. Because vowels are not as easy to differentiate as consonants, there are specific reference points, along those imaginary lines I talked about. Any vowel, at any point in that space, can then be defined in relation to those reference points. It's a bit like using grid references on a map. The terms *front*, *back* and so on are used to identify various points on the lines, and then a particular vowel can be defined as being a little bit to the left or right of the line, for example. Rounding in vowels is handled in the same way as voicing for consonants, with symbols being given in pairs, the unrounded one on the left and the rounded one on the right.

Note that the IPA uses the terms *close/open*, but I'm going to use *high/low*.

4.4.1   Cardinal vowels and the IPA

The most easily identified of the reference points are the ones on the outside edges of the trapezium (the front and back lines) on the four height lines (high, high-mid, low-mid and low). These have a special status in vowel description, and they are called the **cardinal vowels**. There are 16 cardinal vowels, one pair of unrounded/rounded at each point. They are divided into primary and secondary cardinal vowels according to roundedness, but just to make it a bit more confusing, it's not the case that all unrounded vowels are primary or vice versa. The **primary cardinal vowels** are the unrounded front vowels and the unrounded low back vowel together with the other three rounded back vowels: [i, e, ɛ, a, ɑ, ɔ, o, u]. Why? Well, those are the ones that are most commonly found in the world's languages. There are rounded front vowels and unrounded (non-low) back vowels, but they're rarer. They are the **secondary cardinal vowels**: [y, ø, œ, Œ, ɒ, ʌ, ɤ, ɯ]. The primary cardinal vowels are numbered from 1–8 and the secondary cardinal vowels are numbered from 9–16, in each case starting at the top left-hand corner and going round, ending at the top right-hand corner. Don't worry about those numbers, though, as here I just use the IPA symbols.

4.4.2   IPA for English

As I said earlier, vowels are a bit trickier to identify than consonants. As you'll see in the next section, there are ways of measuring vowels very accurately, but for most purposes there's no need to get into using specialist software just to do a transcription. In fact, for most purposes there's no need to be very precise about exactly where on the vowel chart any particular pronunciation lies. For English there is a set of conventional vowel transcriptions which is used, even when the actual pronunciation doesn't quite match. Figure 4.3 shows all of the vowels of the IPA. The cardinal vowels on the outer lines and other symbols for non-cardinal vowels. Table 4.1 shows the conventional vowels for SSBE together with a word containing that sound. In the full table, I have used words that are as similar as possible, except for their vowels (including diphthongs and triphthongs). In this section I am going to focus on the vowels in SSBE, but the table also includes the vowels for the standard American accent, known as **General American** (**GA**).

   The short vowels are the vowels in *bit, bet, bat, pot, put* and *but*. The first of these is not one of the cardinal vowels. It's just to the right and a bit lower than the high front unrounded vowel and has the symbol [ɪ]. It is called *near-high, near-front*. The second one is the low mid-front unrounded vowel, represented with the symbol [ɛ]. Sometimes you might see this written as [e], because English doesn't have both vowels, so there's no need to distinguish between them, and the [e] is easier to type. The third is another one that isn't a cardinal vowel. It's just above the low front unrounded vowel and uses the symbol [æ]. Those are all the short front vowels in English. Note that they are all unrounded. The next two are both rounded and back. The vowel in *pot* is low back rounded and is written as [ɒ]. Note that GA doesn't have this vowel – [ɑ] is used instead. The one in *hood* is another one that is not a cardinal vowel. This time it's near-high, near-back and is written as [ʊ]. Try saying the first three vowels, [ɪ], [ɛ], [æ]. Can you feel that they get progressively lower? Now say the other two, [ɒ] and [ʊ]. Can you feel them getting higher? The last one is a bit odd. This sound is transcribed as the cardinal vowel [ʌ], but it's not really how it is pronounced. The English vowel is more central and lower.

SSBE	GA	Example	Description
Short vowels			
iː	iː	*beat*	long front high unrounded
ɪ	ɪ	*bit*	short front (near-)high unrounded
ɛ	ɛ	*bet*	short front mid unrounded
æ	æ	*bat*	short front (near-)low unrounded
ʌ	ʌ	*but*	short central (near-)low unrounded
ɑː	ɑ	*Bart*	long back low unrounded
ɒ	ɑ	*pot*	short back low rounded (in SSBE only)
ɔː	ɔː	*bought*	long back mid rounded
ʊ	ʊ	*put*	short back (near-)high rounded
uː	uː	*boot*	long back high rounded
ɜː	ɹ̩	*bird*	long central mid unrounded
ə	ə	*again*	short central mid unrounded
Diphthongs			
eɪ	eɪ	*bait*	
əʊ	oʊ	*boat*	
aɪ	aɪ	*bite*	
aʊ	aʊ	*bout*	
ɔɪ	ɔɪ	*boy*	
Centring Diphthongs			
ɪə	iɹ̩	*beer*	
eə	ɛɹ̩	*bear*	
ɔə	oɹ̩	*boar*	
ʊə	uɹ̩	*boor*	
Triphthongs			
aɪə	aiɹ̩	*buyer*	
aʊə	auɹ̩	*bower*	

TABLE 4.1   THE VOWELS OF SSBE AND GA

As well as these short vowels, English has long vowels. Long vowels are transcribed with a symbol a bit like a colon after, for example, [iː]. The long vowels in SSBE are not simply longer versions of the short vowels, however. There are five long vowels, which are found in the words *heed, hard, hoard, who'd* and *heard*. Only one of these is a front vowel, the one in *heed*. This is transcribed as [iː]. As you can see, this is a high front unrounded vowel, not just longer than [ɪ], but higher and fronter. It is also more tense. The vowel in *hard* is a back vowel, in fact, the unrounded version of the [ɒ] in *hod*. It is transcribed as [ɑː]. The third long vowel is back and rounded and low-mid, one line higher than in *hard*, and is transcribed as [ɔː]. The vowel in *who'd* is the high back rounded vowel written [uː]. Like [iː] this is also more tense than the short near-high, near-close vowel [ʊ]. Finally, there's the vowel in *heard*. This is a bit like a long version of schwa (see subsection 4.4.3), but it's slightly lower. You can see from the chart that there are two vowels just below schwa, rounded and unrounded. The vowel in English is the unrounded [ɜː].

So that deals with the short and long vowels, but English also has a lot of diphthongs, shown in figure 4.2. These are found in the words *bait, boat, bite, bout* and *boy*. The way these are transcribed doesn't necessarily reflect the pronunciation very accurately, so it's best to just think of them as conventional ways of transcribing the sounds in those words. As well as these five, there are four more that are called the **centring diphthongs**. This is because the second part of all of these is the schwa, the most central vowel. These diphthongs only appear in accents that are **non-rhotic**. If you look at table 4.1, you can see that SSBE has these centring diphthongs where GA, which is a rhotic accent, has a vowel followed by an *r* sound.

There are just two more vowels that I want to mention here: the two triphthongs. I said earlier that not everyone has triphthongs in their pronunciation, but if someone does, they are transcribed as [aɪə]} (*fire*) and [aʊə] (*hour*).

4.4.3   The mighty schwa

The schwa is a vowel which has a special status. In many ways it's quite like the glottal stop we saw in the consonant chapter. If you look at the IPA vowel chart, the schwa is the vowel right smack bang in the middle. It's a mid central vowel, not on either of the mid height lines. If you think of that vowel space as representing movement of the tongue from a neutral position to higher or lower and more or less forward in the mouth, then the schwa represents the position of the tongue without it moving at all. If you just open your mouth slightly and leave your tongue relaxed, this is the vowel that comes out. It doesn't take much effort to say a schwa, and that's why it has the special status it has.

What about lip rounding? If you look at the IPA chart again, you can see that the schwa is there in splendid isolation. It doesn't have a partner, so lip rounding is never a distinguishing feature. The schwa is technically neither rounded nor unrounded, as the lack of any articulatory effort means that either rounding the lips into a kiss shape or spreading the lips into a smile doesn't happen. The lips, like the tongue, remain neutral, unmoved.

The symbol for the schwa is [ə] – get used to it because you're going to see a lot of it later on!

So what is so special about the schwa? Well, as you'll see later on in the book, syllables and the vowels in them can either be stressed or unstressed (don't worry about exactly what that means – I come to that in chapter 7). When a syllable is stressed, the vowel in it will be pronounced with some degree of effort, moving away from that central neutral position. But when a syllable is unstressed, the vowel in it will often come out without much effort, and so it is a schwa. I talk a lot more about how, when and why this happens in English in chapter 7, but for now you just need to know that, when you hear a vowel which doesn't seem to involve any effort with either lips or tongue, it's probably a schwa.

4.5 Lexical sets

One way that linguists find to talk about the vowels of English without having to get too tied up in the precise articulation is by using what are called **lexical sets**. These were proposed by John Wells (1982) and are very widely used to refer to vowels. The idea is that it is possible to identify sets of words which always have the same vowel, even though the actual vowel may be different in different accents. Table 4.2 gives the lexical sets with their head word in small capitals and a few example words with each vowel.

For most people there are pairs of sets which have the same vowel, but that is the point. With these sets it is possible to talk about the differences between different accents. For example, most SSBE speakers have different vowels for BATH and TRAP, but speakers with northern English accents usually have the same vowel for those two sets. For some, the words in one or more of the sets might not have the same vowel (CURE is particularly problematic here). This is more of a problem, and shows that pronunciation changes over time and can affect different words in different ways. O'Grady (2013, p. 154) has a nice table with the typical vowels for all of the sets in 10 different accents of English.

4.6 Acoustics

Unlike consonants vowels can be very accurately identified and mapped by taking acoustic measurements. If you think about singing a musical note and holding the note for a time, it's a vowel sound that you'll hold the note on (usually). That means that it's possible to detect the tune, or pitch, of vowel sounds. It also means that it's possible to measure the frequencies of the sound. Now, the actual speech sounds you hear all have frequencies that can

Keyword	Example words
KIT	ship, kid, limp, myth, build
DRESS	step, neck, edge, shelf, friend, ready
TRAP	tap, back, badge, scalp, hand, cancel
LOT	stop, sock, dodge, romp, possible, quality
STRUT	cup, suck, budge, pulse, trunk, blood
FOOT	put, bush, full, good, look, wolf
BATH	staff, brass, ask, dance, sample, calf
CLOTH	cough, broth, cross, long, Boston
NURSE	hurt, lurk, urge, burst, jerk, term
FLEECE	creep, speak, leave, feel, key, people
FACE	tape, cake, raid, veil, steak, day
PALM	psalm, father, bra, spa, lager
THOUGHT	taught, sauce, hawk, jaw, broad
GOAT	soap, joke, home, know, so, roll
GOOSE	loop, shoot, tomb, mute, huge, view
PRICE	ripe, write, arrive, high, try, buy
CHOICE	adroit, noise, join, toy, royal
MOUTH	out, house, loud, count, crowd, cow
NEAR	beer, sincere, fear, beard, serum
SQUARE	care, fair, pear, where, scarce, vary
START	far, sharp, bark, carve, farm, heart
NORTH	for, war, short, scorch, born, warm
FORCE	four, wore, sport, porch, borne, story
CURE	poor, tourist, pure, plural, jury

TABLE 4.2   WELLS'S LEXICAL SETS

be measured, but vowel sounds (and some consonants, actually) have very regular patterns of loudness at certain frequencies. These patterns are down to the shape of the human vocal tract – remember how I compared it to a trombone earlier? All humans have basically the same shaped vocal tract and so produce sounds with similar acoustic properties. In the case of vowels, there are four bands of darker lines on the spectrogram that indicate greater loudness at or around four different frequencies. If you look at the spectrogram in figure 4.4, you should be able to see four lines of white dots. Those four lines are called **formants**. Two of these in particular are important for identifying vowels, the ones I have highlighted in white and marked as F1 and F2.

4.6.1 Formants

The four formants I mentioned are named F1, F2, F3 and F4, from the bottom of the spectrogram up. F3 and F4 determine the absolute pitch – that's the tune I mentioned – and F3 is important in identifying the kind of consonants we call liquids. They're not really relevant for identifying vowels. The really important ones here are F1 and F2. Formant F1 is the one nearest the bottom. It indicates how high or low a vowel is. If F1 has a relatively high value, then it is a relatively low vowel. You can see that the two [iː] vowels and [ʊ] have low F1 values because they are high vowels, but the low vowel, [ɑː], has a higher F1 value. Formant F2 is the next one up on the spectrogram. It indicates how front or back a vowel is. The higher the F2 formant frequency, the further forward the vowel is. The [iː] vowels have high F2 values because they are front, and [ʊ] has a lower F2 value because it is relatively back, but the [ɑː] has the lowest F2 value because it is fully back.

With these measurements it's possible to draw a graph, with the x-axis representing the F2 value and the y-axis representing the F1 value. These axes need to be reversed in order to plot the vowels according to their F1 and F2 frequencies in a way that matches the vowel chart as seen on the IPA chart. This chart can be used to plot the actual frequencies of vowels, rather than just listening or feeling how high or back a vowel is.

So how can you find out these frequencies? Fortunately there is software that will do it for you. One package that is used by a lot of linguists is Praat. This is freely available software that you can download to your computer

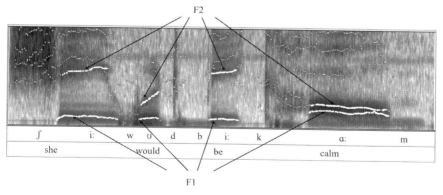

FIGURE 4.4 A SPECTROGRAM FOR 'SHE WOULD BE CALM' WITH FORMANTS MARKED

and use to measure formant frequencies. It's not exactly the most user-friendly piece of software, but once you get the hang of how to measure the formants, it's really quite easy to use. Appendix B gives a brief introduction to using it.

There are some other complications. I've talked about the height and backness of vowels being measured by the F1 and F2 formants, but what about lip rounding? Earlier, I said that back vowels (at least, non-low back vowels) tend to be rounded and front vowels tend to be unrounded. Although this isn't always the case, it does hint at a relationship between rounding and backness, and it is no coincidence that the F2 formant is the one affected by lip rounding as well as backness. Basically, a rounded vowel will have a lower F2 value than an equivalent unrounded vowel, so if there are two vowels that are identical except for their lip rounding, it will appear on the chart as though the rounded one is further back than the unrounded one.

So far in this section I've only talked about monophthongs. What about diphthongs? These can be mapped onto the vowel space as well, but you'll need to measure (at least) two points. That makes it a bit trickier. With a monophthong, you can choose a point to measure that is right in the middle, so you know it's not being influenced too much by the sounds either side of it. For a diphthong you need to measure the start and finish, but you can't go too close to the sounds surrounding the vowel. The standard way of doing this is to measure points in the whole duration of the vowel that are one fifth of the distance from the start and the end. Once you've measured these two points, you can plot them on the chart as an arrow going from the start point to the end point. This is what my student, Kate, had to do when she studied Mick Jagger's accent, because she was looking at three diphthongs. Figure 4.5 shows the measurements of all three diphthongs in all of the samples she measured. The grey lines show the vowel in GOAT, the black lines show the vowel in FACE and the grey dashed lines show the vowel in PRICE.

Additional reading

The articulation of vowels is covered in Carr (1999), chapters 3 and 4; Davenport and Hannahs (2010), chapter 4; and Roca and Johnson (1999), chapters 5 and 7. Roach (2000) covers English vowels in chapters 2 and 3, and go to Ladefoged and Johnson (2015), chapters 3, 4 and 12, for a more detailed look at articulatory aspects of vowels, and chapter 5 for acoustic measurement. Ogden (2009), chapter 5; Knight (2012), chapter 6; and Ashby and Maidment (2011), chapter 5, give introductions to vowel articulation and representation. Wells (1982) also gives a lot of detail about how the vowels are different in different accents of English.

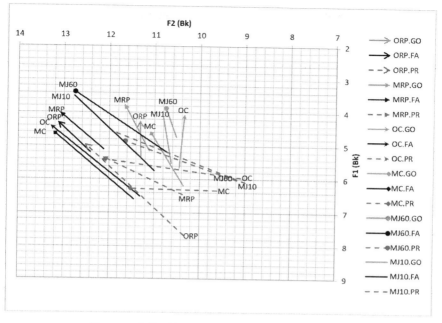

FIGURE 4.5 THE RESULTS OF THE JAGGER STUDY

Exercises

1. Which of these words contain a high vowel?

    sat   suit   got   meat   mud

2. Which of these words contain a low vowel?

    weed   wad   lard   lad   rude   sawed

3. Which of these words contain a front vowel?

    fed   caught   cat   kit   put

4. Which of these words contain a back vowel?

    mat   weep   coop   cop   good

5. Which of these words contain a rounded vowel?

    who   me   us   put   him   her

6. Each of the following sets of cardinal vowels has an odd one out. Identify the odd one out, and say how it is different from the others:

    (a) [a ɑ i ɔ e ɛ]
    (b) [e i a y u ø]
    (c) [ɯ i y e a œ]

7. Write an English word that contains the sounds given, and write the IPA symbols for the vowels:

   (a) Two different high vowels
   (b) Two different back vowels
   (c) Two different rounded vowels

8. Match the IPA vowel symbol on the right with the words on the left. **Note:** these are the vowels in the first syllable and from Standard Southern British English.

1	[iː]	a)	letter
2	[ɪ]	b)	looking
3	[ɛ]	c)	cheerful
4	[æ]	d)	latter
5	[ɑː]	e)	loser
6	[ɒ]	f)	laughter
7	[ɔː]	g)	supply
8	[ʊ]	h)	murder
9	[uː]	i)	later
10	[ʌ]	j)	laundry
11	[ɜː]	k)	lower
12	[ə]	l)	careful
13	[eɪ]	m)	liar
14	[əʊ]	n)	litter
15	[aɪ]	o)	litre
16	[aʊ]	p)	louder
17	[ɔɪ]	q)	lover
18	[ɪə]	r)	lottery
19	[ɛə]	s)	noisy
20	[ʊə]	t)	tourist

9. Transcribe the following words:

   (a) thief
   (b) judge
   (c) bath
   (d) book
   (e) ship
   (f) head
   (g) sign
   (h) cork

Part III

Putting sounds together

So far I've mostly talked about individual sounds, but sounds are rarely pronounced in isolation. Sounds combine to make words, and words combine to make phrases and sentences, and most of the time that's what people use to get meaning across. I'm now going to start looking at how sounds combine and what contributes to the way spoken language is used, in addition to the individual sounds. There are two levels of groups of sounds I cover in this part of the book: syllables and morphemes. Syllables are really important phonetically, but they don't, on their own, contribute meaning. Morphemes, on the other hand, are the smallest units of meaning in language. That is, words are made up of chunks that each carry a bit of meaning, and those chunks are called morphemes.

5   Syllables

5.1   What is a syllable?

Syllables are great! I am biased – my PhD was all about syllables – but they are interesting and they contribute a lot to how sounds are combined and used in language. What I love about syllables is that everyone who speaks a language has an idea of what a syllable is, and is usually able to identify how many syllables there are in a word, but when you try asking them anything detailed about syllables, they suddenly realise that they don't really know very much about them at all, or what they thought they knew turns out to be wrong. This is where you can show off to your friends with your superior linguistic knowledge (well, assuming that you have the kind of friends who are impressed by this sort of thing)!

The Oxford English Dictionary defines a syllable as 'a vocal sound or set of sounds uttered with a single effort of articulation and forming a word or an element of a word; each of the elements of spoken language comprising a sound of greater sonority (vowel or vowel equivalent) with or without one or more sounds of less sonority (consonants or consonant equivalents).' There are two different kinds of definitions here, separated by the semicolon. The first one offers different options at two points. It is a vocal sound or set of sounds – so it is a set which may consist of a single sound. It forms a word or an element of a word – so a word might consist of one or more syllables. All of this is fine, but it doesn't say anything about how to spot whether a word has one or more syllables, nor how many sounds might be combined into any particular syllable. The next part of the definition helps a bit more and gets into the more technical side. A syllable is an element of language that comprises a sound of greater sonority possibly combined with some sounds of less sonority. This is starting to look like something more helpful. It differentiates between vowels and consonants, but crucially it also allows for vowel-like and consonant-like sounds. As you'll soon see, it is important not to be fooled into thinking that vowels and consonants can be easily divided into two clearly distinct, mutually exclusive groups of sounds.

There have been various attempts by linguists over the years to define the syllable. It has been suggested that a syllable is equivalent to a chest pulse – referring to the idea of the amount of effort expended or the activity of the lungs. Other suggestions refer to volume or intensity of the sound, so that each syllable equates to a peak of volume. The second of these is closer to the OED definition, which is the most widely accepted definition of a syllable today. So a working definition of a syllable is that it is a set of (one or more) sounds including at least one vowel-like sound and possibly with other consonant-like sounds surrounding it.

5.2   How many syllables? (And how do you know?)

Quick quiz

1. How many syllables are there in the word *devoted*?
2. How many vowels are there?
3. How many syllables are there in the word *uncritical*?
4. How many vowels are there?

You may remember that I talked about the number of syllables in chapter 1. I asked you about some words where it wasn't obvious how many syllables there are. In the first question, I think it should be pretty clear that there are three syllables. Do you agree? What did you say for question 2? Hopefully you said three. That one is easy because there are three vowel letters and three vowel sounds. One of the apparent defining characteristics of syllables is that every syllable has one vowel. In the first example, this is true. There are three syllables and three vowels; each vowel is in a different syllable and each syllable has one vowel. What about the word in question 3? Hopefully you'll agree that it has four syllables. How many vowels does it have? Once again, ignore the number of vowel letters and think about how it sounds. If you said four, you may well be right, depending on exactly how you pronounce this word. If you said three, you probably pronounce it the way I do. I would pronounce this word [ʌŋkɹɪtɪkl̩]. It is possible, though that you might pronounce it something like [ʌŋkɹɪtɪkəl]. What's important for us in this chapter is that, in terms of the number of syllables, it doesn't matter. This tells us that it is not necessarily the case that a syllable has to have a vowel. This is what the definition meant by 'vowel-like'. If you say the word *uncritical* like I do, the [l] sound is the vowel-like sound in the final syllable.

What does it mean to be vowel-like? And how vowel-like does a sound have to be for it to be able to play this role in a syllable? The answer to that depends on the language, and in some cases the sound doesn't actually have to be very vowel-like at all. I look at this in more detail in section 5.4.1. It's understandable that the OED would want to make the definition something that ordinary (non-linguist) people will understand, but linguists need to be a bit more specific. It's not the case, in all languages, that every syllable has to have a vowel-like sound, but it is the case that, in a sequence of sounds, the ones that are the most vowel-like form the centres of the syllables. So how do linguists measure the vowel-like-ness of a sound? That's where the idea of **sonority** comes in.

5.3 Sonority

What exactly is sonority? It relates to the word *sonorous*, and they're both from the Latin word meaning 'sound'. That's not particularly helpful – I've said that the Greek word for 'sound', *phone* has been used in one way, and now I've said that the Latin word for 'sound' has been used in a different way. The way *sonorous* and *sonority* are used in English, they generally refer to specific qualities of sound, usually referred to as 'loud', 'deep' or 'resonant'. If you think about the quality, and especially the volume, of different speech sounds, it becomes easy to spot which are the sonorous sounds. Try singing a note to a vowel sound like [ɑ]. It's quite easy, isn't it? Now try singing a note to a nasal sound, like [m]. That's not too difficult either, although I'd probably call it humming rather than singing. Now try with a fricative, like [z]. How is that? It's not too difficult, I'd say, but try with [s] instead. That's trickier. Finally, try with the plosives [b] and [p]. If you managed that, well done! The reason the vowel is the easiest is that it's a resonant, or sonorous, sound. When I talked about the acoustic properties of vowels and consonants in chapters 3 and 4, I said that vowels have regular wave forms that represent resonance. Plosives and fricatives don't have any regular wave forms, but other consonants like nasals and approximants do. This all relates to their sonority. The other thing that is important here is voicing. Sounds that are voiced are more sonorous than sounds that are voiceless. The vowels, nasals and approximants are all voiced. The fricatives and plosives can be either voiced or voiceless and for these, the voiced ones are more sonorous than the voiceless ones. On a really simple level, it is possible to just measure the volume. Of course, the volume of speech can be controlled and changed, but all other things being equal, the loudest sounds are the most sonorous.

With all of this information, it's possible to define a **sonority hierarchy**. I start with a quite simple version:

Vowel > Approximant > Nasal > Fricative > Plosive

So far so good, but there are a lot of sounds I've talked about that are not included there, and a lot of finer grained distinctions that are going to be needed later in this chapter. Starting at the right-hand end with the voicing distinction I've already mentioned, voiced fricatives are more sonorous than voiceless ones and the same for plosives:

> Vowel > Approximant > Nasal > Voiced Fricative > Voiceless Fricative > Voiced Plosive > Voiceless Plosive

There are also different kinds of approximants. I talked about the [j] and [w] sounds being called 'semi-vowels' or 'glides'. The first of these alternative names gives a clue that they are actually very similar to vowels, and they do, indeed come next to vowels in the hierarchy:

> Vowel > Glide > Approximant > Nasal > Voiced Fricative > Voiceless Fricative > Voiced Plosive > Voiceless Plosive

It is also possible to distinguish between the other approximants that are found in English, [l] and [ɹ]. It might not be clear, but take my word for it that [ɹ] is more sonorous than [l]. There is one more group of sounds that I've ignored so far: the affricates. Where do you think they fit in this hierarchy? They have aspects of both plosives and fricatives, so it probably won't surprise you to hear that they come in between them in the hierarchy:

> Vowel > Glide > Approximant > Nasal > Voiced Fricative > Voiceless Fricative > Voiced Affricate > Voiceless Affricate > Voiced Plosive > Voiceless Plosive

There are also some other distinctions that can be made. I'm not going to put all of this detail in the hierarchy specification, but it is worth noting for future reference that vowels have their own sonority hierarchy relating to both height and centrality:

> Low [a],[ɑ] > Mid [e], [o] > High [i], [u] > Mid central [ə] > High central [ɨ]

Consonants also have further distinctions relating to place of articulation:

> Velar > Alveolar > Bilabial

If you think about these, it's actually quite natural. When you want to make a loud, resonant sound, you open your mouth wide. It makes sense, then, that vowels pronounced with the mouth wider open, that is the low vowels, are more sonorous than the high vowels. That's why it is easier to sing an [ɑ] than an [i]. It is also not surprising that consonants that involve the greatest degree of opening, where the tongue is raised towards the back of the mouth, are more sonorous than consonants pronounced with the lips closed.

The importance of sonority and the sonority hierarchy in syllables is reflected in a principle called the **Sonority Sequencing Principle** (SSP). This is a principle that applies across all languages (more or less – nothing's ever quite that simple!) and just says that sounds rise in sonority from the beginning of a syllable to the middle and fall in sonority from the middle to the end of a syllable. Basically it says that if you plot the levels of sonority on a graph, they should always form little hills, with an incline from the beginning of the syllable up to the middle and a descent from the middle down to the end of the syllable.

5.3.1   Peaks of sonority

With this way of ranking individual sounds in terms of their sonority, it is possible to identify, for any string of sounds, how many syllables there are. This is done by identifying the **peaks of sonority**. To see how this works, I'd like you to think about two words that have the same sounds but in a different order. The word *filled* can be transcribed [fɪld], while the word *fiddle* can be transcribed [fɪdl]. The same sounds, but the last two are in a different order. How many syllables do you think each has? Hopefully you said one for *filled* and two for *fiddle*. That seems a bit odd, given that they have the same sounds, with only the two consonants at the end being swapped. Why is that?

Peaks of sonority can be identified by mapping out the levels of sonority of the sounds in question. This can be done by using a simple graph, with the sonority hierarchy on the vertical axis. Figures 5.1 and 5.2 show the sonority curves for the two words. I've simply put a star for each sound in the box above it that corresponds to the type of sound and then joined the stars to see the shape of the curve.

What these diagrams show is that in each word, the vowel [ɪ] has the highest sonority. That is, it forms a peak of sonority. In the first diagram, this is the only peak, with the sonority rising from the left, or start, of the word and falling towards the right, or end, of the word. The diagram effectively looks like a hill, with the peak at the [ɪ] and the rest sloping nicely downwards. Now look at the second diagram. There is still a peak at the [ɪ], but there isn't

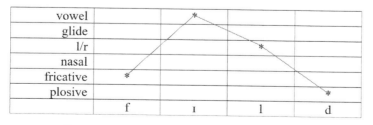

FIGURE 5.1   THE SONORITY CURVE FOR *FILLED*

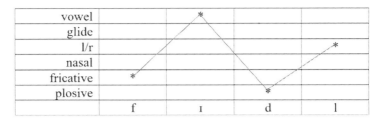

vowel			*	
glide				
l/r				*
nasal				
fricative	*			
plosive			*	
	f	ɪ	d	l

FIGURE 5.2   THE SONORITY CURVE FOR *FIDDLE*

a nice slope down towards the end of the word. There is a drop followed by another rise towards the [l] at the end. This gives two peaks of sonority, and that explains why *fiddle* has two syllables, whereas *filled* only has one.

When a consonant takes on this role in a syllable, that is, when it is deemed to be vowel-like enough, we call it a **syllabic consonant**. There's a special symbol for that in the IPA. It's a little vertical line underneath the consonant symbol. So *fiddle* is transcribed [fɪdl̩].

5.4   The different parts of a syllable and phonotactics

So far I've said that syllables have a vowel-like or more sonorous middle, with optional consonant-like, or less sonorous, sounds on either side. This leads to the other way that syllables can be defined – the structural definition. All syllables have to have that vowel-like sound, and that is called the **nucleus** or the **peak**. I'm going to use the term *nucleus*, but you'll find both, and they are completely interchangeable, although nucleus seems to be more popular now. The consonants on either side have different names: the ones that come before the nucleus are called the **onset**, and the ones that come after are called the **coda**. The nucleus and the coda together are called the **rhyme**. That means that syllables have the structure in figure 5.3.

The nucleus is quite straightforward. It's just the vowel or vowel-like sound at the heart of the syllable. It's the only part of the syllable that is obligatory – every syllable in every language has to have a nucleus. The onset may have one or more consonants, but if there is more than one, then those consonants have to rise in sonority from the start to the nucleus. The coda similarly may have one or more consonants, but in the coda the sonority has to fall. The rhyme is separate from the onset because it plays an important role. If you think about its name, that gives you a clue about one of the reasons it is important. Think about the words *cat* and *bat*, or the words *sing* and *ring*. These are pairs of words that rhyme. If you think about their syllabic structure, you can see that in each pair the words have an identical nucleus and coda, but different onsets. In *cat*, [kæt] the onset is [k], the

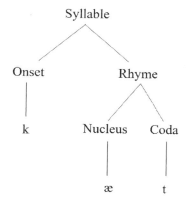

FIGURE 5.3 THE STRUCTURE OF THE SYLLABLE [kæt]

nucleus is [æ], and the coda is [t]. In *bat* the onset is [b], the nucleus is [æ], and the coda is [t]. So their nucleus and their coda are the same – that is the same as saying that their rhymes are the same, and that's the definition of words (or syllables) that rhyme.

These are the simple definitions of onsets, nuclei and codas, but each language has its own rules about how syllables are made up. These rules are the **phonotactics** of the language. The phonotactics of a language tells us what kinds of sounds can be in the nucleus and how many and what kinds of sounds can be in the onset and coda.

5.4.1 Nucleus

As I said earlier, this is most often a vowel, but it can be another sound, which is technically a consonant, but which plays the vowel role in a syllable. Sometimes there are two vowel-like sounds next to each other, and it can be a bit tricky to work out whether they are actually a single sound, that is a diphthong, which I talked about in section 4.2, or whether there are two separate vowels in two separate syllables. To help you think about the difference, try saying the words *tour* and *doer*. Some of you might pronounce *tour* to rhyme with *for*, but if you pronounce it [tʊə], then you probably still pronounce it as a single syllable with a diphthong. For *doer*, on the other hand, you probably pronounce it as two separate syllables, [du.ə]. Note here the full stop or period – that's what is used to indicate a syllable boundary. You won't always need to include that in transcriptions, but if you do, it just goes in between the syllables of a **polysyllabic** word, that is, a word of more than one syllable.

Different languages allow different kinds of sounds to form the nucleus of a syllable. All languages allow vowels, and some only allow vowels, for example, Hawaiian and Chickasaw (a North American language spoken in Oklahoma). The sonority hierarchy says a lot about which sounds can be syllabic consonants in different languages. For example, if you know that a language allows nasals, then you also know that it will allow all of the sounds that come above nasals in the sonority hierarchy. That applies to English. There are words in English like *button* [bʌt.n̩] and *sexism* [sɛk.sɪz.m̩] which have nasals as syllabic consonants, so it follows that English must also allow the glides [j] and [w] as well as the liquids [l] and [ɹ]. In fact, it's quite difficult to distinguish between the glides and their closely related vowels, [j]/[i] and [w]/[u], so glides aren't often transcribed as syllabic consonants.

5.4.2   Onset

Some languages, like Arabic, only allow syllables that have an onset. In those languages there are no words that begin with a vowel. Quite a lot of languages only allow one consonant in an onset (Arabic is also one of these, but there are lots, including Japanese and Hawaiian). Other languages, like English, allow more consonants in an onset. English allows up to three as well as syllables without an onset, so there are words like *at* [æt], *sat* [sæt], *spat* [spæt] and *splat* [splæt], all of which have just one syllable. English is quite unusual in allowing three, but there are languages, like Georgian, that allow up to six.

I said that the SSP states that the consonants in an onset should always rise in sonority. That means that there are words in English like *train* [tɹeɪn], where the [t] is the least sonorous sound followed by [ɹ], which is more sonorous, but we don't get words like **rtain* [ɹteɪn], where the more sonorous sound comes before the less sonorous one. There is a problem with English, though, that is seen in all syllables that have three consonants in the onset. Look at the list of words below that all have three consonants in their onsets:

strength	[stɹɛŋθ]
spray	[spɹeɪ]
scream	[skɹiːm]
splat	[splæt]
sclerosis	[skləɹəʊsɪs]
squash	[skwɒʃ]
skew	[skjuː]

What do you notice about all of these words? They all begin with [s]. That's the only possible sound at the beginning of an onset of three consonants in English. Can you work out what the second consonant has to be? In all of these words the second consonant is one of [p], [t] or [k]. Can you work out what they all are? In chapter 3, I said that those sounds are all the voiceless plosives of English. Now what sounds can be in the third consonant position? There are four different ones in these words: [ɹ], [l], [w] and [j]. They are the glides and liquids, or together, the approximants. It's not a coincidence that these words all have these patterns of sounds in their onsets. Try to think of any English word with three consonant sounds in the onset that has any other combination. I guarantee that you won't be able to. There is a very strict rule about three-consonant onsets in English which says that it must consist of [s] followed by a voiceless plosive followed by an approximant.

There's something very inconvenient about these three-consonant onsets in English, though. Look at the sonority graph for one of the words, *splat*, shown in figure 5.4

Can you see that there is a problem here? A syllable is supposed to have a single peak of sonority, but in the word *splat* there are two. The first sound, [s], has higher sonority than the following sound, [p], so the onset does a little dip before rising to the nucleus. I'd love to be able to tell you that there's a simple explanation for this, but I'm afraid there isn't, and it's one of those phenomena that linguists propose theories about and discuss. Probably the most popular explanation is that sounds like the [s] here are not really a proper part of the syllable. They are kind of optional extras that can be stuck on the front, but they don't have to follow the SSP. That does cause some problems when you start looking at what syllable structure tells us about what happens to different sounds when they are in different parts of a syllable, but I'll ignore that for now. What is interesting is that this isn't just a weird English thing – the same thing happens in other languages. Whatever specific explanation is given for it, it is at least only one sound that misbehaves like this in English. Only [s] can do it. Note, though, that

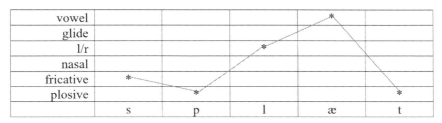

vowel				*	
glide					
l/r			*		
nasal					
fricative	*				
plosive		*			*
	s	p	l	æ	t

FIGURE 5.4 THE SONORITY CURVE FOR *SPLAT*

it's not only onsets with three consonants. The same sonority problem occurs with [spæt].

There are lots of possible words of English that are not actual words. That is, you can make up new words which obey the rules of the language. *Plenk* is an example of this. As far as I know, it is not an actual word of English, but there's nothing to stop it becoming a new word if someone chooses to assign a meaning to it. *Lpenk*, on the other hand, is not a possible word of English. Why do you think that is? If you look at the sonority, you can see that the [l] and the [ɛ] both form peaks of sonority, but that doesn't necessarily mean that it isn't a possible word. Why can't it just be a word with two syllables? The answer is that although English is perfectly happy to have consonants (the ones that are sonorous enough) as the vowel-like sounds in syllables at the ends of words, it doesn't allow them at the beginnings of words.

5.4.3   Coda

Codas are like the mirror image of onsets. Where onsets have to have rising sonority, codas have to have falling sonority. Codas also have some sounds that can be added that mess up the nice neat sonority hills. In the case of codas, it can be a few different sounds, although curiously they are all alveolar sounds in English.

There are quite a few languages that don't have codas at all. All their syllables just have a nucleus and (possibly) an onset. That isn't just a random coincidence either. There appear to be strong tendencies for languages to prefer consonants in onsets to consonants in codas. That not only has an impact on what kinds of syllable are found in monosyllabic words, but also affects how to work out where the syllable boundary is in words of more than one syllable. The highest number of consonants in a coda is probably six, which is allowed in Georgian, although it has been suggested that eight consonants are possible. I'm not going to go into the arguments about this question – it has something to do with morphology which I talk about in chapter 6, but imagine pronouncing a syllable that has eight consonants after the vowel! You can see why there aren't many languages that allow that many, can't you?!

5.5   Syllable weight

One important role that rhymes have is deciding whether a syllable is considered **heavy** or **light**. In the next chapter I talk about stress, which is related to **weight**, but syllable weight is something that can be determined completely separately from stress. A heavy syllable is one which has at least two slots in its rhyme. What that means is that it must either have a coda with at least one consonant or a long vowel or diphthong. I suspect you might be starting to think I'm deliberately trying to confuse you here with long and short vowels and whether they count as single sounds. I'm not – it's just a bit confusing because there are two different ways of deciding whether something counts as one sound or two. Earlier I was only concerned with whether the sounds should be classified as a single entity that had potentially more than one quality. That meant that diphthongs (and affricates) were counted as single sounds. Now length is important, and that means thinking about diphthongs as well as long vowels differently from single consonants and short vowels. So when you're transcribing long vowels and diphthongs, you should be thinking about them as single entities and using the appropriate symbol or pair of symbols. When you're thinking about syllables, and especially syllable weight, though, you need to think of long vowels and diphthongs as occupying two slots. This means that a syllable with a short vowel in its nucleus and a single consonant in its coda, such as *cat* [kæt], has two slots in its rhyme, and so counts as a heavy syllable. The first syllable in a word like *become* [bɪ.kʌm] only has a short vowel and no coda, so it is a light syllable. A word like *be* [biː] has a long vowel, and so it is heavy. Note that you won't find any (content/lexical) words in English that have only one syllable that is a light syllable.

A brief aside on moras ...

There's another way of talking about syllables, and especially syllable weight, that uses a thing called a **mora**. Moras (or morae) are quite difficult to define, which is why I've stuck this bit in a separate box which you can ignore if you want to. When a syllable has a long vowel, a diphthong, or at least one coda consonant, it's called a heavy syllable. Otherwise it's a light syllable. One definition of a mora is simply 'Something of which there are two in heavy syllables and one in light syllables.' A long vowel or diphthong has two moras; a coda consonant has one; and a short vowel has one. Onset consonants don't count as moras at all. So in a syllable with a short vowel and a consonant, there are two moras. In a syllable with just a short vowel, there is only one. Unfortunately, it isn't always that simple. It seems to work differently in different languages. A coda consonant apparently represents a mora in English and Japanese, but not in Irish Gaelic. Even in English, it's not quite clear whether the same is true of stressed and unstressed syllables. So moras are a bit tricky and can't be reliably defined across all languages. They can be helpful for talking about syllable weight and stress, which I look at in the next chapter, but what really needs to be said about syllables, especially in English, can be said without worrying too much about moras. If you're interested in Japanese poetry, on the other hand ...

5.6   Where do they begin and end?

Identifying the peaks of sonority shows how many syllables there are in a word. It also shows which sounds are playing the role of the 'vowel-like' sounds referred to in the definition at the start of this chapter. What it doesn't always show, though, is which consonants (or 'consonant-like' sounds) belong to which syllable. In the examples earlier there was only one syllable, so this problem didn't arise, but think again about one of the words in the quick quiz: *uncritical*, [ʌŋkɹɪtɪkl̩]. I have already said that there are four syllables, and I identified three vowels and one vowel-like, or syllabic, consonant, that form the centre of the syllable. Have a look at this on a sonority graph, shown in figure 5.5.

This clearly shows the four peaks of sonority, but which of the consonants belong to which sonority peak or syllable? There are three consonants all together after the [ʌ]. There could be a syllable boundary at any of four possible positions:

1. [.ŋkɹ]

2. [ŋ.kɹ]

3. [ŋk.ɹ]

4. [ŋkɹ.]

The first of these would mean a first syllable with just a vowel. That's not a problem in itself, but look at what it would mean for the second syllable. Starting from the [ŋ], there isn't a nice slope up towards the vowel [ɪ], but a slope down and then back up. That doesn't fit with the nice slopes in the single syllable, and indeed it shows that the syllable boundary can't be there. (Remember, that's only allowed if the first consonant is [s] and it's at the beginning of a word.) The same thing applies to the last possibility. There isn't a nice smooth slope down, but a drop and then rise to the [ɹ]. So that possibility can be counted out as well. That leaves two possibilities. Do you have any instinct for which one is correct? Do you think you say [ʌŋ.kɹɪtɪkl̩] or [ʌŋk.ɹɪtɪkl̩] (ignoring the other syllable boundaries for now)? It is usually said that the first one is the right one.

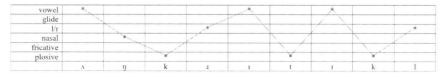

FIGURE 5.5   THE SONORITY CURVE FOR *UNCRITICAL*

What's happening here is something called the **Maximal Onset Principle** (MOP) or the **Onset First Principle**. This is a principle which applies in English, and indeed in most languages of the world, which says that, as much as possible, consonants should belong to onsets rather than codas. When there is a word with a cluster of consonants in the middle, as many of those consonants as possible go in the onset of the following syllable rather than in the coda of the preceding syllable. When I say 'as many as possible', it isn't always possible to stick all of them into the onset. The SSP says that consonants can only go in an onset together if they rise in sonority up to the nucleus. There are actually other constraints on what can be in an onset, and they are different for different languages. In English, I said that there are certain sounds that can be in first, second and third position in an onset. This is because it isn't enough to have a rise in sonority across the onset. There has to be a certain degree of rise in sonority. That means that even in a cluster with rising sonority the consonants might not actually be a legal onset of English. There are some other more specific constraints as well. For example, the sound [ŋ] never appears in an onset. That's nothing to do with sonority, or anything strictly phonetic at all, it's just an accident of history.

So when deciding where the syllable boundaries are, there are two principles to think about – the maximal onset principle (MOP) and the sonority sequencing principle (SSP) – as well as any language specific constraints on what can be in an onset. Think back to the example word: [ʌŋkɹɪtɪkl]. I identified the peaks of sonority, giving the nuclei. Looking now at the various consonants, they can be assigned to onsets or codas. Starting from the end of the word, the [k] before the [l] isn't in a cluster, so the question is whether [k] is a legal onset of English. Is it? Yes, there are lots of words that have a [k] as their onset, like *cat* [kæt], *kick* [kɪk] and *count* [kaʊnt]. So the [k] goes in the onset of the final syllable. Now for the [t] before the [ɪ]. Once again, there are lots of words that have [t] as the onset, such as *top* top, *tooth* [tuːθ] and *teach* [tiːʧ], so [t] here is also in the onset of the third syllable, not the coda of the second. Finally, look at that cluster of consonants: [ŋkɹ]. They can't all go in the onset of the second syllable for two reasons. The sonority falls from the [ŋ] to the [k] before rising to the [ɹ], so it's not a consistent rise up to the nucleus. Also, it's got [ŋ], which I said earlier can never be in an onset in English. So the [ŋ] must go into the coda of the first syllable. That then leaves [kɹ]. Is that a legal onset of English? Yes, it is. Again, there are words that start with those two sounds, such as *crust* [kɹʌst], *cream* [kɹiːm] and *crystal* [kɹɪstl]. So those two consonants can go in the onset of the second syllable. That gives the syllable structure in figure 5.6.

There are some cases where it seems that maximising the onset, according to what is allowed in the language, is more important than sonority. The

A brief aside on the history of [ŋ] in English . . .

The sound [ŋ] in English is a bit weird. Not weird as a sound, but in where it can appear. It's also weird in the way people, as native speakers rather than linguists, tend to think about it. There's an important relationship with the spelling here. There are three nasal sounds in English, [n], [m] and [ŋ]. Back in the depths of history, there were only two nasal sounds that could distinguish meanings, [n] and [m]. The [ŋ] only appeared before the velar sounds [k] and [g]. Gradually, English started to lose a lot of the consonants at the ends of words. You can still see where some of these consonants were, because they are still there in the spelling. Words like *lamb* [læm] and *plumb* [plʌm], for instance. If you have a Birmingham accent or one of the nearby accents, you might still pronounce the [g] in words like *sing* [sɪŋg], but most English accents pronounce it [sɪŋ]. The nasal is more sonorous than the plosive, and so it can only come in that order in a coda, not in an onset. Because all of the [ŋ]s in English were originally only before plosive consonants, this means that they were all in codas, so there are still no words with [ŋ] in an onset. There's no phonetic reason why there shouldn't be a word like [ŋæt]. It's perfectly possible to pronounce it, and other languages do, but English doesn't. This history of the sound [ŋ] means that there isn't a separate letter for it, so English speakers think of the letter pair *ng* as representing the sound. In fact, the *g* here is really representing a [g] sound that used to be pronounced but isn't any more, just like the *b* in *lamb*, but the *g* is now the only way to tell us that [sɪŋ] is pronounced differently from [sɪn]. What this means is that speakers of English still often think that there is a [g] sound there, so when they hear someone who pronounces words like *eating* with [n] at the end instead of [ŋ], they think they're dropping a [g] sound. They're not – they're just using an alveolar nasal [n] instead of a velar nasal [ŋ]. It might not seem very important, but if it is viewed as dropping a consonant, it's easy to think that it's a kind of laziness. If it's viewed as substituting one consonant for another, it seems less like laziness and more like just an accent difference. Of course, there are all sorts of prejudices about different accents that have nothing to do with actual linguistic differences and everything to do with the associations between the accents and the people who speak them, but this is a very specific area where even well-meaning linguistics students can sometimes get confused about whether there is a [g] at the end of a word. Just check that you understand the difference between [sɪn] and [sɪŋg], and know which one you say when you're trying to do a transcription.

word *extra* [ɛkstɹə], for example, could be syllabified as either [ɛk.stɹə] or [ɛks.tɹə]. Sonority would suggest the second, but actually the first seems to be correct. This shows that allowing the onset to be [stɹ], which is legal at the start of a word, trumps following the sonority sequencing principle.

5.7 Syllables and spelling

Syllables are very important in phonology, but what about spelling? In English there isn't any way of representing syllables in writing. The only way in which syllables might be explicitly represented in writing is if syllable boundaries are used rather than morpheme boundaries as possible places to hyphenate words if they go across more than one line. However, some languages and writing systems use syllables as the main unit that is represented by a character. Japanese has a rather complex system that has three different levels – *kanji*, which are like Chinese logograms (and indeed historically come from Chinese), *romaji*, which are based on the Roman alphabet and are especially used for borrowed words, and *kana* (the two systems known as *hirigana* and *katakana*), which are based on syllables. Each possible syllable of Japanese is represented by a character, and these characters are combined to form words. Think about what I said about Japanese syllables earlier. Can you think of why it is possible for Japanese to have this kind of system, whereas it would be impractical for English?

Japanese only allows syllables that consist of a consonant followed by a vowel. That means that the number of possible syllables is the number of consonants multiplied by the number of vowels. There are nine consonants that can appear in the onset of a (native) Japanese syllable, and five vowels, but three of the logically possible combinations don't occur, so that leaves 42 syllables. There are a few more characters, one for each vowel on its own and one for when a [n] appears in a coda (that is the only consonant that is allowed in the coda of Japanese syllables). So in total, for the *hiragana* system there are 48 characters. Now think about English. What kinds of syllables are allowed in English? There are at least 24 consonants in English and around 21 vowels (I'm not going to go into the arguments about how

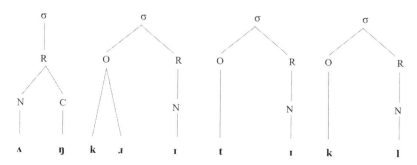

FIGURE 5.6 THE SYLLABIC STRUCTURE OF *UNCRITICAL*

they should be counted here). Even if English only had syllables like in Japanese, that would lead to a lot more possible syllables than Japanese has. But what do you know about English syllables? I've said that it's possible to have up to three consonants in the onset and up to four consonants in the coda of syllables in English. Now, it's certainly true that not all combinations of consonants are possible, but even so, if you start multiplying, it soon becomes clear that you would need a lot of different characters to represent every possible syllable of English. (I did some sums, and by the time I'd considered all of the syllables that are consonant-vowels (CVs), vowel-consonants (VCs) or consonant-vowel-consonants (CVCs), I'd already got to 12,579!)

Another type of syllabic writing system is the Korean system, called **hangul**. This is particularly interesting because it uses characters that can be broken down into the sounds in different parts of the syllable. Each character is a kind of box, with different parts representing the sounds of the initial, medial and final parts of the syllable. The writing system thus explicitly shows both the individual sounds and the syllables.

Syllables are relevant in English spelling as well. I look at this in more detail in the next chapter when I talk about what happens when morphemes are joined together, but think about the words *mat* and *matting*. You will remember that a monosyllabic word has to be heavy. That is, if it has a short vowel, then it has to have a consonant as a coda. In *mat*, the nucleus is the short vowel [æ] and the coda is [t]. In *matting*, however, there are two syllables. The consonant [t] should be the onset of the second syllable, but that would leave a stressed syllable with a short vowel and no coda, and that's not allowed. So that means that the [t] is said to be **ambisyllabic**. Ambisyllabic consonants in the pronunciation are considered to be part of both syllables. They are both in the coda of one syllable and the onset of the next. This is represented in the spelling in English by having two written consonants. The word *mating*, on the other hand, doesn't need two consonants. That's because the vowel is a diphthong, so the syllable is heavy and does not need a coda consonant. The consonant can be solely the onset of the following syllable, rather than ambisyllabic, and so there is only one written consonant. This is a case where syllable structure is represented directly in English spelling.

There is another curious relationship between English spelling and syllable structure. Remember that the least sonorous sounds appear at the edges of syllables, and the most sonorous in the middle. The least sonorous sounds are the plosives, and they are generally represented in English spelling with the letters *p, t, k, b, d, g*. The most sonorous sounds are the vowels and they are usually represented in English spelling with the vowel letters, *a, e, i, o, u* (and combinations of them). What do you notice about the letter shapes here? All of the plosive letters have either an ascender or a descender – a bit that goes above or below the main letter position. None of the vowels do. This means that written syllables tend to have a particular shape. They are taller at the edges than they are in the middle. This doesn't completely work across the sonority scale. Nasals are obligingly like vowels with no ascenders or descenders, but *l* is annoyingly tall for such a sonorous sound. However, it is a pattern that works more often than not.

Additional reading

Gussenhoven and Jacobs (2005), chapter 10, gives a more theoretically oriented introduction. Kenstowicz (1994), chapter 6, and Blevin's chapter (6) in Goldsmith (1996) give fairly advanced discussions. More about syllabic spelling can be found in Sampson (2015). The Korean and Japanese writing systems are described in more detail there and also in Coulmas (2002). Knight (2012), chapter 8, has a good introduction to syllables.

Exercises

1. Here are some one-syllable words. Divide them into:
   (a) words with a zero onset
   (b) words with one *C* in the onset
   (c) words with two *Cs* in the onset
   (d) words with three *Cs* in the onset

act	bald	blame	chain	crisp	dog
drip	dwarf	faith	edge	flaw	ice
home	grasp	lend	ox	screw	skin
snow	split	spring	squat	stretch	twin
world	use				

2. Draw syllable structure trees for the following (and work out the transcription for b and c):
   (a) reason [ɹiːzn]
   (b) computer [???]
   (c) carbuncle [???]

3. The following are the pronunciations of some words by a two-year-old American child. Look at the initial consonant clusters, and think about how they compare to the adult pronunciation of these words.
   (a) What constraints on syllable structure are there in the speech of this toddler?

(b) How are words 'repaired' to conform to these constraints? Try to account for the data as precisely and accurately as possible.

stop	[sɑp]	spoon	[pun]
sleep	[sip]	small	[mɑl]
step	[sɛp]	sky	[kaɪ]
stay	[se]	school	[ku]
stand	[san]	skip	[kɪp]
snack	[sak]	swipe	[waɪp]
slide	[saɪd]	spring	[pɪŋ]
stretch	[sɛt]	scrub	[kʌb]
plate	[pet]	please	[pis]
truck	[tʌt]	cracker	[kaka]

6   Morphemes and words

Chapter 5 showed that sounds can combine together to make syllables that are important for how the individual sounds behave as well as aspects like stress and tone. What I haven't really addressed so far is how to combine sounds into chunks that actually have a meaning. When it comes down to it, after all, it would be pretty pointless making sounds if they didn't carry meaning. When I talk about combining sounds to make meanings, the first thing that comes to your mind is probably the **word**. Words obviously have meanings which, can be found in dictionaries. Words are important for how sounds behave, but they are not the smallest unit of meaning. The smallest units of language that carry their own meaning are called **morphemes**. Now, in a lot of cases in a language like English, a word is a single morpheme. Words like *cat, idea, happy, swim* and *swallow* are all **monomorphemic**, that is, they only have one morpheme, and that's true of about a quarter of English words. The words *cats, ideas, unhappy, swimmer* and *swallowed*, on the other hand, all have two morphemes. In this chapter I'm going to look at the ways morphemes combine to make words and what implications this has for the pronunciation and spelling. The world of morphology is not really difficult to understand, but there are a lot of different terms to explain what happens to words. I'm going to explain those terms, because it does make it easier to explain some of the things that happen in the phonology, and also because every self-respecting linguist should know about morphology.

6.1 Morphology

Quick quiz

1. What is the difference between *cat* and *cats*?
2. Which bit of the word means 'plural'?
3. What about *man* and *men*?
4. How many different bits with different meanings are there in the word *internationalists*?

First of all, I want you to think about what the bits of language I'm talking about here really are. I've said that words are made up of morphemes, and that a morpheme is the smallest unit of meaning in language, but what does that really mean? The first three questions in the quiz address this issue. Did you say that *cat* is singular and *cats* is plural? That's the difference between the two words, which means that the answer to question two must be that the *s* at the end means 'plural'. Linguists say that this word has two **morphemes** and often write the word with a '+' in between the morphemes: *cat + s*. So there are two morphemes here, but they're not the same kind of thing. The first morpheme, *cat* is the most important part as it carries the most information. It tells you what I am talking about. The *s* just adds more information to tell you that there is more than one. The core morpheme in words like this is called the **root** morpheme. The *s* is an **affix**. Another way to distinguish between these kinds of morphemes is with the terms **free** and **bound** morphemes. Free morphemes can stand on their own, or be a word in their own right, and don't have to be attached to another morpheme. So *cat* is a free morpheme. Bound morphemes, on the other hand, have to be attached to another morpheme and can't be a word on their own. So the *s* is a bound morpheme. Roots (in English, at least) tend to be free morphemes, whereas affixes (in all languages) tend to be bound morphemes.

A brief aside on cranberry morphs

The distinction between free and bound morphemes is a useful one, and it applies to most morphemes fairly reliably. However, as is so often the case in linguistics, there are morphemes that don't fit neatly into these categories. One of these is a particular type of morpheme called a **cranberry morph**. The reason for the rather colourful name is that the word *cranberry* includes a good example of one. To explain this, you need to think about other kinds of berries. There are lots of different berries in English, including *blueberry, blackberry* and *strawberry*. These words are all made up of two words that are recognised as free morphemes. That is, *blue, black* and *straw* can be used on their own, with their own meanings. For these types of berry, the words are made up of two parts, and each part can be a word on its own. Now think about the word *cranberry*. This obviously has the same *berry* part as the others, but what does *cran* mean? In terms of its etymology, the *cran* comes from the German word for *crane*, but it's not the case that the word *cranberry* is actually *crane + berry*. So can *cran* be used on its own? Well, actually there is a word *cran*, but it means a basket for catching fish, and as well as being apparently completely unrelated to the berry, it's also probably not a word that most English speakers are familiar with. Are there any other words that have this particular *cran*? No, there aren't. So that gives the morpheme *cran* a special status. It can't be called a free morpheme because it isn't used on its own (in this sense). But it doesn't really make sense to call it a bound morpheme either, because it only appears in that one word. And that's why it's called a cranberry morph.

Affixes come in different forms as well, depending on where they attach. When an affix is attached to the beginning of a root, it is called a **prefix**. There is a prefix in *un+happy*. When an affix is attached to the end of a root, it is called a **suffix**, and that's what the *s* is in *cats*. These are the most common types of affix. English has mostly suffixation, but some prefixation. In other languages, however, there are other kinds of affix. **Infixes** are inserted inside a root. English doesn't have proper infixes, but they are sometimes used in casual speech. The song 'Wouldn't It Be Lovely' from *My Fair Lady* has the example *abso-bloomin-lutely*. (This is called 'expletive infixation' because when this happens in English, the thing that is infixed is always an expletive or a swear word. This example is one of the more polite ones!) Finally, there are **circumfixes**, which go around the outside of a root. This is basically the same thing as simultaneously prefixing and suffixing.

Now have a look back at question 3. What is the difference between *man* and *men*? Once again, it is singular and plural, but this time there isn't a plural suffix like in *cats*. What is it that shows that it is plural? You might say that it's the *e*, and in a way you'd be right. However, the *e* here doesn't act like the *-s* suffix. When you see an *e* in the middle of a word, you don't immediately think that it's plural, as you can see with words like *bed*, *mess* and *pen*. What's happening here is something that we call **ablaut**. There are a few words in English that use ablaut, or vowel changes, to indicate things like plural (*man/men, goose/geese, mouse/mice*) or different tenses (*swim/swam/ swum, meet/met, sit/sat*). The reason these words behave like that in English is down to some peculiar phonological processes that used to happen in Old English and which have left their mark on the morphology. I look at this in more detail in chapter 13.

Clitics are another type of bound morpheme, but they're a bit different from affixes. Affixes always attach themselves to the same kind of word. A plural affix will attach to a noun, but a past tense affix will attach to a verb. Clitics also attach to words, but they aren't as picky about what they attach to. It's probably best if I give you an example. The possessive marker in English is usually written as *'s*. I'm going to ignore the issue of what to do when a word ends with *s* for now (as in *Charles'* or *Charles's*). If I ask you where you can add a possessive marker, you'll probably say on a noun, and that's where most of them end up. So you might talk about *the cat's whiskers* or a *dog's dinner* or *Lee's book*. Apart from the apostrophe, it looks just like a plural suffix really, doesn't it? Now think about a slightly more complex example. If I want to talk about a cat that belongs to a president I can say *the president's cat*. But if I want to specify which president, I can say *the president of France's cat*. Now the possessive marker has moved away from the president and onto *France*. It hasn't changed the meaning in terms of who owns the cat (if anyone can ever really own a cat). You don't think that the cat is owned by France; you know that it's owned by the president, and yet the marker is not on the word *president*. This is what we call a clitic. Phonologists are interested in what happens to the sounds that make up morphemes when they get put together, and they're often not too bothered about whether they are free morphemes, bound morphemes, affixes or clitics, but it can be important when they start thinking about the difference between what happens inside words and what happens between words.

6.2   Inflectional versus derivational morphology

There are two different types of morphology: **inflectional** and **derivational**. The examples in questions 1 to 3 in the quick quiz are cases of inflectional morphology. Inflectional morphology, also sometimes known as **grammatical morphology**, roughly speaking involves adding information that is grammatical, such as number (singular or plural) and tense (present or past). Derivational morphology, on the other hand, involves making new words, and is sometimes called **word formation**. To make new words, either the meaning (making *happy* into *unhappy*) or the word class (making *happy* into *happiness*) changes. The last question shows that both inflectional and derivational morphology can occur in a single word. The *s* at the end is an inflectional ending, but the other bits are all derivational. I look at exactly what's happening in section 6.2.2.

6.2.1   Inflectional morphology

I said earlier that inflectional morphology involves grammatical information. That means things like marking nouns as singular or plural (*cat* vs *cats*), marking verbs for tense (*swallow* vs *swallowed*) and marking adjectives for comparative (*big* vs *bigger*). In different languages there are a lot of different kinds of inflectional morphology. If you know anything about Latin, you might be aware that Latin nouns have a lot of different endings for different cases (nominative, accusative, genitive, dative and ablative) which English doesn't have. German also has different cases for nouns, including nominative, accusative, genitive and dative. The key point to remember with inflectional morphology is that it doesn't fundamentally change the meaning or change the word class. There are some complications in that, actually, but those are something for a grammar book, not a phonological one.

Inflectional morphology in English is interesting for phonologists because of what happens to the pronunciation when inflectional affixes are added. For example, the plural *-s* that is added to nouns is always spelled the same, but is pronounced differently depending on the stem it's added to. Think about the pronunciation of the words *cats, dogs* and *horses*. Can you hear that the sound at the end of *cats* and *dogs* is different? What is the difference? If you remember how to describe consonants from chapter 3, you should have noticed that the first is voiceless and the second is voiced. Can you work out why this might be? What is different about the ends of the stems *cat* and *dog*? If I transcribe them, you can see that [kæt] ends with a voiceless consonant, and [dɒg] ends with a voiced consonant. So the affix is voiceless when it follows another voiceless sound, but voiced when it follows another voiced sound. What about *horses*? That's a little bit more complicated. The stem is pronounced [hɔːs], which ends with a voiceless sound, so why is the plural not [hɒːss]? Try saying that. It just sounds like a long [s] at the end, rather than two separate sounds, doesn't it? That's why it's pronounced [hɔːsɪz]. It doesn't only happen with [s], but with all sibilant consonants.

6.2.2   Derivational morphology

Going back to the quick quiz, have another look at the last question. The example word in question 4 of the quick quiz has both inflectional and derivational morphology. It is made up of five morphemes in total: *inter+nation+al+ist+s*. The root (free morpheme) is *nation*. This can be a word in its own right. The other parts can't, so they are bound morphemes, or affixes. The morphemes *inter-, -al* and *-ist* are all derivational affixes, one prefix and two suffixes. They change either the meaning or the word class (or both). The word can be built up a bit at a time:

1. Root = nation
2. Add *-al* = national (derivation)
3. Add *inter-* = international (derivation)
4. Add *-ist* = internationalist (derivation)
5. Add *-s* = internationalists (inflection)

So there are roots, which are like the foundation stones of words, and a variety of different kinds of affixes that can be added to the root. The other important term needed here is **stem**. A stem is what inflectional affixes are added to. In a word like *cats*, the root *cat* is also its stem. In a word like *internationalists*, the root is *nation*, but its stem is *internationalist*.

I said earlier that inflectional affixes can be affected by the stem that they attach to, and the same goes for derivational affixes. Think about the words *undone, unbridled* and *unkind.* They all have a stem and the derivational prefix, *un-.* How is the prefix pronounced, do you think? If you say them normally, you should have something like [ʌndʌn], [ʌmbɹaɪdəld] and [ʌŋkaɪnd]. Can you hear that the nasal is pronounced differently in each of them? Can you see why each nasal sound is the way it is? Each time, the nasal has the same place of articulation as the consonant that follows it. This is like the voicing in the plural suffix. I come back to these examples frequently in the rest of the book.

6.2.3   Compounding

Derivational morphology can be a bit confusing because it is often divided again into **derivation** and **compounding**. Derivation involves taking a single root and adding affixes to it. Compounding, on the other hand, involves taking two roots and putting them together. An example of compounding is *blackbird*, when it refers to a particular species of bird rather than one that just happens to be black.

Compounding is a little bit different from other forms of derivation. Crucially it involves more than one root. When derivational affixes are added to a root, it is always written as a single word with no spaces and usually no hyphens. (There are a few exceptions to that, but mostly just because of slightly strange orthographic conventions. For example, you might write *co-operate* with a hyphen, because having two *o*'s together is confusing and could be interpreted as the *oo* pronounced as [uː] or [ʊ].) Compounds, on the other hand, can be written as single words, with hyphens or with spaces between them. Have a look at the following list:

- blackbird

- greenhouse

- long-term

- follow-up

- food poisoning

- lone wolf

These are six examples of compounds formed from two roots. Two of them are (normally) written as single words, two with hyphens and two as separate words. These differences are not important for this book, but compound words are interesting because of the way stress behaves in them. I talk about this in section 7.3.2.

One thing that is important here is that once an inflectional affix has been added, nothing more can be done to the derivational morphology. Any word that has an inflectional affix in English is therefore not a stem, but a fully inflected word. This is supposed to be a universal rule, although there is some evidence that it isn't always obeyed.

A brief aside on trouser presses and toothbrushes ...

There are some words in English that are always plural, like *trousers, scissors, shears* and so on. These are usually things that are considered as always coming in kind of pairs, but where you never want to refer to each individual part of the pair. You've probably never had cause to refer to one part of a pair of scissors, and even though these are often referred to explicitly as a *pair of scissors, pair of trousers* and so on, they are not really thought of as consisting of two identifiable separate parts. So if I ask you what a scissor is, you'll probably look at me a bit strangely. These kinds of words are especially interesting for what they show us about how morphology works. I said just now that derivation has to happen before inflection. The flip side to this is that only uninflected stems can be used in derivation. So compounding, which is a kind of derivation, should happen to uninflected stems. With words like *trousers* and *scissors,* this means that the singular form is used, even if it's never used on its own. So the thing that is used to press trousers is called a *trouser press*, not a *trousers press.* Another type of example is the *toothbrush.* It's not quite the same kind of thing as the *trouser press*, because the word *tooth* in the singular is used. What's interesting here is that the brush that is used to clean teeth generally cleans several teeth at a time. Unless you are unfortunate enough to only have one tooth, it's unlikely that your brushing will be confined to one tooth at a time. That makes it interesting that it's called a *toothbrush* and not a *teethbrush.* There are some exceptions to this. Way back in 1983 there was a paper discussing this which referred to 'Jets fans' and 'Raider Rooters' (Churma, 1983). These are terms used to refer to the supporters of two sports teams, the teams being known as *the Jets* and *the Raiders.* One of the terms for the supporters obeys the rule to use uninflected forms (*Raider Rooters*), but the other one doesn't. I may be mistaken, but this seems to be a thing that is happening in English more often now ...

6.3 Words

Right at the start of this chapter, I said that morphemes rather than words are the smallest units of meaning. That doesn't mean that words are unimportant, though. Words are the cornerstones of language in many ways. You can look them up in dictionaries, and they have a special status in written language, where they are separated by spaces. In spoken language, however, the status of words is a bit less obvious. You may remember from the spectrograms of actual speech in chapters 3 and 4 that there is no obvious break between words in normal speech. That doesn't mean that there are no pauses in normal spoken language, and indeed, usually when there are pauses, it is in between words rather than in the middle of a word. However, separate words are not marked reliably in speech. This begs the question of whether words are really interesting in terms of pronunciation at all. There is a sense in which morphemes are really more important, but words are also important. The key point is that spoken language involves creating new sentences on the fly by choosing the appropriate words and organising them into a grammatical sentence of the language. What this means is that the pronunciation of any particular word may be affected by its position in the sentence. Sometimes there are changes that happen to sounds only when they are at the beginning or end of a word. Sometimes it's difficult to tell whether it's word, morpheme or syllable that's important.

What happens in the words I talked about, where one of the sounds in an affix is different depending on the stem that it attaches to, can also happen when words are combined into phrases. In spoken language at normal speed, words tend to run together, and sounds affect other sounds around them. I say a lot more about this in chapter 13.

In chapter 1, I talked about different types of writing systems. One type of system which doesn't reflect pronunciation directly is the logographic system. I said then that there are a number of languages, especially East Asian, that have this type of writing system. One of the interesting questions about this type of writing system is whether it genuinely reflects words or morphemes. It is sometimes claimed that these languages (e.g. Mandarin, Vietnamese) don't have any morphology, that they only have monomorphemic words. If that is the case then there is no issue about whether a character represents a morpheme or a word, as every morpheme is a word and vice versa. However, that claim is not taken very seriously by linguists, and the generally accepted view is that characters represent morphemes which can be combined into words.

So what exactly was the point of this diversion into the world of morphology? Well, there are three main reasons why it's important to know this. The first is that, as you start looking in more detail at how sounds behave in real speech, you have to take into account what happens around morpheme boundaries and word boundaries (that is, where morphemes and words begin and end). The second reason is that morphology and phonology are actually very closely connected. There are often alternations that appear to be a part of morphology in a language today that are the result of alternations that used to be part of the phonology. It's also the case that doing morphology (as speakers, not linguists, that is, producing the words) is where the interesting aspects of the phonology of a language can most easily be seen. The final reason is that understanding what's happening in the morphology can often reveal a lot about why English spelling isn't a nice neat reflection of its pronunciation. One of the fundamental principles of English spelling is that, as far as is reasonably possible, it tries to spell morphemes in the same way if they are related, even when they are not pronounced the same. That's why there are sets of words like *electric* [ɛlɛktɹɪk], *electricity* [ɛlɛktɹɪsɪtiː] and *electrician* [ɛlɛktɹɪʃən]. The second *c* in these words is pronounced differently, because of processes that have happened after adding suffixes, but they are all spelled the same so that they can be recognised as coming from the same root.

Additional reading

Lieber (2015) is a good, up-to-date introduction to morphology. Although they are quite old now, Matthews (1983) and Bauer (1984) are excellent places to learn more about morphology. Knight (2012) has a chapter (16) on liaison.

Exercises

1. In the following words, work out how many different morphemes there are and whether they are inflectional or derivational:
   (a) discontented
   (b) unwarily
   (c) kindnesses
   (d) unhappier

2. What are all of the inflectional affixes that can be added to nouns and verbs in English?

3. How many derivational affixes can you think of that are used in English?

4. For each of the following derivational affixes, state what kind of words it can attach to and what its function is:
   (a) -ness
   (b) un-
   (c) -age
   (d) pseudo-

Part IV

Rhythm and tune

The last part explained how sounds are combined into syllables, morphemes and words. This part now looks at other aspects of pronunciation that affect syllables rather than individual sounds. Two main types of thing affect syllables in particular: stress and tone. They roughly mean the volume and the pitch, although it can be a bit more complex. In the first chapter of this part, I look at stress. I then look at tone in chapter 8. The final chapter in this part looks at length and duration. These three things together are called prosody. The word *prosody* comes from the Greek, meaning 'song sung to a tune'. The original Greek word refers much more to tone or pitch than to stress or rhythm, but in modern linguistics it is used to mean all aspects of the pitch and rhythm of an utterance.

7 Stress

7.1 What is stress?

Quick quiz

1. Which word do you think has the most prominence when you say 'You need to walk home'?
2. How do you know?
3. Are there any other differences in prominence among the other words?
4. Can you imagine saying the sentence with different words being more prominent?
5. How does that affect the meaning of the sentence?

I have mentioned stress at a few points already in this book. For example, I said that vowels in unstressed syllables often become schwa ([ə]). I also talked a bit about the difference between the English verb and noun *record*: [ɹɪ'kɔːd] versus ['ɹɛkɔːd] in Chapter 1. But what exactly is stress? In many ways, it's a bit like the idea of syllables. Just as speakers of a language know how many syllables there are in a word, without really knowing exactly what a syllable is, they usually know which syllable in a word is stressed, but they don't really know what that means.

Think about what you mean when you talk in a non-linguistic way about stressing something. 'He stressed how important it was,' for example. This means that he made sure that his audience heard or understood how important it was. Stressing a syllable is similar in that it is made more noticeable. Question 2 asks about what makes a syllable or word more stressed. You may have mentioned it being louder or the speaker using more effort in articulating the stressed word, and that's getting to the right answer. There are actually three characteristics that make a stressed syllable more noticeable:

- It is louder (or has more intensity).

- It has a higher pitch.

- It is longer.

The loudness or intensity is probably the most important and most consistent way of picking out the stressed syllables and also relates to the idea of effort. Pitch is affected by tone and intonation, which I look at in the next chapter, and duration also depends on exactly what sounds make up the syllable to some degree.

Stress is used in language in different ways, some of which you're probably more aware of than others. Going back to the non-linguistic way of talking about stressing things, one of the ways stress is used is really very much the same idea. Which word did you say was the most stressed (or prominent) when you said the sentence in question 1? I would expect that for most people the answer would be *home*, so this word would sound a bit louder, have the highest pitch, and its vowel would sound longer than the other words. This is probably the most neutral way of saying the sentence, athough, as you can see below, other ways of stressing it give slightly different meanings. What did you answer for question 4? Apart from the word *to*, it is possible to imagine situations when any of the other words might actually have the greatest prominence. Say the sentence again, with each of the words in italic stressed:

- *You* need to walk home.

- You *need* to walk home.

- You need to *walk* home.

- You need to walk *home*.

In one sense they all have the same meaning, but giving the different words stress means that they appear to be responses to different questions or situations. The first one seems to make the point that it is 'you' and not 'me' or someone else that needs to go home. The second seems to say that this really is a necessity rather than just something that might be a good idea. The third one seems to contrast with another way of getting home – you need to walk, not drive (because you have had too much to drink or you need the exercise maybe). And the final one, the one that I said is probably the most neutral, emphasises the direction – you need to go home, not to work or the pub, for example. These all have the effect of making a contrast between what's being said and another option. That's why this kind of stress is known as **contrastive stress**. Stress is used in this way to make one particular idea more prominent or to draw attention to it. When it is used in this way, absolutely any word can be stressed. It's more unusual to stress a function word, but it can be done in certain situations. Imagine you're talking to someone who is not a native speaker of English and who says, 'I need for go home.' You might well correct them by saying 'You need *to* go home.' These situations are quite rare, but it shows that it is possible to stress any word when using stress contrastively.

7.2 Lexical stress

The example sentence had words that only had one syllable (they are **mono-syllabic**). When words have two syllables (**disyllabic**) or more (**polysyllabic**), there are different patterns of stress within those words. Content (or lexical) words all have stress on (at least) one syllable. If they are monosyllabic then they have stress on that syllable. If they have more than one syllable, then they have one syllable that is stressed more than any of the others. However, in words with several syllables, there is not simply one stressed syllable and a lot of unstressed ones. There may be more than one syllable that has some degree of stress. Linguists therefore talk about **primary** and **secondary** stress. Just like in the examples in the previous section, it is possible to place stress on different syllables within a word for contrastive purposes, but all words have a neutral or default stress pattern.

7.2.1   Primary and secondary stress

The syllable with primary stress is the one that has the greatest prominence or loudness. It's not always easy to work out where the primary stress falls, especially if you try just saying the word out loud over and over. One reason for this is that, as I just showed, it is possible to stress any syllable for contrastive purposes. Let's start with some fairly easy ones with only two syllables.

rabbit	giraffe
table	lagoon
butter	delight

Can you hear that the words in the first column have the primary stress on the first syllable, but the words in the second column have it on the second? What you might not be aware of is that the words in the second column are all words that have come into English from other languages. That's not surprising because the normal stress pattern in English is for the first syllable in disyllabic words to be stressed. This doesn't necessarily help the typical native speaker, who might not be aware of the etymology of many words.

Spotting where the primary stress is can be even more tricky with a long polysyllabic word with secondary stress as well. Think about a word like *information*. Which syllable do you think has the primary stress? Did you say the third one? If so, you're right. Did you maybe say the first one? If so then don't worry. You're not right about the primary stress, but you are right that it is stressed. In this case there are two syllables that are both stressed, but one of them is stressed a bit more than the other: the third syllable has **primary stress** and the first has **secondary stress**. The other two syllables are unstressed. So you can see now that syllables aren't just stressed or unstressed – there are at least three different degrees of stress.

In all of these examples, the syllables that are unstressed share some characteristics that are different from the stressed syllables (whether they have primary or secondary stress). The unstressed syllables tend to have reduced vowels. That is, the vowels are usually short, so no long vowels or diphthongs, and often become more central and lax. The epitome of a reduced vowel is the schwa, and that's what is often found in unstressed syllables, but it isn't always a schwa. The high lax vowel [ɪ] is also often found in unstressed syllables of English and sometimes other vowels, depending on other factors like exactly where in a sentence the syllable/word is and how quickly or slowly you are speaking. Another thing that is associated with unstressed syllables is light syllable weight, but, as I explain shortly, this relationship can work in both directions.

Transcribing stress is fairly simple. There are two little vertical lines, one at the top which is placed before a syllable with primary stress and the other at the bottom, which is placed before a syllable with secondary stress. The word *information* is transcribed: [ˌɪnfəˈmeɪʃən].

7.2.2   Stress and syllables

The relationship between stress and the structure of syllables is very important and works in both directions. Sometimes the position of stress in a word is determined by the nature of the syllables. Most often this involves the idea of syllable weight (section 5.5). For example, some languages have a rule that says that if a syllable is heavy, then it can be stressed, but if it is not, then the stress has to move to a syllable that is. On the other hand, syllables that are unstressed tend to be reduced, either by the vowel becoming shorter, or by the loss of consonants in the onset or coda, or sometimes by all three. This means that because a syllable is unstressed, it can become light.

There is another important interaction between stress and syllable structure and that affects the syllabification process, and in particular which consonants go in onsets or codas. Chapter 5 showed that the spelling of words with consonants between vowels in the middle often have a double consonant, which reflects the fact that that consonant is ambisyllabic. This, I said, was because a stressed syllable has to be heavy in English, and so where a stressed syllable has a short vowel, it needs a consonant in the coda, even if it has to share that consonant with the following onset. So when you're deciding what the syllable structure of a word is and where the syllable boundaries are, you need to consider not just the sequence of sounds but also where the stress falls in the word.

7.2.3 Rules (or guidelines) for stress assignment in English

Some languages have really simple stress rules. For example, in Icelandic the primary stress always falls on the first syllable. In English it isn't that simple. This is clear because there are words that have different primary stress depending on whether they're a noun or a verb, like *record* as I mentioned earlier. There are some rules, though, that apply to a lot of nouns, verbs and adjectives in English. These rules don't apply to all words. Some stress is affected by the morphology, which is described at the end of this section. Other words have different stress patterns because they come from different languages.

Look at the following set of nouns (some of these are proper nouns, or names, but they still count):

co.ró.na	[kə.ˈɹəʊ.nə]	re.lá.tion	[ɹɪ.ˈleɪ.ʃn̩]	com.mú.ter	[kə.ˈmjuː.tə]
neu.ró.sis	[ˌnjuː.ˈɹəʊ.sɪs]	h.orí.zon	[hə.ˈɹaɪ.zn̩]	po.tá.to	[pə.ˈteɪ.ˌtəʊ]
as.bés.tos	[ˌæs.ˈbɛs.tɒs]	Co.lúm.bus	[kə.ˈlʌm.bəs]	di.sás.ter	[dɪ.ˈzɑːs.tə]
ap.pén.dix	[ə.ˈpɛn.dɪks]	e.níg.ma	[ɪ.ˈnɪg.mə]	pro.jéc.tile	[pɹə.ˈʤɛk.ˌtaɪl]
ás.te.risk	[ˈæs.tə.ɹɪsk]	dís.ci.pline	[ˈdɪ.sɪ.plɪn]	pén.ta.gon	[ˈpɛn.tə.gən]
Cá.na.da	[ˈkæ.nə.də]	Gér.ma.ny	[ˈʤɜː.mə.ˌniː]	cá.pi.tal	[ˈkæ.pɪ.təl]

They all have three syllables (they're trisyllabic). These words show that not all nouns have the primary stress on the first, second or third (final) syllable. In fact, though, none of them has the stress on the final syllable. Now have a look at the ones that have the stress on the first syllable (the last two rows). In particular, look at the second syllable of all of these words. Can you see what they all have in common? Every one of these second syllables is a light syllable. That means that they have a short vowel and no coda. Now look at the second syllable of all the words that have stress on the second syllable. Can you see that they are all heavy syllables? That means that they have either a long vowel (or diphthong) or a coda. This is crucial in explaining the stress patterns of English nouns. The rule here is as follows:

1. Ignore the final syllable.

2. If the penultimate syllable is heavy, put the stress there.

3. If the penultimate syllable is light, put the stress on the one before it (the antepenultimate syllable).

I've only looked at trisyllabic words here, because it's easier to see the pattern like this, but it works for words of more than three syllables, too. Think about *information* [ɪn.fə.ˈmeɪ.ʃn̩]. Ignore the final syllable and look at the one before it. Is it heavy or light? It has a long vowel (in fact a diphthong, which is the same thing in this context), so it is heavy. That means it takes the primary stress. Now think about *hippopotamus* [hɪ.pə.ˈpɒ.tə.məs]. Again, ignore the final syllable and look at the penultimate one. Is it heavy? No, it has a short vowel and no coda, so it's light. That means the stress is on the syllable before, [pɒ], even though this syllable is also light. I should say here that it doesn't work for disyllabic words because there isn't an antepenultimate syllable to shift the stress to if the penultimate syllable is light, and there are disyllabic nouns with stress on the final syllable, as in the first set of examples (compare *rabbit* and *giraffe*).

Verbs behave a little bit differently, although not very. Look at the following list of verbs:

de.láy	[dɪ.ˈleɪ]	pro.dúce	[pɹə.ˈdjuːs]	com.póse	[kəm.ˈpəʊz]
ar.ríve	[ə.ˈɹaɪv]	vi.bráte	[ˌvaɪ.ˈbɹeɪt]	re.vérse	[ɹɪ.ˈvɜːs]
re. jéct	[ɹɪ.ˈdʒɛkt]	as.síst	[ə.ˈsɪst]	at.tráct	[ə.ˈtrækt]
pro.nóunce	[pɹə.ˈnaʊns]	in.dúlge	[ɪn.ˈdʌldʒ]	in.vólve	[ɪn.ˈvɒlv]
é.qual	[ˈiː.kwəl]	rát.tle	[ˈræ.tl̩]	con.sí.der	[kən.ˈsɪ.də]
é.dit	[ˈɛ.dɪt]	fí.nish	[ˈfɪ.nɪʃ]	mí.mic	[ˈmɪ.mɪk]

These are mostly only two syllables. Some have the stress on the first and some on the second syllable. It's not quite as easy to see the pattern here, because you have to ignore not the whole of the last syllable, but just the final consonant (if there is one). If the final syllable, without its final consonant, is still heavy, then it gets the stress; otherwise, the syllable before it, the penultimate one, gets the stress. So this is the rule:

1. Ignore the final consonant (if there is one).

2. If the final syllable is still heavy, then stress it.

3. If the final syllable without its final consonant is light, then stress the one before it.

For adjectives there is a mixture of the noun and verb behaviour. Some follow the verb rule:

decrépit	ecstátic	periódic	distínct
ináne	obscéne	corréct	profóund

Some follow the noun rule (e.g. those that end in *-al*, *-ous*, *-ant* and a few others):

crítical	bárbarous	vígilant	dífficult	
suicídal	horréndous	malígnant	éarnest	pérfect

Another complicating factor which these adjective examples shows us is morphology. Chapter 6 explained that some words have affixes: prefixes and suffixes. In English, there are three different kinds of affix when it comes to stress. The first set has no effect on the stress, so the stressed syllable in the stem still has the stress when one of these suffixes is added. The second moves the stress to a different syllable of the stem, and the third attracts the stress itself, so the suffix is stressed, not any of the syllables in the stem. Inflectional suffixes, that is the ones that are there for grammatical reasons like plurals on nouns or past tense suffixes on verbs, never affect the stress. The derviational suffixes, the ones that change the meaning or word class of a word like the ones that turn verbs into nouns, have different effects.

The group of suffixes that don't affect the stress (**stress-neutral suffixes**), in addition to the inflectional ones, include the following:

-ness e.g. ópen – ópenness

-ly e.g. courágeous – courágeously

-hood e.g. néighbour – néighbourhood

-ment e.g. góvern – góvernment

The group of suffixes that moves the stress within the stem (**stress-shifting suffixes**) includes the following:

-ic e.g. átom – atómic

-ity e.g. génerous – generósity

-ous e.g. cóurage – courágeous

-ian e.g. Ítaly – Itálian

In all of these, the stress moves to the last syllable before the suffix, that is, to the last syllable of the stem.

The final group is the one that attracts the stress to the suffix. These are called **auto-stressed suffixes**. Here are some examples of these:

-ee réfuge – refugée

-ese Pórtugal – Portuguése

-esque Káfka – Kafkaésque

-ette báchelor – bachelorétte

Compound words also have different stress patterns, which is compared to stress in phrases in section 7.3.2. So you can see that the way English words get their primary stress is a bit complicated, but not completely random. It gets even more interesting when you start putting words together, though.

7.3   Phrasal stress

I've talked about how stress affects words individually and that it can be used contrastively when those words are combined into phrases and sentences. Whenever speakers utter a phrase or sentence, the relative stress of the individual words results in patterns of stress across the whole phrase. The patterns across these phrases are a bit more complex than just identifying the primary stressed syllable in each content word. Individual words within a phrase can take more prominent stress, so that even the stressed syllables in the other words are less stressed than the stressed syllable in that word. Think back to the examples of sentences with different words stressed at the start of this chapter. It should be clear from those examples that each of the words in italics can be stressed more than the other words. Those examples simplified matters by using only monosyllabic words. The lexical stress described in the previous section is something that is inherent to each word or entry in the dictionary. But stress is used at the level of the phrase or sentence as well, and for a variety of functions. The examples at the start of the chapter show one of those functions – to make a particular word more prominent. This is considered a discourse function, because it has the role of making a particular part of the message appear more important. This is a special use of stress, but even in phrases and sentences that are spoken without any special prominence being given to particular words, there are certain patterns of stress that go beyond the stress patterns of individual words.

7.3.1   Metre and metrical feet

Think about this sentence, spoken normally, with no particular stress on any word:

> Lee and Sandy left together.

There are five words here. The second word, *and*, is a function word and so has no lexical stress. *Lee* and *left* are monosyllabic and so have lexical stress on their only syllable. *Sandy* has stress on the first syllable and *together* has the primary stress on the second syllable with the other two unstressed. That means that there are eight syllables with an alternating pattern of stress

(I've marked stressed syllables here as S for strong and unstressed as W for weak – you'll see why in a bit):

Lee	and	San	dy	left	to	ge	ther
S	W	S	W	S	W	S	W

If you've studied any poetry, this is something you might have come across as **metre**. Poetic metre is described in terms of **trochees** and **iambs**. These refer to pairs of syllables, one of which is strong and the other of which is weak. In a trochee the strong syllable comes first, and in an iamb the strong syllable comes second. The line above, then, is made up of trochees – pairs of syllables where the strong one comes first, followed by a weak one. This is quite normal for English, which is generally considered to be a **trochaic** language. That doesn't mean that it doesn't have iambs at all, but that it tends to have more trochees. A language that has more iambs is known as an **iambic** language. You may remember that in the examples of disyllabic words with initial or final primary stress I gave at the start of the chapter, I said that the ones that had stress on the second syllable (the iambs) were all borrowed words, not native English ones. These pairs of syllables, trochees and iambs, are called **metrical feet** (or sometimes just **feet**).

What is also important here is that it's not the case that each of those S syllables has the same amount of stress. Why not? Well, within a phrase it isn't just adjacent syllables that can be paired up; those pairs, or feet, can be combined into pairs at the next level and upwards. Once again, each of those pairs has a strong and a weak member. In English, in the higher levels the weak comes before the strong. This can be represented in a **metrical tree** like the one in figure 7.1. If you follow the line up from one of the syllables, you can see that each syllable has a different pattern of Ss and Ws. The strongest syllable in the whole phrase, the one with the greatest stress, is the one that

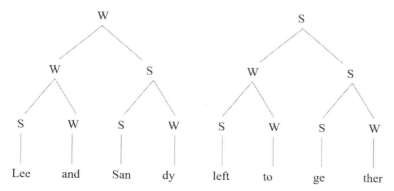

FIGURE 7.1 METRICAL TREE STRUCTURE FOR 'LEE AND SANDY LEFT TOGETHER'

FIGURE 7.2   METRICAL GRID FOR 'LEE AND SANDY LEFT TOGETHER'

has Ss all the way up, which is the second syllable of *together*. The weakest or least stressed is *and*. Now, it's quite possible that when you say this you don't have the same pattern of stress, because there are lots of reasons for using stress patterns differently, but that is the normal way of stressing it. What this shows is that, far from just the simple stressed/unstressed contrast, it is possible to distinguish a range of subtly different levels of stress in the syllables of a whole utterance.

Another way of representing the same information is what we call **metrical grids**. In a grid, rather than a tree, an asterisk is placed above the strong element in each pair at each level. The same sentence is shown in a metrical grid in figure 7.2. With the tree you have to follow the lines up from each syllable to get a path to the top with Ss and Ws. With the metrical grid you can see a bit more directly the relative stress of different syllables by looking at the number of asterisks above each one. However, this representation doesn't give the same amount of detail. For example, there is no distinction here between *and* and *to*.

7.3.2   Phrases and compounds

One of the interesting uses for stress is to indicate whether a pair of words is supposed to be understood as a single word made up of two other words or whether it should be understood as separate words. Let me explain with a few examples. Think about the following:

blackbird	black **bird**
greenhouse	green **house**
light-year	light **year**
darkroom	dark **room**
fun park	fun **park**

Can you see that the ones on the left are compounds – single words made up of two other words? A *greenhouse* is different from a *green house*, because it's made of glass, and not necessarily (in fact not very likely to be) green. A *green house*, on the other hand, is a house which is green. The different position of the stress is helpful in these cases to show whether it is a compound or not, but it's not done deliberately for that purpose. You remember that English is a trochaic language, so words tend to have the stress on the first syllable. That means that when two monosyllabic words are combined into a disyllabic word, the first one tends to take the primary stress. In phrases, on the other hand, the stress tends to fall on the most important word grammatically. In grammatical terms, this is called the **head** of the phrase. In a noun phrase (like 'the black cat' or 'the cat on the table') the head is the noun, *cat*, and so this takes the greater level of stress. This is the third reason for assigning stress – the grammatical or syntactic assignment. As with most ideas about stress in English, there are exceptions, such as compounds like *downstream*, where the stress is on the second part.

So you've now seen the three different and interacting ways in which syllables within words get their different levels of stress:

1. Lexical stress determines which syllable in a polysyllabic word is (by default) stressed.

2. Syntactic stress determines which word in a phrase is (by default) stressed.

3. Discourse stress determines which word in an utterance is stressed for contrastive purposes.

Because these three considerations can require different stress placements, the actual stress pattern of a particular utterance in a particular context can be quite complex to work out. In general, though, lexical and syntactic stress do not conflict, because the syntactic considerations tell you which word has the greater stress, but the stress of individual syllables within that word is not affected. Discourse stress, on the other hand, trumps both of the other two. It is possible to stress absolutely any syllable within any word for contrastive discourse purposes.

7.3.3   Timing

The patterns of phrasal stress I talked about were actually a bit simplified. In English there isn't always a nice, neat pattern of strong and weak syllables. Think about the sentence:

> I talked to the telephone company.

This has a stress pattern that goes W S W W S W W S W W. How on earth are you supposed to pair these off into feet? You could take one of three approaches. First, you could just determinedly pair the syllables up from the left to the right and just deal with the fact that you'll have not only a mix of iambs and trochees but also feet with two weak syllables. Second, you could assume that a foot can have three syllables if two of them are weak. Or, third, you could assume that some of those (weak) syllables just don't get combined into feet. The first of these isn't allowed – I'm afraid it's part of the definition of a foot that it has to have one strong and one weak syllable. The second is sometimes allowed and has a special name – a **dactyl**. That's a foot with one strong and two weak syllables. However, a lot of linguists don't like allowing them either. So that leaves the third option. As English prefers trochees, you start off with an **extra-metrical** syllable, that is, one that doesn't join with a friend to make a foot. You then make a trochaic foot with the S and W and then have another extra-metrical syllable. You keep doing this, with three trochaic feet and four extra-metrical syllables. This all might seem a bit opaque and above all, rather pointless. Well, it isn't really. Apart from the fact that it's useful to understand patterns of stressed and unstressed syllables, if you happen to fancy trying your hand at writing poetry or songwriting, there are also other aspects of pronunciation that are affected by these patterns. One of those is timing.

Languages are described as being either syllable-timed or stress-timed. What that means is that, for some languages, the time between each syllable is the same, regardless of how many sounds there are, how long the vowel is or how stressed it is. In other languages, there is the same time between stressed syllables regardless of how many unstressed syllables there are in between the stressed ones. English is an example of a stress-timed language. French is an example of a syllable-timed language. You probably aren't consciously aware of this, even if you speak both languages pretty fluently. It is, though, the kind of thing that will make someone whose native language is English sound a bit foreign when they try to speak French (and vice versa). The fact that it's so hard to pick up on these kinds of very subtle accent differences is what makes it really difficult to speak a second language without any foreign accent at all. It's also important to note that, if those extra-metrical syllables (or dactyls, if you choose to consider them as three-syllable feet) in the example sentence were not allowed, the timings of English and French would actually be the same because there would always be one unstressed for each stressed syllable, so it would be a case of looking at the timing of pairs of syllables in English and single syllables in French, which would effectively be the same thing. It has been shown that this is something of a simplification, but the main thing to take from this is that different languages have different patterns of stress in their sentences.

7.3.4   Other effects of stress

Chapter 13 looks in more detail at what happens to sounds as a result of whether the syllable they're in is stressed. For now I just want to focus on one particular thing that happens as a result of stress (or rather, lack of it): the reduction of function words. I noted earlier that function words, except in very special circumstances, are unstressed. However, they can still have a bit more or less stress because of where in a sentence they appear or other factors like how slowly and carefully you are speaking. Because of this, there are strong and weak forms of most function words. That includes, for example, articles, conjunctions, pronouns and some prepositions. Table 7.1 shows the strong and weak forms of a few English function words. There are two main changes that happen to these words when they appear in their weak form: there are different vowels and there are fewer consonants. The vowels mostly reduce to schwa in these forms, as they often do in unstressed syllables. Consonants may be lost either at the beginning or the end, and especially when they appear in clusters. In some cases a whole syllable is lost, although most of these words are monosyllabic anyway.

If you look at the example of *and*, you can see that in its strong form it has a vowel (nucleus) and two consonants (coda). In its weak form, it just has the consonant *n*. Now, chapter 5 explained that a sonorant consonant, which [n] is, can be the nucleus of a syllable, so just having this sound left still gives a legitimate syllable. Another thing to note is that sometimes, when people want to represent the pronunciation more accurately, they might spell *and* just as *n*, although this only usually happens in specific types of phrase, and the loss of the other two sounds is indicated with apostrophes, as in *fish 'n' chips*.

Word	Strong Form	Weak Form
the	[ði:]	[ðə]
a	[ɛɪ]	[ə]
and	[ænd]	[(ə)n(d)]
of	[ɒv]	[əv]
to	[tu:]	[tə]
him	[hɪm]	[(h)ɪm]
her	[hɜ:]	[(h)ə]

TABLE 7.1   STRONG AND WEAK FORMS OF FUNCTION WORDS

Additional reading

There are good introductory chapters about stress in Carr (1999), chapter 8; Spencer (1996), chapter 7; Roca and Johnson (1999), chapters 11 and 12; and Kennedy (2017), chapter 10. Ladefoged and Johnson (2015) focuses on the phonetics of stress in chapter 5. Knight (2012), chapter 8; and Davenport and Hannahs (2010), section 6.2, also have descriptions of stress. For English stress, Roach (2000) has three chapters, 10–12, and Spencer (1996), chapter 8; also addresses the specifics of stress in English.

Exercises

1. Transcribe the following words, marking primary stress:
   (a)   i. diplomat
          ii. diplomacy
          iii. diplomatic
   (b)   i. billow
          ii. below
   (c)   i. strategy
          ii. strategic
   (d)   i. notorious
          ii. notoriety

2. Each of the following words has regular stress, according to the principles outlined in the chapter. For each, mark the stressed syllable and explain why stress falls on that syllable.
   (a) delinquent (n)
   (b) equity
   (c) furnish
   (d) arrive
   (e) demure
   (f) picturesque
   (g) proverbial
   (h) compact (v)
   (i) advantageously

3. Draw metrical trees and grids for the following phrases.
   (a) Kim and Sandy left the table.
   (b) He cannot live, I hope, and must not die.
   (c) How the chimney sweeper's cry.

4. Limericks are (usually comic) poems with a particular pattern of metre and rhyme. An example of a limerick follows. Work out what the pattern is in terms of number of syllables, the patterns of feet and the rhyme pattern.

> There was an old man with a beard
>
> Who said, 'It is just as I feared!
>
> Two owls and a hen
>
> Four larks and a wren
>
> Have all built their nests in my beard.'

8 Tone and Intonation

The last chapter looked at how words or syllables can be stressed, that is, given more prominence. One of the ways that stressed syllables differ from unstressed syllables, I said, is that they tend to have higher **pitch**. So what is pitch, and how else is it used in spoken language?

The pitch of an utterance can best be thought of as its tune. Whenever you say something, you give it a kind of tune. It's what makes normal human speech sound so different from (early) robotic speech. If you hear something spoken without any change in pitch, it sounds unnatural and also pretty boring. That's where the word *monotonous* comes from. It literally means 'with one tone', and that leads to the ideas of pitch and **tone**.

8.1 Pitch and tone

Quick quiz

1. Try singing a note while saying a vowel sound. Now sing a lower note and a higher note. Then try doing the same thing while saying a consonant like [k]. What do you notice?
2. Say the sentence 'The cat likes to be stroked' as if you're stating it as fact. Now say the same sentence as if you're questioning it. What are the differences?
3. What do you think happens to your voice when you're excited or angry?

When I introduced spectrograms of speech in chapters 3 and 4, I pointed out the dark lines that are called formants. As I said in section 4.6, the first and second formants show which vowel is being said – F1 indicates the height of the vowel and F2 indicates how front or back it is. The other formants, F3 and F4 are used to identify consonant sounds. There is another formant, though, called f0 (this one has a lower-case f) and this shows the fundamental frequency. Fundamental frequency is the pitch, which is a bit like the musical note. It is easiest to find the pitch of a vowel or similar sound, and that's why it's really hard to sing a collection of consonants. The first question in the quick quiz shows this. The distinction isn't really between vowels and consonants, though. It's between voiced and voiceless sounds. It's perfectly possible to sing [l] or [w], and nasal sounds like [m] or [n] can be sung, although it is called humming when the air goes through the nose rather than the mouth. Plosives are trickier, whether they're voiced or not, but that's because they don't have long enough duration, or if they do, it's a silence. I come back to this in chapter 9.

Of course, different people have different natural pitch. In general, women and children have higher pitch than men, and pitch lowers as we move from being children to becoming adults. For boys this is usually a rather sudden change (there's a special term for this: the voice 'breaking'), but for girls there is also a change. When talking about pitch being used in language, then, it is important to realise that it is **relative pitch** that matters. If children say something with relatively low pitch, the actual pitch of what they say may well still be higher than anything an adult man says, but as long as it's lower than their usual pitch, it will be recognised as being low.

When linguists talk about pitch being used in spoken language, there are two different uses for it: **intonation** and **(linguistic) tone**. They are used differently, as you'll see shortly, but the important thing to note here is that they both refer to relative rather than absolute pitch. Absolute pitch can be measured. Tone (and intonation) are not referred to like this – they are just described as being relatively high or low or of them rising or falling.

8.2 Intonation

English, like all languages, uses pitch to mark intonation over phrases and sentences. That is, the pitch varies over a phrase or sentence to indicate grammatical and discourse information.

Quick quiz

1. Say the sentences 'I like chips' and 'Is that right?' Say them a few times over and try to listen to the tune of each one. What happens to the pitch at the end of each one?
2. Say the sentences 'The students who had finished their work were allowed to go.' and 'The students, who had finished their work, were allowed to go.' What happens to the pitch between the words *students* and *who*?
3. Say the sentence 'The cat with the white bib had kittens.' Now say the same sentence as if it was the answer to the question 'Which cat had kittens?' What happens to the pitch of the word *bib* in each case?

Intonation affects meanings that are associated with phrases or sentences. It can indicate syntactic structure, discourse structure, information structure and emotive meaning. The idea of syntactic intonation is what questions 1 and 2 refer to. Questions usually have a different intonation pattern from statements. In SSBE, there is usually a drop towards the end of a statement but a rise at the end of a question, as in question 2 of the first quiz. Syntactic structure is also important in 2, and it also gets at an interesting relationship between the spoken and written form. First of all, check that you know what the difference in meaning is between the two sentences. The first one, with no commas, says that there were a bunch of students and the ones who had finished their work were allowed to go, but there were some who hadn't finished their work who weren't allowed to go. The second sentence, with the commas, says that the students had all finished their work and were allowed to go. Can you see the difference here? If you didn't appreciate the difference before, go back and read them aloud again, this time bearing in mind the differences in meaning. There should be a drop on *students* in the second sentence, with a rise to *who* that is not there in the first sentence. This is because in the second sentence, the bit between the commas is what we call 'parenthetical'. That is, it could be put in brackets (or parentheses). It's giving us some additional background information that isn't essential to understanding the core meaning of the sentence. Compare that to the first sentence, where those same words are essential in order to understand who was allowed to go. Because those words in the second sentence are parenthetical, they behave as a separate **intonation group**.

What's happening here is quite complex, because these examples, which I said relate to syntactic structure, also reflect aspects of information and discourse. The parenthetical bit in question 2 is syntactically separated, but arguably this is only because it has a different status in terms of how important it is. Question 3 demonstrates the significance to intonation of how important information is. There are a lot of things that go into making a discourse – that is a conversation or a whole coherent text, written or spoken – but when people use spoken language, they use intonation to indicate, for example, whether they mean it to be taken as a statement or a question (or indeed a rhetorical question), which bit of what they say they want the listener to really focus on and which bit or bits are new or surprising information. I talked about similar uses of stress in the previous chapter. Think about the sentence in question 3. Did you feel that you said it differently if it was a response to the question? Again, most people, if they say that sentence with no particular agenda, will not use any noticeable variation in the intonation. If they're saying it in response to the question of which cat, then they'll want to focus attention on the bit about the white bib, and so that will usually have a higher pitch.

I have said that intonation applies over whole phrases or sentences. Each phrase or sentence that has a single **intonation pattern** or **contour** is called an **intonation group**. As you can see from the sentences in question 2, the same string of words might have different intonation groups depending on how the words are grouped together into phrases. In the first sentence the phrase 'who had finished their work' is a relative clause that is part of the noun phrase, so 'the students who had finished their work' is a single phrase and is a single intonation group. In the second sentence the same string of words is a separate phrase (as I said, a parenthetical) which is an intonation group all on its own, breaking up the sentence 'The students were allowed to go,' which is another intonation group. This is also a form of grammatical intonation, and what's interesting here is that it is indicated by means of **punctuation**. Stress and intonation are not generally represented by the spelling of words. There are no letters or accents on letters to indicate when a syllable is stressed or has high or low tone, except when linguists want to talk specifically about them. That is one reason why written language is not an accurate representation of the spoken language. Punctuation is one of the ways the written language tries to address this. Although it's a pretty poor substitute for the amazing nuance used in spoken language, it does at least give some clues about some of the uses that intonation has in spoken language.

8.3 Linguistic tone

Unlike intonation, linguistic tone is not found in all languages. Linguistic tone is when a language uses different tones to indicate different meanings. English is not a **tone language**. That is, English does not use differences in the pitch of a word to indicate a different meaning. If you don't speak a tone language, they can be quite difficult to get the hang of, but there are a lot of languages around the world that do use tone in this way. There are two main types of tone systems: **lexical tone** and **grammatical tone**. Lexical tone is where a single word, or at least a single string of sounds, has different meanings depending on what the tone or tone pattern is. Grammatical tone is where tone differences indicate grammatical information about a word, for example, whether it is present or past tense (if it is a verb) or whether it is singular or plural (if it is a noun).

8.3.1 Lexical tone

Lexical tone is found in many languages spoken in East Asia, including Mandarin, Cantonese, Thai and Vietnamese. In these languages a word which looks and sounds to us like the same word may have very different meanings depending on the tone it is pronounced with. For example, [ma] may be pronounced in Mandarin with high, low (or neutral), rising, falling or rise-fall tone, and have completely different meanings as shown in table 8.1.

Tone	IPA Diacritic	IPA Symbol	Gloss
High	má	m˥a	'mother'
Rising	mǎ	m˩a	'hemp'
Falling	mâ	m˥a	'horse'
Rise-fall	mā	m˦a	'scold'
Low	mà	m˩a	question particle

TABLE 8.1   EXAMPLE WORDS WITH TONES MARKED IN IPA

Different languages have different numbers of tones. Mandarin, as you can see, has five tones, but some languages have only two or three. Tibetan, for example, only has two tones: high and low.

8.3.2   Grammatical tone

Grammatical tone can be more complex than lexical tone. Whereas lexical tone is firmly attached to individual syllables or words, grammatical tone can be more movable. In its simplest form, grammatical tone just appears on a word stem and indicates, for example, the tense of a verb or the number of a noun. However, in many tone languages it is much more complex and operates together with a set of endings, like the ones in English. In these cases the tone marking might happen on either the stem or the ending, and in some cases the tone marking can be on different parts of the word depending on, for example, how many or which endings are there or even what sounds are part of the stem or the ending. Tones can also move across words in phrases. Just for fun, here's an example of a really complicated system of grammatical tone from Gikuyu.

Gikuyu is a Bantu language spoken in Kenya. It has a system of tones that includes high, low, rising and falling. The tones in Gikuyu don't just attach themselves to syllables in a word and stay there, though. They can move across whole phrases. Have a look at the phrases in table 8.2.

Noun	Gloss	Noun + Adj	Gloss
1. [ŋɔɔbɛ]	'cow'	[ɲɔɔbɛ dito]	'heavy cow'
2. [borí]	'goat'	[borí díto]	'heavy goat'
3. [ɲamǒ]	'rabbit'	[ɲamo díto]	'heavy rabbit'
4. [bókó]	'animal'	[bóko díto]	'heavy animal'
5. [hóómǎ]	'fork'	[hóóma díto]	'heavy fork'

TABLE 8.2   TONE IN GIKUYU

The first thing to note here is that low tones are not marked, so every syllable (vowel) that has no accent above it is a low tone. There are two other kinds of tone here – high, marked with the acute accent (á), and rising tone, marked with the breve accent (ǎ). If you look at the first row in the table, you can see that there are no tone marks, so every syllable has low tone. Notice, especially, that the word [dito], meaning 'heavy', has no tones marked. Now look at the next line. In this phrase, the same word, with the same meaning, has a high tone marked. Where has this tone come from? The simple answer is that it has come from the last syllable of the previous word. Because the word [borí], meaning 'goat', has a high tone on its last syllable, that high tone 'spreads' to the first syllable of the adjective that follows. You can see the same thing happening with *rabbit*. Now look at the next two lines. Once again, the first syllable of the adjective has a high tone, but this hasn't come from a high tone on the noun. In both of these examples, the final syllable of the noun has a rising tone. What has happened to the tone on the noun? In examples 2 and 3, the tone on the noun doesn't change. It spreads to the next syllable but stays behind on its original syllable as well. In examples 4 and 5, the final syllable of the noun starts off with a rising tone, but when the adjective is added, the first syllable of that picks up a high tone, and there is no tone (high or rising) marked on the final syllable of the noun. One explanation for this is that a rising tone is actually a bit like a diphthong or an affricate, made up of two bits, in this case, a low tone and a high tone. When there is a high tone on the noun, it can be split into two bits of high tone. One moves to the adjective and one gets left behind, keeping the high tone on the noun. A rising tone can be split into a low tone, which stays behind on the noun, and a high tone, which moves to the adjective.

When you see tone discussed in books, you'll often see a way of marking tone using accents on orthographic words, rather than full phonetic transcriptions with tone marked. This can be a bit confusing because different accents are used in different languages, depending on which tones need to be marked. In a language with high, mid and low tone, it is quite normal to only mark high and low tones, with mid tones being assumed when there's no mark on a syllable. The other problem with this system is that there aren't any really obvious accents that indicate high and low reliably, unless they are next to each other for comparison, so people usually use the acute and grave accents that you find in French. Of course, one of these starts high and ends low, and the other starts low and ends high, so it's not obvious which one should be used for which tone. In fact, the convention is that the acute accent is used for high tone and the grave for low. So a word with a high tone can be written as *má*. It gets even more confusing when you remember that the same accents are used to indicate primary and secondary stress on orthographic words. It's not usually a problem because these notations are only used when either stress or tone is being discussed, but there is a way of avoiding any ambiguity. Yes, it's the good old IPA again. It only applies when you are giving phonetic or phonemic transcriptions, rather than orthographic forms, but if you really want to be clear, then the IPA is the way to go.

In the IPA, there is a special set of symbols for tone, just as there is for stress. I said that primary and secondary lexical stress can be marked for any syllable that is not completely unstressed. I also said that that might not cover all of the information about stress you might want to include, but if you're really keen on representing more than three levels of stress, you can use metrical trees or grids. In the case of tone, the IPA is much more flexible. Figure 8.1 (and table 8.1) show the IPA conventions for representing tone. There are two parallel systems: one which appears as accents over phonetic symbols and one which can be used separately to just represent tone patterns. The second of these is a set of symbols with a single vertical line on the right which represents the full scale of heights and against which the individual tones are plotted. There are five possible **level tones** for situations where there is no tone movement on a single syllable: extra-high, high, mid, low and extra-low. Then there are the **contour tones**. These are for where there is movement between tones during a single syllable. These include rise, from low to high and from mid to high, and falls from high to low and from mid to low. Then there are what are called 'peaking'. These are often called rise-fall or rising-falling. The IPA also gives four more tone symbols. These are where the whole tone pattern takes a step up ('upstep') or down ('downstep') and where the whole pattern or phrase gradually gets higher ('global rise')

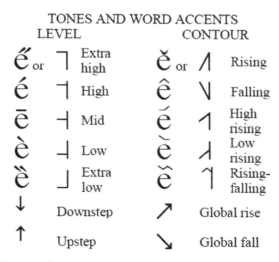

FIGURE 8.1   IPA CONVENTIONS FOR MARKING TONE

or lower ('global fall'). Finally, under the suprasegmentals in the IPA chart, there is the symbol for indicating an intonation group: ‖. This means that the two sentences in the first question of the quick quiz could be transcribed as follows:

'I like chips.': [‖ aɪ laɪk ↘ʧɪps ‖]
'Is that right?': [‖ ɪz ðæt ↗ɹaɪt ‖]

A brief aside on stress, tone and writing . . .

I have said that punctuation is a way of representing, to some degree at least, information about stress and/or intonation. I also said that punctuation is a pretty poor substitute for the range of prosodic variation used in normal spoken language. So how do people understand written language if they can't use the prosodic cues? There are several different kinds of answers to this. One answer is that they don't always. In the modern age of computer-mediated communication, I'm sure you have experienced situations where you see something written and don't understand it, misunderstand it or have to think for a long time before you understand it. Miscommunications are common when you can't pick up on subtle nuances of irony, humour and so on. There are, of course, other ways of trying to get this emotional level across. Many people use emoticons or emoji, for example. Written language is also used in a range of creative ways to try to express the information that is conveyed by prosody in spoken language. Capitals may be used to indicate SHOUTING, or to indicate a particularly stressed word: 'No, I didn't mean the white cat, I meant the BLACK one!' Other devices such as italics, bold font, different font choices or even different colours may be used. People rarely seem to explicitly indicate anything to do with tone or intonation in written language, though. Even using emoji or emoticons only gives an indication of the general emotion intended. That might give an indication of the intonation contour, but it doesn't indicate specifically what the tone, stress or intonation is intended to be. By the way, emoticons are symbols like the smiley face that are constructed from punctuation, such as :-). Emoji are graphical symbols such as 😊. (Oh, and don't be fooled by people who talk about emoji as being a 'language'. If emoji were a language, I would be able to write this whole book using just emoji, and other people who 'speak' emoji would know exactly what I mean!) One reason that it's not always a problem, especially with more traditional forms of writing, is that when people write, they tend to be clearer. They use longer sentences, fewer contractions (like *haven't* or *would've*) and just generally plan what they're going to write more thoroughly than when they're speaking. When it comes to tone languages, they generally don't mark tone explicitly, but there is an interesting project underway in Togo to consider ways in which the alphabet used for the Kabiye language can be adapted to include markers of lexical and grammatical tone.

I said earlier that tone and intonation are harder than some other aspects of pronunciation to accurately analyse, and there are several reasons for that. For one thing, there is the interaction of tone and intonation. In tone languages, where tone indicates lexical and/or grammatical meaning, there is still intonation, where an intonation contour applies over a whole phrase. That means that one 'high' tone may not be much, or even any, higher than a 'low' tone in terms of its actual pitch, depending on where they each fall in the intonation group. Even in languages that only have intonation, the grammatical and discourse functions might get confused, as well as different discourse functions, like indicating a question or drawing attention to a particular part of the sentence. The relation between intonation and stress is also complex, and very often it simply doesn't make sense to separate the two, but to consider the combination together.

The final reason why intonation can be tricky to analyse is the variation across accents. Or maybe I should really put that the other way round and say that different accents of English use intonation differently, but it's quite difficult to study this. There are two well-known accents of English that use intonation differently: SSBE and Australian English. You may be aware that one of the defining features of the Australian accent is the tendency to have rising intonation at the end of all sentences, whether they are indicating questions, statements or anything else. This particular accent feature is known as **HRT** (high-rising terminals). You may have heard it talked about because it is apparently spreading to the speech of young British people, and some older British people seem a bit upset about that. What happens in HRT is that all sentences rise at the end, usually from an already quite high pitch, hence the name. People who mock this accent feature, in particular, say that it sounds as though every sentence is a question, but in reality, it doesn't seem to lead to any major problems of comprehension between Brits and Australians.

I said at the start of this section that all languages use intonation. Unfortunately, there is relatively little research on intonation in languages other than English, but O'Grady (2013, p. 82) gives some examples.

Additional reading

Knight (2012), chapters 19 and 20; Kennedy (2017), chapter 9; and Davenport and Hannahs (2010), section 6.3, cover tone and intonation. Katz (2013), chapters 10 and 11, cover stress and tone. For more detail about English intonation, see Roach (2000), chapters 15 and 18; and Gimson (2001), section 11.6. Tench (2011) has more detail about how to transcribe tone. O'Grady (2013, p. 78–82) gives a more detailed explanation of the different functions of stress and how they interact.

Exercises

1. Transcribe the following sentences with intonation marked:
   (a) The children who liked football played outside.
   (b) The children, who liked football, played outside.

2. Transcribe the following sentences with intonation marked:
   (a) Kim likes eating cake.
   (b) Sandy insisted on it.

   Now transcribe them as if they were spoken as questions.

3. Think about a song that you are familiar with. For a small set of the lyrics, work out what the intonation would be if those words were spoken. Now think about how that compares to the tune that they are sung to. Is there a mismatch? If so, does it affect how easy it is to understand the lyrics? Does it sounds odd?

9 Length and duration

The last two chapters have looked at two of the key aspects of prosody. I said at the start of this part that there are three components of prosody: stress, tone and duration. I'm now going to look at duration. I've already talked a bit about length or duration in a couple of places. I said in chapter 4 that some vowels are short and some are long, and I said that the IPA has a special symbol for indicating length. So there can be a short vowel [i], a long vowel [iː] and even an extra long vowel [iːː]. In chapter 7, I said that the length of the vowel in a syllable affects its weight, and that syllable weight can be important for stress placement. And I also said in chapter 7 that stressed syllables tend to be longer in duration than unstressed syllables. In this chapter I'm going to look in more detail at length and how it relates to different types of sound. I also explain that the idea of 'length' as it relates to specific sounds is not always the same thing as simple duration.

Quick quiz

1. Which is the longer: *strength* [stɹɛŋθ] or *bee* [biː]?
2. How do you know?
3. Is the [n] sound the same in the words *tennis* and *penknife*?
4. Is there any difference in the vowel sound in the words *bin, bid* and *bit*?

When you see words written down, whether in orthographic form or phonetic transcription, it's tempting to think that each individual sound is pretty much the same length. When you look at both the spelling and the transcription of *strength,* it seems quite long. It has eight letters and six sounds in its transcription. Compare that to *bee*, which has three letters and only two sounds. You would naturally expect that *strength* would be quite a lot longer than *bee* when you say it. Is that what you said in response to question 1? Think about saying those two words in the following sentences:

■ We know that he has real strength of character.

■ Look at that amazing bee!

There are a few reasons why I think you probably pronounced *bee* slightly longer than *strength* in these sentences. The first is all about the individual sounds. Although *strength* has a lot of different sounds in it, none of them is likely to be very long. There are a lot of voiceless sounds, which tend to be less drawn out than their voiced counterparts. There are two plosives, which by definition are just short explosive bursts. Finally, the vowel in this word is short. In *bee*, on the other hand, even though we only have two sounds, they are both voiced, and the long vowel, obviously, is quite long. The fact that the vowel in the first word is followed by a consonant (it's in a closed syllable) also tends to make it even shorter, whereas the long vowel in the second word is in an open syllable. There is also the likely stress pattern in each of the sentences. The fact that *strength* in its sentence comes as part of a fixed phrase *strength of character,* where the normal main stress would be on the first syllable of *character,* means it is very unlikely that *strength* will have much stress at all. On the other hand, *bee*, in its sentence, is the most important word in the sentence and is likely to be extremely heavily stressed. That, as I said, means it is likely to be longer than a syllable that is unstressed. Of course, if you really properly stretch out the word *strength,* then it can be made really long, and it is possible to pronounce *bee* really short, but I'm talking about how you would normally pronounce them, all other things being equal.

So length can relate to the length of individual sounds as well as characteristics of syllables, like stress and whether they are open or closed. There are also some length differences that you might not really have thought about before. Did you think that the [n] sounds in the two words in question 3 were different? If you did, what did you think was different about them? The way most English people pronounce the words, the sound is longer in *penknife* than in *tennis*. There's a simple explanation for this. The word *penknife* is made up of two words *pen*, which has an [n] at the end and *knife* which has an [n] at the beginning. When you put those two words together, the two [n] sounds join together to make one long [n] sound. In *tennis*, even though there are two *n*'s in the spelling, there is only a single [n] sound. (In fact, the doubling of the consonant actually indicates the fact that the vowel is short, rather than anything about the length of the consonant.)

The final question in the quiz points to some much more subtle differences in length, or rather duration. The vowel in all three words is the [ɪ] vowel, which is considered a short vowel in English. Do you think it is the same length in those three words? If not, which word do you think has the longest pronunciation of the vowel and which the shortest? I would expect that if you measured the actual duration of these vowels, you would see that the longest one comes in the word *bin* and the shortest in *bit*. Is that what you thought? Again, it is, of course, possible to adjust the length on purpose, but for most people, all other things being equal, vowels are longer before voiced sounds than before voiceless sounds, and longer before nasals than before plosives.

I hinted earlier that there is a difference between length and duration. That might seem a bit strange, but let me explain. In the sense in which these words are used in linguistics, there is a distinction. It's a little bit like the distinction between pitch and tone or intonation. Length is relevant for phonology, where distinctions are made between sounds that are classified as long or short, just as sounds are classified as voiced or voiceless or as rounded or unrounded. Duration is relevant in phonetics, where the actual time taken to pronounce a word, a syllable or a sound can be measured. The two things are not unrelated, of course, but it is possible, as I explain shortly, for a 'short' sound to actually have a longer duration than a 'long' sound.

9.1   Vowel length

Linguistic use of length is mostly associated with vowels. Vowels in English can be classified as either short or long. In some languages there are more different lengths. For example, in Dutch vowels can be short, long or extra long. If you think back to the IPA vowel chart, the positions on that chart only tell us about the height and backness of the vowel. In addition to these, we saw that vowels can be either rounded or unrounded, and this is indicated on the chart by pairs of symbols, with the unrounded one on the left and the rounded one on the right. Length is another way in which vowels can be distinguished. In terms of how this is indicated, it is quite simple. For every one of those vowels on the chart, extra length can be indicated by using the IPA symbol that looks like a colon, ː. So the symbols on the IPA chart are used to indicate the height, backness and rounding, and the length symbol is added if appropriate. The individual vowel symbols on their own are assumed to represent short vowels.

The actual realisation of length in vowels, as I explain in section 9.3, is not always straightforward. You may also remember that when I talked about vowels in chapter 4, I talked about the relationship between length and tenseness. That is important for English, but not for all languages. In English the short and long vowels are described as such, but they are not transcribed as though they only differ in length. For example, the vowels /ɪ/ and /iː/ are considered to be short and long equivalents. However, if they were really only different in their length, they would be written as /ɪ/ and /ɪː/ or /i/ and /iː/. So why are they transcribed the way they are? It's because when they are pronounced, there is a genuine difference in their quality. If you measure their F1 and F2 formants, you will see that /iː/ is higher and more front than

/ɪ/. It is also more tense. Tenseness is not something that is easy to measure, and there are vowels that tend to be long in English that are not tense, such as /ɜː/. However, where there are pairs of vowels that appear to differ in their length, this can often be viewed as a difference in their tenseness.

There is a further complication here, especially in English, and that is the diphthongs. The diphthongs in English today started emerging some time around the twelfth century, mostly developing from combinations of a short vowel and one of the glides, [j] or [w]. Sometimes people who are not phonologists might still talk about the diphthongs as long vowels. For example, when learning spelling rules of English, the diphthong /eɪ/ might be referred to as the 'long a', to contrast it with the 'short a' when an *e* is added in words like *plan/plane*. Diphthongs, not surprisingly, tend to be longer than short vowels. Diphthongs are transcribed as two distinct sounds, indicating the beginning and end points, so there has to be sufficient time for the transition from the beginning point to the end point to take place. In fact, all other things being equal, diphthongs are usually longer than long vowels. However, note that they are not transcribed with the length mark because the two characters already indicate additional length. The actual duration of various vowels is discussed in section 9.3.

9.2 Consonant length

Just as vowels can be either short or long, so can consonants. A long consonant is called a **geminate**, from the Latin word for 'twin', as in the star sign Gemini. It's not as common for languages to have length distinctions in consonants as it is in vowels, and there's a very simple reason for that. Because of the way they are articulated, vowels are easy to sustain for a long time. Consonants involve more effort and so are harder to sustain. It isn't really difficult to pronounce a really long [n] sound, though, or a really long [s] (although you sound like you are hissing like a snake). It's just a bit more effort than pronouncing a long vowel sound. In fact, it's quite possible to pronounce a long plosive. That might sound a bit strange, because a plosive is just a closure followed by a sudden release, but a long plosive just involves keeping the closure, and therefore actually the silence, for longer than usual.

Some languages have distinctions between long and short vowels and consonants. Norwegian and Italian both do, for example. I said that English also has long consonants in some situations, although it isn't usually the only thing that differentiates words. In Italian, there are pairs of words where the only difference is the length of consonants. For example, the word [pala] means 'shovel', but [palːa] means 'ball'.

9.3   Length versus duration

As I have said, the length of a sound is not simply its duration. There are lots of things that affect the actual duration of a sound. Most obviously, if I speak very quickly, then all of the sounds will have shorter duration than if I speak very slowly. That's not very interesting from a linguistic perspective, but there are lots of other factors that are. I said in chapter 7 that stressed syllables tend to have longer duration, and so it follows that sounds within stressed syllables are likely to have longer duration. But it's not the case that all sounds in a stressed syllable will be lengthened to the same degree. Think about a word (syllable) like *bound*. Say it aloud. Now say it again, deliberately stretching it out. Did all of the sounds become longer? Think back to what I said in the previous section about consonant length. You probably made the vowel sound very long, and you may also have made the [n] sound longer, but you probably didn't make the [b] or [d] longer. So you can see that a vowel in a stressed syllable is likely to be longer than one in an unstressed syllable. It's not just a simple distinction between stressed and unstressed either. There are different degrees of stress, including primary and secondary lexical stress, but also the contrastive stress within phrases and sentences, so that results in syllables with a range of different levels of stress and therefore durations.

There are other reasons why some syllables and sounds might be longer. When you're speaking, you don't always know what you're going to say. Sometimes (actually, quite often in normal conversation) there might be pauses while you're thinking about what word you want to say, or you might fill the pause with *um* or *er*. People do this because they don't like there to be too much silence, or they don't want to lose their 'turn' in the conversation. Another tactic they sometimes use is to elongate words to use up some time while they're thinking about the next word they want to say. This is a matter of choice. Some people tend to do this a lot (try listening to the journalist Robert Peston when he's being interviewed rather than when he's saying a prepared piece), but others don't really do it at all. Again, this is something that affects the duration of individual sounds, but not phonological length.

Another factor that affects the duration of sounds again relates to stress and something I talked about in chapter 7. That is whether your language is stress timed or syllable timed. You may remember that some languages, including English, are stress timed, which means that the length of time between the stressed syllables tends to be roughly equal, whereas some languages, including French, are syllable timed, which means that the length of time between each syllable is roughly equal, regardless of whether they are stressed or not. This means that the duration of unstressed syllables in

A brief aside on making words looooonnnnngggggeeeeerrrr …

Have you ever tried to write a word as if you were really stretching it out? It often happens in some forms of computer-mediated communication (CMC) to give the impression of spoken language and people try to indicate things like speaking loudly (BY USING CAPITALS), pauses or hesitant speech (like … er … this) or elongating words. The most obvious way to do this is by repeating letters, like in the example in the heading here. There are a couple of interesting facts about how people do this. The first is the fact that, when they do it, they don't always take into account the fact that letters are often pronounced differently when they are doubled. This is a problem if they want to indicate that a [ɒ] is long, because if they just repeat the letter *o* and make it *oo* or even longer, that tends to suggest the sound [uː], which can be confusing. The other thing that is interesting is which letters people choose to repeat. One of my students a few years ago did a project looking at how people used letter repetition and found that, contrary to what she expected, people would often repeat random letters in a word, not reflecting the actual lengthening of the sounds. Remember what I said about the word *bound*? I said that if you wanted to really stretch it out, you would probably only actually stretch the vowel and the [n]. So how would you write that? The first thing to think about is how to represent the [aʊ] sound. If you think about the diphthong as a single sound, then you might think it's reasonable to repeat the letter pair, *ououou" ouou*. I think that gives the impression of saying the sound several times, though, rather than just saying it for longer. So maybe you should write *oooouuuu*, but that doesn't really look right either, because it seems to suggest two long but separate sounds. The other question is which of the consonant sounds is elongated. I said that it is probably only the [n] that would be pronounced longer, so that suggests that the *b* or the *d* should not be repeated. My student, however, found that people often do repeat the letters that represent plosive sounds, which tend not to be pronounced long. Her conclusion was that people just find a variety of ways of representing the fact that the word as a whole is stretched out, and don't worry too much about the detail of which sounds are elongated and which are not.

English will tend to be affected more than unstressed syllables in French. In a situation where English has two or more unstressed syllables in between the stressed ones, this is even more extreme. The example I gave in chapter 7, *I talked to the telephone company*, has three sequences of one stressed followed by two unstressed syllables. Those unstressed syllables are likely to be even shorter in duration than an unstressed syllable in between two stressed syllables.

Finally, the duration of a sound can be affected by the other sounds around it. This is especially true of vowels and the sounds that follow them. As a general rule, vowels are longer when they come before a voiced sound and shorter when they come before a voiceless sound. The quiz question 4 showed this. Because it's quite easy to measure duration of sounds, this can be demonstrated scientifically. Research done right back in 1965 (Wiik, 1965) measured the durations of different types of vowels followed by different types of consonants. The results are shown in table 9.1. What you can see here is that different vowels have different durations that do not simply reflect the long/short distinction. Look, for example, at the results for [æ], which is considered a short vowel, compared to the other short vowels. The other thing that is really interesting in this table is that the duration of the short vowels when they come before a voiced sound is actually longer than the duration of the long vowels when they come before a voiceless sound. It showed that there were four distinct types of vowel in English when it came to duration: the short vowels ([ɪ, ʊ, ɛ, ɒ, ʌ, ə]), the long vowels ([iː, uː, ɔː, ɜː, ɑː]), the diphthongs ([eɪ, aɪ, əʊ, aʊ, ɔɪ]) and [æ]. Technically, [æ] is a short vowel, but in the study it was shown to behave differently from the other short vowels.

9.4   Representing length in transcriptions

So I've shown that there are various ways in which length is used in spoken language and I've also talked about the complex relationship between length and duration. I've talked about how length is used in English, but I'll just sum it up here, with some advice on how to represent length if you're trying to transcribe English.

The typical way to represent the vowels of English is to mark the vowels in *heed, hard, hoard, who'd* and *heard* as long. That is, they're transcribed as [iː, ɑː, ɔː, uː, ɜː]. The other vowels and the diphthongs don't have the IPA

	Before Voiced Obstruent or Ford-Finally	Before Nasal	Before Voiceless
Short vowels (not æ)	172 ms	132 ms	103 ms
[æ]	234 ms	196 ms	158 ms
Long vowels	319 ms	233 ms	165 ms
Diphthongs	357 ms	265 ms	178 ms

TABLE 9.1   VOWEL DURATIONS IN ENGLISH, FROM WIIK (1965)

length mark. If you want to really focus on length, or duration, and mark it more accurately, then you can use the length mark on any vowel that is actually pronounced longer, or write the typically long vowels without the length mark to indicate whether they have been pronounced shorter. There are also other ways of indicating differences in length. The symbol · is used to indicate 'half-long', and you can use multiples as well. So if someone really pronounces a vowel very long, you might transcribe it as i꞉꞉꞉. On the other hand, you can also indicate that a sound is particularly short with a diacritic over the top: ĭ. And remember, you can do this for consonants as well as for vowels. Going back to the brief aside about indicating length in writing, there are no such problems when using the IPA. If I want to accurately represent the elongated pronunciation of the word *bound*, I can write [baʊ꞉꞉꞉n꞉꞉d]. The only detail that is missing here is how long the different parts of the diphthong each last, but that's not reflected in the normal transcription of diphthongs, either.

9.5 Spelling

Representing length in English spelling is, as I said above, a bit tricky. However, there are some aspects of English spelling that are designed to reflect certain differences in length. In the case of consonants, the lengthening of consonants is not consistently reflected in spelling, as I showed in the case of words like *penknife* and *tennis*. The doubling of a consonant letter in English doesn't tell us anything about the length of the consonant, but, somewhat bizarrely, it does often indicate the length of the vowel before it. Compare *tennis* with the word *scenic*. The *e* in *tennis* is the short vowel [ɛ], but in *scenic* it is the long vowel [i꞉].

Additional reading

Carr and Montreuil (2013), chapter 10, is a good source on the relations between length andother factors. For more detail on transcribing length, see Tench (2011).

Exercises

1. Which of the following words have long vowels:
   (a) bit
   (b) beat
   (c) bite

(d) boot

(e) book

(f) birth

(g) both

2. Order the following words according to how long you would expect the vowel to be in each one. You will need to consider the type of vowel and the sound that follows it.

bit	bean	bide
pine	bad	bin
beat	bid	bat
bite	ban	bead

3. Have a look at the spectrogram in chapter 4.

(a) Which vowel is the shortest?

(b) Which is the longest?

(c) Is that what you would expect?

(d) Why do you think the two [iː] vowels have different durations?

4. Which of the following words have geminate consonants?

(a) eighty

(b) eighteen

(c) patter

(d) pity

(e) pitta

(f) pizza

(g) rattrap

Part V

Phonology

So far I have talked about real sounds. I explained how sounds are produced, how they are described and transcribed. I explained various ways that they are combined in speech. Mostly I've talked about English, but I have also mentioned other languages. Every language has its own set of rules that determines what sounds there are in a language, how they can combine and a range of changes that can happen when they combine. In this part of the book, I look at these changes. This is the area called **phonology**, as opposed to **phonetics**. The first chapter looks at how to describe sounds in terms of the specific features they have and how they can be grouped into classes. I then look at a very important idea in phonology: the phoneme. This is basically a way of thinking about how sounds are organised in languages. Finally, I look at some of the problems with the idea of the phoneme and some solutions.

10 Phonological features and classes

One thing it is important to consider when talking about features is that they are used not for phonetic description, but for **phonological** description. This is an important distinction that I haven't really talked about yet. So far in this book I've just talked about phonetics – that is, describing the actual sounds. Those sounds are not just sounds that are made in isolation or in random combination, though. They are used in very clearly defined ways depending on the language spoken. Changing one sound for another, even if that other sound is very similar, can give a whole new meaning. The study of how sounds are used in individual languages is called **phonology**. When you start thinking about phonology rather than phonetics, it gets a bit more abstract, so you need to start thinking about sounds in a different way. It's like any kind of scientific study. If I ask you to describe whales, dolphins and sharks, you might say that they are very similar and describe the characteristics that they share, like being large creatures that live in the sea. If, however, you know a bit about marine biology, you might say that whales and dolphins are mammals, but sharks are fish. Phonetics treats sounds like the first of these, looking at the obvious characteristics that they share, like whether they are voiced or not. Phonology looks at aspects that might not be as obvious, but that are important for the classification of sounds – how they group together in their natural environment, that is, language.

One thing that makes the distinction a bit tricky is that linguists use a lot of the same words for the phonological features and classes as they do for the phonetic descriptions. In this case, it's a bit like the problem with consonants and vowels. With letters, there are five vowels in the English alphabet, and the other 21 letters are all consonants. With sounds, though, the difference is not as clear-cut, and letters that are consonants can represent sounds that are vowels (think back to the example of *y*, which is a consonant letter, but represents a vowel sound in the word *sky*). In chapters 3 and 4, I talked about how different sounds are articulated and described. The articulation of the sounds – which bits of the mouth move and exactly how – gave a set of terms that can be used to describe the sounds. These ways of describing sounds can be viewed as ways of both breaking individual sounds down into smaller parts (**features**) and grouping together sounds that share features (**classes**).

I'm going to go back for a moment to letters rather than sounds. Letters have different shapes, and they can be put together in different ways. There are different aspects or features of individual letters and also groups of letters that behave in similar ways.

Quick quiz

1. How would you describe the letter *p*?
2. What other letters would you group it with?
3. What do the letters *b, d, h, k, l, t* have in common?
4. What do the letters *a, e, i, o, u* have in common?
5. How would you describe the difference between *a* and *A*?

You probably don't often think much about letters in the ways I've asked you to here, but I think it's a helpful exercise to get you thinking about sounds in a similar way. What did you say for the first question? I imagine you could have given one of three rather different kinds of answer. You might have just said something like 'It's a small (or lower-case) *p*.' That's a perfectly fine answer on one level. It's certainly true, but it doesn't really *describe* it. If you said something like 'It has a vertical line with a round bit on the right at the top,' then you're thinking in terms of features. If you're familiar with handwriting teaching, you might have referred to things like 'descenders'. That's the term for vertical lines going down below the line you're writing on. If you said something like 'It's a consonant,' then you're thinking in terms of classes. Most people know that there's a difference between vowels and consonants, although, as I mentioned, the difference between letters and sounds is very important. But when you're talking about letters, it's true to say that *p* is a consonant. (Actually, there's no real problem with *p* as a consonant sound either, but that's not true for all letters.)

If you think about *p* as a consonant, you might have answered question 2 by mentioning other consonant letters, such as *b, c, d, f* . . . . If you were focussing on the physical shape of *p*, you may have grouped it with *g, j, q, y*, other letters that have descenders, or even with *b, d, q* as letters that have a straight line and a round bit. In that case, you probably had no trouble identifying the letters in question 3 as being letters that have ascenders – lines going higher above the line. You will no doubt have identified that the answer to question 4 is that they are all vowels. That is, they all belong to the group or class of letters called vowels. Finally, the two letter shapes in question 5 are interesting because in some sense you would probably say that they're the same letter – they both represent a letter *a*. But they don't look at all alike, do they? You might have answered question 5 in a number of ways, again referring to how you'd classify it ('small/lower-case *a* ' vs 'capital/

upper-case *a*'), describing their physical attributes or even how and where they are used (at the beginning of sentences and in proper names for *A*, e.g.).

10.1   Features

So what does this have to do with sounds? First of all, let me make clear that I am not talking about the symbols used to represent the sounds. They really are just like letters. I'm talking about the actual sounds themselves. Sounds can be described as I did in chapters 3 and 4, and each of the different parts of the descriptions of the sounds can be seen as a feature of that sound. Let's take the sound [p]. I described it as a 'voiceless bilabial plosive'. There are three features there – the feature of being voiceless, the feature of being bilabial and the feature of being a plosive. These relate to the three main parameters of description: voicing, place of articulation and manner of articulation. So it is always possible to talk about consonants as having three features that represent those three parameters. What about vowels? Vowels have three parameters of description, too: height, backness and rounding. The vowel [i], for example, is a high, front, unrounded vowel. That means that it has three features: high (height), front (backness) and unrounded (rounding). So far that all looks pretty uninteresting, doesn't it? But there's more that can be done with features.

10.1.1   The major parameters

Consonants

The most obvious features are the ones that represent the ways of describing the articulation of sounds. These are basically the terms used in the descriptions in chapters 3 and 4. There are three parameters for describing consonants. Voicing is usually just represented by voiced and voiceless. Manner of articulation and place of articulation are a little more complex.

For manner of articulation I start from the categories on the IPA chart: plosive, nasal, trill, tap/flap, fricative, lateral fricative, approximant, lateral approximant. One approach would be to say that each one of these is a feature, but just looking at the names, it is clear that there might be some other ways of assigning features. For example, the fricative and lateral fricative categories surely want to both have a feature 'fricative', and the lateral approximant and lateral fricative surely both want a 'lateral' feature? So another approach would be to suggest a set of features such as plosive, nasal, fricative, lateral, approximant, trill, tap/flap, which can be put together to get the lines in the IPA consonant chart. There is also a class of consonant that is not in that table. Do you remember what it is? There are two of them in English: the affricates. Affricates are a combination of a plosive part and a fricative part, so their feature description can be made up out of the other features. What about nasals? In some respects they are quite reasonably represented by a feature 'nasal', but they also involve a complete closure in the mouth, just like plosives, so it might be helpful to have a feature that they both share to reflect this. If the feature 'stop' is used for both plosives and nasals, then that can be used for affricates as well and leave the feature 'plosive' for just the plosives.

For place of articulation, I again refer to the IPA chart. There are 11 places distinguished: (bi)labial, labiodental, dental, alveolar, post-alveolar, retroflex, palatal, velar, uvular, pharyngeal and glottal. Once again, looking at the names suggests some sharing of features, for example with labial, dental and labio-dental. It's also important to note that the distinction between dental, alveolar and post-alveolar only applies to fricatives. For all other manners of articulation, there is no distinction between these three places of articulation. This is a useful example to really explain the idea of phonology rather than phonetics. In terms of phonetics, there are plosives in some languages (English included) that are phonetically alveolar. That is, most speakers of (at least British) English produce the sounds [t] and [d] by placing their tongue against their alveolar ridge. In some other languages, for example Punjabi and Basque, these plosive sounds are produced by placing the tongue against the teeth. What is really important to note, and what is reflected in the IPA classifications, is that there is no known language where there are both alveo-lar [t] and [d] *and* dental [t̪] and [d̪] and where they can change the meaning of words. That is, there is no language where there are two words with two different meanings that are identical apart from one having a dental [t̪] and the other having an alveolar [t]. This does leave an interesting decision. Should those three places of articulation be distinguished for every manner of articulation, even though it's only relevant for fricatives? Or should they be collapsed into a single place feature and find another way to distinguish the fricatives? I come back to this shortly.

Another question that needs to be addressed in relation to place of articulation is whether to represent more in the features than just the main point of articulation. When I talked about the way consonants are pro-duced, I mentioned the fact that, in most cases, there are two articulators, often one active and one passive. For most of the sounds I described, the active articulator is the tongue, so that is ignored, and the description just includes what the tongue is moving towards or touching. That's fine for phonetic description – you can think of it as just a bit of an abbreviation. When I say that a sound is alveolar, I'm really saying that it involves the

---

A brief aside on dental plosives . . .

I said that there are no languages that distinguish words by having both alveolar and dental consonants. In case you're interested in some rather obscure languages that do use dental plosives, I'd like to tell you about two. The first, Temne, is a Niger-Congo language, spoken widely in Sierra Leone. It is the only example I am aware of of a language that may distinguish these sounds. It has both a voiceless alveolar plosive [t] and a voiceless dental plosive [t̪]. However, in some descriptions of the language the dental sound is described as a fricative rather than a plosive. The other language is Pazeh. This is really obscure, and is technically extinct, the last speaker having died in 2010. It was spoken in Taiwan and is an Austronesian language. Pazeh apparently had both dental and alveolar plosives, but the voiceless plosive is dental [t̪] while the voiced plosive is alveolar [d]. Most of the other languages that are believed to have dental plosives actually have sounds that are more accurately described as 'laminal denti-alveolar'. That is, they have plosives that are produced with the blade of the tongue touching somewhere in between the teeth and the alveolar ridge, or even touching both simultaneously. There are many languages that have this sound, including Punjabi and Basque. You may remember from chapter 3 that I speculated on the fact that there aren't many languages that use genuine dental plosives, or many dental consonants at all, and saying that it's probably because not everybody has teeth. Another purely physical explanation is that even people who do have (front) teeth often have gaps between the teeth, so however tightly the tongue is pressed against the teeth, there's no guarantee of a complete closure.

---

tongue and the alveolar ridge, but I just don't need to explicitly mention the tongue. But there are some types of classification that benefit from saying not only that the tongue is involved, but which part of the tongue. Try saying [s] followed by [θ]. Which part of your tongue touches the alveolar ridge for [s]? Which part touches your teeth for [θ]? Can you feel that it's different? What about [k]? Which part of your tongue touches the velum? When I was describing the articulation, I didn't bother with these details, but when it comes to looking at how sounds can affect the other sounds around them, they can be important. It's also important for some of the kinds of classes or groups of sounds I talk about later, so when considering the features used to describe consonants, it may well be important to include, for example, whether it is produced with the tip, blade, front or back of the tongue.

Just like with the other parts of the mouth, Latin terms are used to refer to the different parts of the tongue. The tip is also known as the **apex**; the blade is known as the **lamina**; and the back of the tongue is known as the **dorsum**. The lamina is not often referred to, but there is another term, the **corona**, which refers to the tip and blade together. These terms give the adjectives **apical**, **dorsal** and **coronal**. It is now possible to talk about all sounds that use the blade of the tongue as having the feature coronal. That includes dental, alveolar, post-alveolar and palatal sounds. What this shows is that sounds can have more features than just the three basic parameters of description from chapter 3.

There are lots of other kinds of features as well, reflecting ideas I've talked about in other contexts before. I said that consonant sounds can be considered to be either obstruent or sonorant. That's another feature that can be applied to consonant sounds. Actually, it can be applied to all sounds, with vowels always having the feature sonorant. In section 3.1.5, I talked about a particular type of fricative and affricate sound that has a hissing quality. I said that they were called sibilants. That's another kind of feature that can be used in phonological description.

Vowels

When I talked about how to describe vowels, I again identified three parameters: height, backness and rounding. Like voicing for consonants, rounding is a fairly straightforward case of either rounded or unrounded. Actually, this is a nice example of the difference between phonetic and phonological features. In section 4.1.3, I asked you to say a list of words with different vowels while looking in the mirror, or to look at a friend saying them. I said then that it's not a simple case of some sounds being fully rounded and some being fully unrounded. As you moved from *heed* through the list to *who'd*, you passed through different degrees of rounding in words like *hard* and *hod*. You may remember that those two words were where I said that the cut-off is between what is called unrounded (*hard*) and what is called rounded (*hod*). In phonetic (articulatory) terms, it's most accurate to say that *hard* is more rounded than *heed* but less rounded than *hod*, but in phonological terms the sounds up to and including *hard* are unrounded, and the sounds from *hod* onwards in that list are rounded.

The other parameters for vowels are a bit more tricky. According to the IPA chart, there are four different heights: high, high-mid, low-mid and low. But what about schwa? There are also other vowels on the chart that don't lie on any of those height lines. How are they categorised? This is a case, like the place of articulation of consonants, where it really does depend on the language you're trying to describe. Any individual language will have its own set of vowels, and the number of different heights that particular language has tells you how many features you need to distinguish them all. For

English, there are three different heights. I said in chapter 4 that the English vowels [ɛ] and [ɔ] are low-mid, and phonetically, that's true. But there aren't any vowels that contrast with them in English that are high-mid, so there's no need to specify whether they are high-mid or low-mid; they can just be defined as mid. That means there is no problem with schwa either, which is not on the low-mid line, but is still in the mid area.

The situation for backness is actually a bit more complicated because of real physical factors. When your tongue is high in your mouth, it has much more room to move backwards and forwards than when it's lower in your mouth. That's why, as you can see from the IPA vowel chart, the shape of the vowel space is narrower at the bottom than it is at the top. What this means is that high vowels can be front, back or central, but low vowels can only be front or back. In fact, it gets even more complicated than that, because in a lot of languages, low vowels don't have any distinctions between front and back – regardless of what their strict phonetic realisation is, they either behave as front vowels or, more often, as back vowels.

In addition to these basic features, I have talked about other aspects of vowels. I said in chapter 4 that vowels can be either tense or lax. If there is a tenseness feature, then this can be used to distinguish different mid vowels. Another aspect of vowels, which is related to tenseness, at least in English, is length. As length isn't always related to tenseness, a length feature will be needed.

10.1.2   Mixed features

Thinking about features in this way also makes it possible to identify features that might be shared by both vowels and consonants. The parameters of phonetic description make it seem as though consonants and vowels are completely different kinds of sound that need completely different sets of features to describe them, but that's not quite true. I said in chapter 4 that vowels are technically approximants, so they have a manner of articulation feature that is shared with consonants. They are also voiced. Although I didn't worry about this when I was describing vowels, because they are all voiced, it is often important to recognise that they have the voice feature when talking about what happens around voiced sounds, as these tend to happen whether the sound is a voiced consonant or a vowel.

Think about vowel descriptions. They are all about two parts of the mouth – the lips and the tongue. The lips in vowels are either rounded or unrounded. Now think about some of the consonants. Which consonants use the lips? You should have mentioned [p], [b] and [m]. They involve only the lips (not counting the glottis). But there are other sounds that use the lips to different degrees. The [w] sound is called a labial-velar and involves both the lips and the velum/tongue. Say the sounds [w] and [u]. Can you feel that they are very similar? I said in chapter 3 that the two glides, also known as semi-vowels, [w] and [j], are very similar to the vowels [u] and [i], and it's no coincidence that the letters *w* and *u* and the letters *y* and *i* are used interchangeably to some degree. This is seen in some non-standard spellings, like *Kwik Fit*, but also in standard spellings, like *bowl* versus *soul*. There are also two more sounds (in English) that use the lips, or at least one lip: the labio-dentals [f] and [v].

It's not unusual for there to be sounds that are very similar and that tend to be mixed up or substituted for each other, but when it happens with two sounds where one is a consonant and the other a vowel, it is clear that care is needed when expecting the features for vowels and consonants to be completely independent.

The other factor here is what is, in many ways, the true core of phonological study, and that's how sounds that are next to each other can influence each other. As it's very common (in fact, it's very much the norm in many languages) for consonants and vowels to alternate, that means the sounds next to a consonant will often be vowels, and vice versa. Linguists often want to talk about particular features spreading from one sound to a neighbouring sound, and that's not going to work if the sets of features used for consonants and vowels are completely different. I come to some of these in chapter 13, but for now you just need to know that it sometimes makes sense for consonants and vowels to have at least some overlap in the features used to classify them.

So the lips are used for sounds that have a 'labial' in their name. So far, so unsurprising. Say the words *key* and *cue*. Try saying them in front of a mirror (or get a friend to help out), and look at what your lips are doing right at the start of each word, while you're saying the [k] sound. Can you see that when you say *key* your lips are unrounded, but when you say *cue* they are rounded? This is an example of the vowel feature of rounding apparently appearing on a consonant.

The other part of the mouth involved in making vowels sounds is the tongue. The tongue can be (relatively) high or low and to the front or the back of the mouth. Think again about the [w] sound. What is happening to the tongue when you say it? I've already said that it's a labial-velar sound, and I've dealt with the labial part, so what does the velar part tell us? The tongue is raised quite high towards the velum, which is at the back of the mouth. So the back part of the tongue is high in the mouth. Now think about what kind of vowel sound [u] is. It's a high back vowel, meaning that the tongue is raised high, and the highest point is the back of the tongue. So this really explains the similarity between [w] and [u]. One is a consonant, so it's called a labial-velar (approximant); the other is a vowel, so it's called a high back rounded vowel – but those descriptions are actually saying more or less the same thing.

So consonants and vowels are not completely different types of thing, but rather points on a scale. Once you realise that, it's not difficult to see that there might be some benefit of using the same (or at least overlappping) features to define these sounds.

A brief aside on Latin spelling ...

A lot of the strange spelling in English came about because of the use of a lot of Latin words and the fact that early writing in England was almost all in Latin to start with. One of the things you might have noticed, if you've ever seen genuine Roman writing, is that it only uses one letter, *I*, for both [j] and [i]. There was no letter *J*. The situation with [w] and [u] is complicated, with the letter *V* representing the sound [w] and the letter *u* representing the sound [ʊ]. Actually, there is some debate about exactly how these sounds would have been produced in Ancient Roman Latin, because there are no recordings around, but the fact that there is confusion and debate just backs up my point that these sounds can be confused very easily.

Another feature which can be used for both consonants and vowels is the nasal feature. There are consonants that have nasal as their manner of articulation, but there are also vowels which are called **nasalised**. That means that they have the normal relatively minor obstruction in the mouth, but air also escapes through the nose. In English, as you will see later, vowels tend to be nasalised when they are next to a nasal consonant, but in other languages nasalised and non-nasalised vowels are treated as different sounds.

10.1.3   The purpose of features

So far I've shown that there are some really straightforward ways of thinking about features as well as some areas where they're a bit more tricky. What I haven't really talked about is what these features are going to be used for. In the rest of the book, I talk about what happens to sounds when they get together. There are two key reasons for needing to know about features for doing that. The first is to be able to say, for example, 'If a sound has feature X, then something will happen to it.' The second is to be able to say, for example, 'In this particular situation, feature X of this sound changes.'

For the first of these, it is often possible to express what needs to be said quite simply in English by saying something like 'if the sound is rounded' or 'if the sound is unrounded'. Sometimes you might want to say, for example, 'if the sound is a plosive' or 'if the sound is anything other than a plosive'. These might not seem to be very different, but actually they are. Think about all of the vowel sounds in English. Every one of them can be viewed as being either rounded or unrounded. There are just two possibilities, and every sound fits into one of two groups, so it is possible to talk about how each group behaves very simply. Now think about all of the consonant sounds. They all have a manner of articulation. Some are plosive, some are fricative and so on. There are several different possibilities. If you want to talk about something that happens to just one group, then there's no problem. The problem comes when you want to talk about the other sounds. There are two possibilities here. You can somehow express the idea of 'not plosive', which applies to all of the other sounds, or you can express the idea of a set of groups, including the fricatives, the approximants and so on. There are good reasons for doing both of these, but it depends on what exactly you are doing. In fact, as you'll see when I talk about classes in section 10.2, you're not likely to need to talk about all of the non-plosives, for example. I'm now going to look at how these two approaches translate into different kinds of features and what each type is good (and not so good) for.

10.1.4   Boolean and non-Boolean features

The term 'Boolean' comes from maths. A Boolean feature is just a feature that can have only one of two values. They are usually thought of as being + or −, but they can also be 0 or 1, and another term for them is **binary features**. For some phonological features, Boolean values make perfect sense. For example, consonant voicing is generally considered to be either present or absent. A consonant is either voiced or it is not (unvoiced or voiceless). So it makes sense to think about the feature [voice] as having two possible values: + or −. In this way, the sound [b] is said to have the feature [+ voice], whereas the sound [p] has the feature [− voice]. That one's nice and simple, but what about some of the other features? For manner of articulation I said that the manner features are [plosive], [nasal], [fricative], [lateral], [approximant], [trill], [tap/flap]. Does it make sense to think about these as Boolean features? If they are, then each sound would have to have a value of + or − for every feature. A fricative, for example, would be [− plosive], [− nasal], [+ fricative], [− lateral], [− approximant], [− trill], [− tap/flap]. It all seems a bit redundant. Apart from a few cases, where there might be + values for two features, every feature except for one has the value '−'. The same thing applies to the place of articulation.

In the case of vowels, there is a similar situation, with rounding apparently being a nice simple case of a Boolean feature, with [u] having the value

[+ round] and [i] having the value [− round]. But there is a similar problem to the consonants with height and backness. It's not quite as complex with vowels because there aren't as many different possible heights and backnesses, and that's probably why a lot of people have tended to suggest that it's possible to get away with Boolean features for height and backness of vowels. The argument goes that four values for height and three for backness need to be distinguished. Assuming two features for height, [high] and [low], there are four different possible combinations of + and −. High = [+ high], [− low]; low = [− high], [+ low]; high mid = [+ high], [+ low] and low-mid = [− high], [− low]. That is a way of distinguishing the four heights, but it does mean claiming that one height is both high and low and another is neither high nor low, and there's no obvious reason for choosing which of those is which. In fact, for English and a lot of languages, it is not necessary to distinguish four different heights, so it is possible to say that vowels are either high ([+ high], [− low]), low ([− high], [+ low]) or mid ([− high], [− low]). But why not just have a single feature [height] which can have one of four values: high, high-mid, low-mid and low? Or, going back to the consonant example, a feature [manner] which has values: plosive, fricative and so forth?

There isn't a single straightforward answer to that question. It really depends on what you want to do with your features. There are real advantages to having only Boolean features, especially if you want to use them to provide very precise classifications that might be used by a computer program, for example. Computers love Boolean things. They are basically just machines designed to process Boolean features. All computer programs (from the systems used by NASA right down to the apps on your phone) are built on millions of virtual switches that are either on (1) or off (0). The simplest type of computer program to write is one that works like one of those decision charts, where you answer a question with a yes or a no and follow the appropriate branch to the next question. Using only Boolean features allows us to do that kind of description and processing. It is possible to classify all sounds in this way, by asking, for example, whether it is a consonant or a vowel. Consonant, okay – is it voiced or voiceless? Voiced, okay – is it bilabial or not? And so on, until you get to the sound in question. There are still some problems with this, though. Why did voicing come before place of articulation? Why bilabial before alveolar? The decisions have to be ordered when there might not really be any obvious reason for that order. It also makes it difficult to make the most of the fact that features are shared among different groups of sounds. If there's a decision between consonants and vowels first, which seems sensible, then the decision about whether they are labial (labial place of articulation for consonants and rounded for vowels) has to be made separately.

Another important use of features that you're going to need later on is using **variables** in place of feature values. Imagine that you want to say that the voicing value of one sound is the same as whatever sound comes before it. You want to say that if the sound before it is [+ voice] then it will be [+ voice] and if the sound before it is [– voice] then it will be [– voice]. You can just say those two things, but it's easier and quicker to say that the sounds will have the same value for [± voice], whatever that value is. This is done by using a variable. That's just a symbol that stands for any value. Usually Greek letters are used for this, so the sound is [α voice] when the sound before it is [α voice]. Then if α is + the sound also has + and if α is – then the sound will have –. Different Greek letters can be used as variables to say that the two sounds have different values for a feature.

In the next section I tell you a bit about some of the sets of features that phonologists have suggested. Then I say a bit about the features that I use in the rest of the book.

10.1.5   Some possible feature systems

Back in the early twentieth century, phonologists came up with a theory known as **distinctive feature theory** (see chapter 14.3). The idea behind this theory was that all sounds could be classified in terms of Boolean features, but for any particular language, it was only necessary to use the features that actually distinguished sounds in that language. The idea of **contrast** is a very important one, and one that I come back to in chapter 11.

How might that apply to English? In English there are voiced and voiceless consonants. Are there any examples of two sounds that are only different in their voicing? Yes, there are lots, actually. Think about [p] and [b]. There are words that have different meanings that are distinguished only by these two sounds, such as *pit/bit*, *nip/nib* and so on. And there are loads of other consonant pairs like this: [t]/[d], [k]/[g], [f]/[v], [s]/[z], [tʃ]/[dʒ] and more. So it's fair to say that the feature [± voice] is **distinctive** in English.

Place of articulation is also distinctive, because consonants with a different place of articulation can distinguish words, as in *pit* and *kit*. But how many features are needed to distinguish the different places of articulation in English? The traditional distinctive feature approach doesn't use labels like 'alveolar' and 'velar', but distinguishes the places of articulation with features that say whether the front part of the tongue (corona) is used or not ([± coronal]), whether the articulation is in the front or back of the mouth ([± anterior]) and whether the lips are used or not ([± labial]). So an alveolar sound uses the corona, is in the front of the mouth and doesn't use the lips. A velar sound doesn't use the corona, is in the back part of the mouth and doesn't use the lips. When it gets to the different places of articulation for the fricatives, though, there are difficulties. Dental [θ] and [ð] are distinct from alveolar [s] and [z], but these three features aren't going to distinguish them.

Both pairs of sounds use the corona, are in the front of the mouth and don't use the lips. The solution that was suggested was to use another feature, in this case one referring to the fact that the [s] and [z] are sibilants.

Distinctive feature theory was adapted in Noam Chomsky and Morris Halle's book *The Sound Pattern of English*, published in 1968. In spite of its title, their approach to phonology was intended to apply to all languages. They took the distinctive feature theory approach and devised a set of features which they believed could be used to define any language's set of sounds. Their set of features is still talked about today, but modern phonology has largely moved away from the exact approach.

More recent work takes a more sophisticated approach to features, as I explain in chapter 14.3, but for our purposes a relatively simple set will do.

10.1.6 A simple set of features

In this book I use the features that are the most familiar. I'm not too strict about defining a single set of features and sticking with them. I use what is needed as I go along. For example, when I need to specify that a sound or set of sounds is labial, I just use [+ labial]. For most of what is needed in the remaining chapters, the articulatory features will suffice. So for consonants I use features relating to voicing, place and manner, and for vowels I use features relating to height, backness and rounding. I also refer to some of the other characteristics mentioned in previous chapters. For consonants I use a feature [± sonorant] to distinguish obstruent and sonorant consonants, and I use [± sibilant] to refer to the sibilant sounds. For vowels, I use features to indicate length and tenseness.

Where I want to say, for example, that two sounds have the same place of articulation, I do that using variables and use an umbrella feature, [place]. For example, I use [α place] to indicate any place of articulation, without having to give a long list of place features. I do the same thing for manner of articulation.

10.2 Classes of sounds

In the last section I talked about how sounds can be broken down into their component parts, or features. In this section I look at how sounds can be grouped together into classes of sounds. The two ideas are really very much two sides of the same coin. If you think about animals, for each different type of animal it's possible to identify its own particular characteristics or features. So a cat has four legs, fur, a tail and miaows. A dog has four legs, fur, a tail and barks. A lizard has four legs, scaly skin, a tail and doesn't make a noise. A snake has no legs, scaly skin, a tail and hisses. All of these things can be considered as features that define those animals. These features can also be used to group the animals into classes, such as animals with four legs (cat, dog, lizard), animals with fur (cat, dog), animals with scaly skin (lizard, snake) and so on. The same thing applies to sounds. For each of the features I talked about in the previous section, classes of sounds can be identified that have that feature (and maybe classes that don't). For example, all sounds that have the feature [plosive] are in the class of plosives. For features that are naturally Boolean, it makes sense to think about classes both with and without the feature. So there is a class of voiced sounds and a class of voiceless sounds. On the other hand, for features like [plosive] it doesn't necessarily make sense to think about a class of non-plosive sounds.

What are classes for? Well, as with features, they are useful for looking at how sounds work together, but in the case of classes it's also helpful even at the level of phonetic description to think in terms of classes. When I talked about how to articulate different sounds, I was already talking in those terms. How is a plosive articulated? There is a complete closure followed by a release. That is true for all members of the class 'plosives', regardless of where they're produced or whether they're voiced or not. How is a voiced sound articulated? The vocal chords vibrate. Again that is true of every sound in the class 'voiced sounds', regardless of where they are produced or whether they are plosives, fricatives or so forth. So treating sounds as belonging to classes is something I've already been doing. In this chapter I look in more detail at different types of classes.

10.2.1   Natural classes

The idea of **naturalness** is something that is not only found in phonology. There are certain linguistic forms and behaviours that are very common across different languages that suggest that some belong in languages more naturally than others. There are lots of different theories about how and why this happens. In the case of sounds, these theories generally refer to things like how easy sounds are to articulate or how easy they are to distinguish. In chapter 3, I said that the click sounds are rather difficult to produce, and not surprisingly, they are not found in many of the world's languages. On the other hand, they are very easy to distinguish from other sounds, and that probably explains why they have survived at all. Alveolar sounds are pretty much universal. There is no known language that doesn't have at least one alveolar sound. This idea of some things being normal, natural, common or in some cases universal is important in lots of different areas of linguistics. The opposite of naturalness is known as **markedness**. Linguists say that sounds, or the ways in which they behave, are either natural or marked. I'm now going to focus on one particular theory in the area – that of natural classes.

Quick quiz

1. How many different classes would you group the following sets sounds into?

    (a) [b, d, g, p, t, k, f, θ, s, v, ð, z]
    (b) [iː, ɪ, ɛ, æ, uː, ʊ, ɔː, ɒ]

2. Would you want to group any of the sounds from (a) with the sounds from (b)?
3. Why or why not?

The idea of natural classes is not quite the same as what I said about types of sounds that are common or rare. Natural classes are groups of sounds that behave in similar ways and, crucially that would be expected to behave in similar ways because of something that they fundamentally share. It might be the case in a particular language that a few sounds, let's say [f], [d], [h] and [w] all get deleted when they occur at the end of a word. It might be reasonable to treat these sounds as a class because of this behaviour, but they do not make a natural class. They don't make a natural class because there are no features that they all share that are not shared by other sounds. There are two fricatives, one plosive and one approximant. Two of the sounds are voiced and two are voiceless. They all have different places of articulation. The only thing that they have in common is that they are all consonants, but that is not enough to make them a natural class unless they are the only consonants in that language (and it would be a very strange set of consonants for a language to have). So what is an example of a natural class? To take a very simple example, voiceless sounds might make up a natural class. Voiceless sounds often behave in similar ways, such as becoming voiced in certain positions. Getting more specific, voiceless plosives could be a natural class. In English, voiceless plosives that are at the beginning of words are aspirated, that is, they're pronounced with a little puff of air. Try saying *pit* and *spit* with your hand in front of your mouth. You should be able to feel that there's more of a puff of air with *pit* than there is with *spit*. The same thing happens with [t] and [k] as well, but not with voiced plosives, [b], [d], [g] nor with voiceless fricatives, [f], [θ], [s], [ʃ].

The sounds in question 1 form two obvious naturals classes: consonants and vowels. How many smaller groups did you think you would group them into? This is a bit like those questions where you have to say how many triangles you can see in a picture. The more you look at it, the more triangles you can see, when you realise that you can connect two or three triangles to make another bigger one, and so on. There are many different groups that you could divide the consonants into. You could say plosives and fricatives.

You could say bilabial, alveolar, velar, labio-dental and dental. You could say voiced and voiceless. Or you could break some of those groups down more. For example, you could have a group of voiced plosives, one of voiceless fricatives and so on. Alternatively you could have a group of voiced bilabials, one of voiced alveolars and so on. And you could break it down even further and have a group of voiced alveolar plosives, one of voiceless alveolar plosives and so on. How many members would each of those groups have? They would only have one. It might seem odd to have a class of sounds that only has one sound in it, but there's nothing to stop us doing it if it is useful. One situation where it might be helpful to do it is if there is a set of groupings which has some classes with more than one sound and one or more classes with only one sound. Grouping the consonants of English into classes by manner of articulation, which is a perfectly sensible thing to do, will give a lateral class that has only one member, [l].

Natural classes also change together when the sounds of a language change. Speakers of a language aren't always aware of changes that happen to their language, because they happen gradually, but if you compare the way English is pronounced today with how it was pronounced a few hundred years ago, you can see the changes. What is interesting is that changes don't often happen to individual sounds; they happen to classes of sounds. In the case of consonants, for example, there are points in the history of English where a whole class of voiceless plosives became fricatives (well, actually this was way back in Proto-Indo-European – the ancestor of English and many European and Indic languages). In the case of vowels, there are examples of changes like low vowels all becoming higher. This is what happened in what is known as the Great Vowel Shift.

A brief aside on English and Germanic sound changes . . .

There was a point in the history of English, or more accurately its ancestor language, when a whole group of voiceless plosives became fricatives. A similar thing also happened in German. There is a set of words in English, German and Dutch which are very similar because they come from the same word in their common ancestor language, Germanic. The English and Dutch words all have bilabial plosives, but the German words have either fricatives or affricates. These are words like English *ape, hope, pound, penny*, Dutch *aap, hopen, pond, penning* and German *Affe, hoffen, Pfund, Pfennig*. The Great Vowel Shift happened around 500 years ago and involved the long vowels. Roughly, what happened is that the low and mid-low vowels raised and the high vowels, which were being pushed out of their space by those vowels, became diphthongs. This is one of the reasons why a spelling like *bite* represents a diphthong in modern English. Originally this would have been the long vowel [iː].

10.2.2   Consonant classes

Pretty much any of the features I talked about in the last section could be the basis for a group of sounds.

What happens if all the sounds that share a value for a single feature are grouped together? Think about the key features for the consonants, based on the articulatory descriptions. The classes of sounds that have the value '+' for each of these features are as follows:

[+ **voice**]: b, d, g, v, ð, z, ʒ, m, n, ŋ, j, w, ɹ, l

[+ **plosive**]: p, t, k, b, d, g, ʔ, tʃ, dʒ

[+ **fricative**]: f, v, θ, ð, s, z, ʃ, ʒ, h, tʃ, dʒ

[+ **nasal**]: m, n, ŋ

[+ **approximant**]: j, w, ɹ, l

[+ **lateral**]: l

[+ **labial**]: p, b, m, f, v, w

[+ **dental**]: f, v, θ, ð

[+ **alveolar**]: t, d, s, z, n, ɹ, l, tʃ, dʒ

[+ **palatal**]: ʃ, ʒ, tʃ, dʒ, j

[+ **velar**]: k, g, ŋ, w

[+ **glottal**]: ʔ, h

These all make a lot of sense. But there are some other groupings that would be good to have as well. For a start there is a nice natural class of voiced sounds, but not one of voiceless sounds. I've already talked about a situation where voiceless sounds seem to behave in similar ways, so a [− voice] class is definitely useful as well. What about the other features? Does it make sense to think about a class of sounds that are [− labial]? The sounds that are [− labial] include all the dental, alveolar, palatal, velar and glottal sounds. That doesn't seem like such a natural class.

In the previous section I talked about the voiceless sounds and then voiceless plosives. So there can also be any combination of two features defining a class. Does this actually make sense? There are three parameters of description: voicing, place of articulation and manner of articulation. Let's assume the features for place and manner from the last section.

The use of more than two features to define some places of articulation also leads to questions about whether the groups for each single feature are correct, or at least whether some other groups might be needed. I'm not going to go through all of the possibilities of combining two features because there are hundreds, but I will just say now that when I look at phonemes in chapter 11 and what happens to sounds in chapter 13, a range of combinations are relevant. Just as a little taster, I have already talked about voiceless plosives: [– voice], [+ plosive]. Voiced fricatives might also be interesting: [+ voice], [+ fricative]. So it does seem that smaller classes could be useful, as shown in relation to the first question in the quick quiz.

10.2.3   Vowel classes

Vowel classes, just like consonant classes, can be defined according to the features the sounds share, and once again, it makes sense to turn to the three parameters of description. A class of rounded vowels and one of unrounded vowels, for example, is likely to be useful. When it comes to the other parameters, it is important to bear in mind the actual set of vowels in the language in question. For English, for example, high, mid and low vowels are recognised, but it might be better for some purposes to group them into only two heights. For example, high and non-high (including low and mid) or low and non-low (including high and mid). The same thing applies to backness and with the added complication of low vowels that I have discussed before. Low vowels often behave as though they are back vowels, even if they are phonetically front. This is another example of where phonology doesn't always follow the phonetics.

The other features I talked about in the previous section can also define classes, for example tense or lax vowels and long or short vowels. Once again, as with the consonants, classes can be broken down in different ways. It might be useful to talk about rounded front vowels and rounded back vowels, for example.

Additional reading

Giegerich (1992) covers the features and classes of English well. All introductory phonology books will have chapters on features, although they will give different sets and different types. Kennedy (2017), chapter 6, combines features and classes, as does Carr (1999), chapter 3. Katamba (1999) has separate sections: chapter 3 on features and section 6.2 on classes. For a deeper look at the phonological issues, Lass (1984), chapters 5 and 6, is a good traditional source. Clark and Yallop (2006), chapter 10, is also a good traditional source on the issues of distinctive features, and Zsiga (2013), chapter 12, gives a more recent perspective.

Exercises

1. For each of the following sounds, state all of the features you think it has and all of the natural classes you think it belongs to.
   (a) [g]
   (b) [ʧ]
   (c) [w]
   (d) [iː]
   (e) [l]

2. Below are pairs of groups of sounds. For each one work out what feature or features the sounds in each set share and what feature or features are different between the two sets. Does each set form a natural class?
   (a) [y i ɛ œ] versus [u o ʌ ɒ]
   (b) [i u y ʉ] versus [e o ɤ ø]
   (c) [i ɑ e a] versus [u o ɒ y]
   (d) [y e u o] versus [ɪ ɛ ɔ ʊ]
   (e) [p d k g] versus [ʃ s v x]
   (f) [t s g d] versus [d v z g]
   (g) [t f s k] versus [d v z g]
   (h) [l ɹ ʎ ɾ] versus [m n ŋ ɳ]
   (i) [m d r f] versus [i y a œ]
   (j) [t s n l] versus [k g x ŋ]

3. For each of the following, say what natural class is represented by each set of sounds. What feature or features change if the sounds in the first set become the sounds in the second set?
   (a) [b, d, g] → [β, ð, ɣ]
   (b) [f, s, ʃ] → [v, z, ʒ]
   (c) [p, t, k] → [pʰ, tʰ, kʰ]
   (d) [i, y, u] → [e, ø, o]
   (e) [e, o] → [ɛ, ɒ]
   (f) [k, g] → [ʧ, ʤ]

11   Phonemes

At the start of this part of the book, I explained about the difference between phonetics and phonology. I'm now going right to the heart of phonology. That is, I'm now going to look at how sounds are used in languages and how they behave, rather than looking at how they are produced and described.

The most important concept when it comes to individual sounds and how they behave is the **phoneme**. Like all of these words that begin with *phon-*, it's from the Greek word for a sound. In phonology, there is a distinction between **phones** and **phonemes**. Phones are the actual sounds. They are real. You can feel and see how they are articulated; you can measure their frequencies and find their acoustic properties; and you can hear them. Phonemes are not measurable things out in the real world. They exist only in speakers' minds. That doesn't make them unimportant; it just gives them a different status and makes them a bit harder to really pin down. A phoneme is an abstract sound which can be realised in different ways, depending on where it occurs.

Quick quiz

1. Where would you use A and where would you use *a*?
2. What is the difference between the two sentences below?

   (a)   A cat called Alan sat on the mat.
   (b)   a cAt cAlled alAn sAt on the mAt.

3. Does the different use of A and *a* change the meaning?
4. Can you hear any difference between the *p* in the words *pit* and *spit*?

First of all, I'm going to go back to letters again. Back in chapter 10, I asked you to think about the relationship between *a* and *A*. I came back to this in the quiz. I hope you will agree that in some sense they are the same thing. That is, they are both the letter *A*. But they're rather different, aren't they? Question 1 asked where you would use each one. You hopefully said that the upper-case, or capital, *A* is found at the beginning of sentences and the beginning of names (or proper nouns, to give them their technical term) and the lower-case, or small, *a* is found in all other places. You would not (normally) expect to find a lower-case *a* in either of the places where you find

A and, unless it was a piece of writing all in upper-case, you wouldn't expect to find the upper-case *A* anywhere other than those places. If you want to choose a letter *A* to put in a piece of writing, you will ask yourself (probably not consciously – that would make the process all rather long-winded), 'Is it the beginning of a sentence or a proper noun?' If the answer is yes, then you put an upper-case *A*; if it is no then you put a lower-case '*a*'. It's pretty straightforward, but it's not the same for all languages. Even forgetting about languages that are written with completely different scripts, there are languages that use the Roman alphabet but use capitalisation differently. German, for example, puts capitals at the beginning of all nouns, not just proper nouns. So the rule about where to put upper- and lower-case letters is **language-specific**.

This idea that there are things that are different, but kind of the same thing, and that language users know where to use one and where to use another is very much the idea behind phonemes. Think about the example in question 4. I have mentioned this before. Say the words *pit* and *spit* with your hand in front of your mouth. Can you feel that there is a little puff of air when you say *pit*, but not when you say *spit*? When transcribing the exact pronunciation, this can be reflected by using a diacritic in the IPA. So *pit* is transcribed [pʰɪt] and *spit* is [spɪt]. The superscript *h* indicates that little puff of air or aspiration. These two sounds can be thought of as different sounds. They can have different features (at least, different values for the feature 'aspirated') and one can be said to belong to the set of aspirated sounds and the other to the set of unaspirated sounds. In this way, aspiration could be treated in just the same way as voicing. I didn't do that, though, in chapter 10. Why not? In that chapter I stressed that I was focusing on features that are **distinctive**, that is, differences that can produce different words. This, like the upper- and lower-case letters, is language-specific. In English, aspiration doesn't distinguish different words, but in other languages it does.

The two sentences in question 2 have their upper- and lower-case *a*'s swapped round. The second sentence looks a bit odd, doesn't it? Question 3 asked if they have different meanings? No, they don't, do they? It's exactly the same if you swapped the aspirated ([pʰ]) and unaspirated ([p]) versions of *p*. If you can say *pit* without aspiration and *spit* with aspiration, it won't change their meanings; it will just make them sound a bit odd. That's because they are both realisations of the same **phoneme**.

So what is a phoneme? It's an abstract representation (in your mind) of a set of sounds. The phonemes of a language are all of the sounds that can be used to differentiate words, and each phoneme may be phonetically realised in different ways in different places.

11.1 Minimal pairs and sets

One of the simplest ways of working out which sounds in any particular language are separate phonemes is by identifying **minimal pairs**. A minimal pair is a pair of words that are the same apart from one of their sounds and which have different meanings, If two words that only differ in one of their sounds have different meanings, that tells us that the two sounds in question must be different phonemes. Here's a simple example. The words *bat* /bæt/ and *cat* /kæt/ mean different things. They each have three sounds (in this case represented fairly straightforwardly by their three letters). This simple comparison tells us that /b/ and /k/ are different phonemes. (You may have noticed that I've used slashes // here. I explain why shortly.)

It's possible to compare words with different sounds in any position. For example, using the same two sounds, there is another minimal pair: *tab* /tæb/ and *tack* /tæk/. This shows the same thing as the other pair.

It doesn't have to stop at pairs either. It's possible find whole sets of words that all only differ by one sound: *bat, cat, mat, gnat, sat, vat, fat, rat, hat, that*. This is called a **minimal set** (for obvious reasons). This is a nice, efficient way of identifying groups of distinct phonemes. This set shows that English has (at least) the phonemes: /b/, /k/, /m/, /n/, /s/, /v/, /f/, /h/, /ð/. One thing to be careful about here is that finding minimal pairs or sets relies on finding actual words in the language. But there are lots of possible words that just don't happen to exist, like [*gat*]. This can't be included in the minimal set, because it doesn't actually exist, but there are other sets that show that /g/ is also a separate phoneme of English, such as *get, bet, set, met, let* and so on. So it's necessary to try to find several sets in order to identify all of the phonemes of English.

It doesn't only apply to consonants either. In chapter 4, I asked you to think about lip rounding. The set of words I gave for you to see the difference in rounding was actually a minimal set of words that had the same beginning and ending consonants, but different vowels. So the set *heed, hid, head, had, hard, hod, hoard, hood, who'd* show that the vowels /iː/, /ɪ/, /ɛ/, /æ/, /ɑː/, /ɒ/, /ɔː/, /ʊ/ and /uː/ are all phonemes of English.

For some pairs of sounds, there are minimal pairs with the sounds in one position, but not in another. There are two different kinds of situation where this happens. Some sounds just don't appear in some positions for historical reasons (I look at some examples of that in the next chapter). In English, for example, the consonant /h/ never appears at the end of a word and the consonant /ŋ/ never appears at the beginning of a word. That means that there are pairs of words where these sounds contrast with other consonants in one position, but not the other. For example, *sin* and *sing* show that /n/ and /ŋ/ are separate phonemes, but there are no pairs of words with those sounds contrasting at the beginning. There is no matching word for *nip, not, net* and so on. The other situation is where two (or more) sounds contrast in some words, but not in others. An example of this is the word *either* in English. The first vowel can be either /i:/ or /aɪ/, and it doesn't change the meaning. However, in the words *beat* and *bite* those two sounds do change the meaning, so they must be different phonemes. These are both interesting situations which I look at in more detail shortly, but the important thing to remember here is that it only takes one example of a minimal pair to prove that two sounds are separate phonemes.

Important note: When linguists write IPA symbols, they are enclosed in either square brackets, [], or in forward slashes, //. The difference is important. When writing a phonetic transcription, brackets are used, and when writing a phonemic transcription, slashes are used. I say more about different types of transcription later, but note that where I use slashes, I'm talking about phonemes, and where I use brackets, I'm talking about phones.

11.2 Phonemes and spelling

One of the really important uses for phonemes is for working out how to write languages. In chapter 1, I talked a lot about the problems of writing language, and especially about the difficulties of representing the actual pronunciation with normal alphabetic writing. Phonemes offer us at least part of a solution to those problems, and the whole idea of phonemes is behind many of the writing systems in use for the world's languages today. In fact, they are often referred to as, 'phonemic writing systems', although care is needed about exactly how far to push that definition. Here's a quick recap of the reasons why spelling doesn't represent pronunciation accurately:

1. **The strict one-to-one problem:** a single sound might be represented by more than one letter, and vice versa.

2. **The variation problem:** different pronunciations might be represented by the same letter (or pair/group of letters), and vice versa.

3. **The cross-linguistic problem:** different languages that use the same (basic) alphabet have different sets of sounds that need to be represented.

4. **The accent problem:** different accents within a single language have different pronunciations but the same spelling.

So which of these problems can the phoneme help with? Certainly the second of these. Given that a phoneme is an abstract representation for a set of different, but non-contrasting, sounds, using a single symbol, or letter, for that set helps with this problem. It doesn't entirely solve it, though. There are a lot of cases of sounds represented by a single letter that don't belong to a single phoneme. Even just looking at the set of phonemes, rather than phones, of a language like English, there are more instances than there are letters in the alphabet, so the phoneme idea isn't going to completely solve the problem. It's a similar situation with the first problem. It is possible, in part, to get round the second problem by using pairs (or groups) of letters to represent different phonemes, but then that leads to the first problem. The third problem is not really helped by using phonemes, because different languages have different sets of phonemes as well as different realisations of those phonemes. The question of accents is more interesting. There is an assumption in a language like English that even across a wide range of accents, the same set of phonemes can be defined, although the exact realisation of those phonemes will be different in different accents. That works up to a point. Someone with a Southern English accent will generally pronounce a /k/ as [k] (or [kʰ]), whereas someone with a Liverpool accent might pronounce it as [x]. However, there are lots of other accent differences that can't be defined in this way. For example, the North/South divide in English accents in words like *luck*, and *look*. For Southern English speakers the two are pronounced differently and so reasonably have different spellings. For Northern English speakers, though, they are pronounced the same, so it's not clear why they should be spelled differently.

The idea of alphabets as phonemic writing systems is perhaps best seen as the ideal, which is only rarely achieved. Even languages that have clearly transparent writing systems, like Spanish, don't really have fully phonemic writing systems. It is also something of a myth that languages like English have a spelling system that was once phonemic, until various changes happened to mess the system up. There is no evidence that the spelling of English has ever been fully phonemic. The only situation where genuinely phonemic writing systems might be found is where modern linguists are developing writing systems for languages that don't have an existing system. In those cases the linguists in question are likely to try to get as close as reasonably possible to a system that is based on phonemic analysis. However, as I show in chapter 12, there are lots of aspects of pronunciation that phonemes don't actually represent, which might be needed in the writing system of a language. That means that even a thorough phonemic analysis of a language still might not provide what is needed for the writing system.

11.3   Phones, allophones and phonemes

I've said that there is a difference between phones, which are actual speech sounds, and phonemes, which are abstract representations of sets of sounds. The set of different sounds which are established as belonging to one phoneme are called the **allophones** of that phoneme.

A brief aside on -emes and allo-s ...

Linguists use the idea behind phonemes and allophones for lots of different things. The most commonly used other ones are **morphemes** and **allomorphs** and **graphemes** and **allographs**. Allomorphs are different ways of pronouncing the same morpheme, so the plural morpheme in English is pronounced differently in *cats* and *dogs*. Can you hear the difference? The s in *cats* is voiceless but the -s in *dogs* is voiced. The example of the letter *a* is an example of a grapheme, with the upper- and lower-case versions being the allographs. There are also lexemes. This is the word used for the idea of a dictionary entry which represents all the different forms of a word, so the lexeme *cat* has two possible forms, *cat* and *cats*. The *allo-* part is not generally used here, though – we just talk about word forms rather than allolexes. Some people use the term *grammeme* for grammatical units (e.g. 'plural' or 'past tense') or the alternative tagmeme. There was also briefly the *chereme*, which was the equivalent of the phoneme, but in sign language. That didn't catch on, though, and now linguists use the term *phoneme* for sign language, too. The phoneme was the first of these and the others were then created by analogy. The suffix *-eme*, doesn't really mean anything; it just comes from the Greek word *phonema*, meaning 'that which is sounded'. The *allo-* prefix, however, means 'other' and is used in other areas of science, such as chemistry. The terminology has been extended so that some people talk about 'emic units' and 'etic units'. Emic units are abstract, whereas etic units are real. The idea was even extended to other areas of behavioural science, with emic accounts based on 'insider knowledge' and etic accounts based on observation.

11.4   Complementary distribution

One of the key ideas about phonemes is that the allophones of a single phoneme are in **complementary distribution**. That means that they appear in different places or contexts. The example of the letter *A/a* is a case of complementary distribution. I said that the upper-case is used at the beginning of sentences and proper nouns. The lower-case is used in other places, but never in those. This is complementary distribution. Going back to the example of aspirated and unaspirated plosives in English, it is possible to state where the aspirated allophone appears and where the unaspirated allophone appears. The aspirated allophone is found at the beginning of words, and the unaspirated allophone in other places, like after /s/. The crucial thing about complementary distribution is that the two sounds can never occur in the same environment. That is, there is never an unaspirated plosive at the beginning of a word and never an aspirated plosive in other places.

The idea of complementary distribution is really the other side of the same coin as minimal pairs. Minimal pairs show that two sounds do occur in the same position or context, so by definition the two distinct sounds in a minimal pair are not in complementrary distribution. They are said to be in **overlapping distribution**, sometimes known as **parallel distribution**. That is, they share some positions they can occur in. They don't have to share all of their contexts – it is enough for them to share only one context for them to be in overlapping distribution.

In some cases it's quite easy to work out whether two sounds are in complementary distribution, like the example of aspirated and unaspirated plosives. In other cases it can be a bit more tricky. There are several different considerations when you're trying to decide whether sounds are in complementary distribution. The simplest are, for example, whether the sounds are at the beginning or end of words. You may also need to think about syllables – is it really that a sound can occur at the beginning of words, or is it actually the beginning of syllables? If you think about it, it should be quite obvious that if a sound can occur at the beginning of a syllable, then it can also be at the beginning of a word, but the other way round isn't necessarily true. So when you're looking at where sounds occur, you need to think about syllables as well as words. You might need to think about other things, too, like whether the syllable a sound occurs in is stressed. Sometimes one allophone occurs in stressed syllables and another in unstressed syllables. It's also important to think about what other sounds can be before or after it. Does it always come before or after a consonant or a vowel, for instance? But sometimes more detail is needed. If there are two sounds both occurring before vowels, it's possible that they are still in complementary distribution if, for example, one of them occurs before front vowels and the other one before back vowels, In these cases it is often helpful to think about how and why the allophones are different. For example, if you find that a consonant has one allophone that is pronounced further back and one that is pronounced further forward, then it would make sense if the one further back occurs before (or after) back vowels, and the one further forward occurs before (or after) front vowels. As the case study in section 11.7.1 shows, doing a phonemic analysis is a bit like solving a logic puzzle, like a sudoku, but it does help to think about exactly what is happening and why, to see if the solution you come to makes sense. A bit of linguistic intuition can help you towards the right answer!

11.5 Phonetic similarity

The other criterion to consider when deciding whether two sounds are allophones of a phoneme is phonetic similarity. Lots of pairs of sounds are in complementary distribution, but that's not enough to decide that they are allophones of the same phoneme. For example, to return to the aspirated plosives again, it is true to say that [p] and [tʰ] are in complementary distribution, but you would not claim that they are allophones of a single phoneme, because they are not similar enough, phonetically. The idea of phonetic similarity is fairly simple, but it's not easy to pin it down to a strict definition. If you think about the aspiration example, it is clear that aspiration is never contrastive in English, so if two sounds only differ in this feature, then it's fair to say that they are phonetically similar. So the [p] and [pʰ] sounds are phonetically similar because they share all of their other features, such as place and manner of articulation and voicing. The trouble is that often sounds are genuinely allophones of a single phoneme but are actually quite different and differ in their place or manner of articulation or voicing, features can distinguish different phonemes. Once you are a reasonably experienced linguist, you'll be able to spot the kinds of features that are most likely to distinguish allophones, because you'll know about how and why sounds vary and change.

11.6 Free variation

I talked earlier about the word *either*, which could be pronounced with two different vowels – vowels which must be distinct phonemes in English because of other words that form minimal pairs. In this word (and a few others, for example *neither*) these sounds are in **free variation**. Sometimes there are sounds in a language which are always in free variation. That is, they never form minimal pairs, but can occur in the same environments. An example of this from English is the different kinds of *r* sound, which might be down to your accent or just how you feel. In terms of our example of the different letter *A*'s free variation is like choosing a different font style, so a, ɑ and ɑ are free variants of the letter. Free variation is not very common and tends not to affect many sounds in a language, but it is important to be able to recognise it when it does occur.

11.7 Phonemic analysis

Working out which sounds occur in a language and how they are grouped into phonemes is vital to understand the pronunciation of that language. You can get some way down the road of finding out what phonemes there are by identifying minimal pairs or sets, but they can't tell you about all of the different allophones of those phonemes. To do that, you first need a good, reasonably detailed phonetic transcription. Then you need to do a phonemic analysis for all of the sounds of the language. In my description I may have given the impression that phonetic similarity is something you only think about after you've considered the other questions, but in practice, it's likely to be the first thing you'll look at. That is, when you start out on a full phonemic analysis of a new language, you'll start by looking for sounds that seem to be very similar and then test to see if they are in complementary distribution.

Figure 11.1 is a flow chart which shows how to go about testing two (or more) sounds. In a typical phonemic analysis that you may be asked to do as

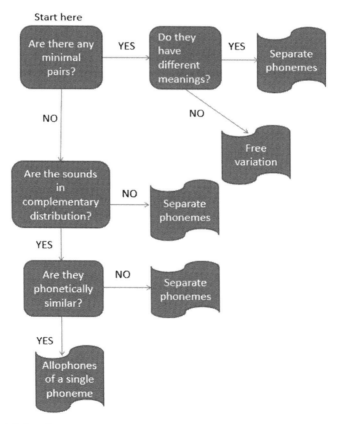

Figure 11.1   A flow chart for testing sounds for their phonemic status

an exercise, the last part, that is, identifying which sounds it is worth testing against each other, will normally have been done for you. You'll be given a set of data in the form of phonetic transcriptions of words, together with their meanings. Can you see why you need to have the meanings? You might think that it's not important because you're only interested in the pronunciation, but it is necessary to see whether having different sounds actually changes the meaning.

Mostly you'll be given data from a language that you're not familiar with, but you don't need to know anything about the language in order to be able to do a phonemic analysis. In the following subsection, I run through a phonemic analysis for a pair of sounds in English. In some ways, it's harder to do this kind of analysis for your own language because you are so used to using it, and especially to writing it, that it's hard to think consciously about the different pronunciations.

11.7.1   Case study: [l] and [ɫ]

First I'm going to compare two ways of pronouncing *l*. Try saying the words *lull, loll* and *label*. Listen very carefully to the way you pronounce the /l/ at the beginning and at the end, and try to feel what your tongue is doing. These different pronunciations have special names. The sound at the beginning is called 'clear *l*' and at the end it is 'dark *l*'. The technical phonetic word for the dark *l* is **velarised**. and it is transcribed as [ɫ]. The transcriptions for those three words, and a few more that include those sounds, are as follows:

word	transcription
lull	[lʌɫ]
loll	[lɒɫ]
label	[leɪbəɫ]
lick	[lɪk]
loop	[luːp]
pool	[puːɫ]
call	[kɔːɫ]

Thinking back to the flow chart, are there any minimal pairs? No, there aren't. Are the sounds in complementary distribution? Look at the collection of words. For each occurrence of either [l] or [ɫ], describe where it appears. One simple way to do this is to say what comes before and after it, including word boundaries, which can be indicated with the hash symbol: #. The first word, *lull* has the [l] with a word boundary before it and the vowel [ʌ] after, so that can be written as #_____ ʌ. It also has [ɫ] with the same vowel before and a word boundary after, ʌ _____ #. You can make a list of all of the occurrences of each sound and what comes before and after:

[l]		[ɫ]			
#_____	ʌ	ʌ_____	#	lull	
#_____	ɒ	ɒ_____	#	loll	
#_____	eɪ	ə_____	#	label	
#_____	ɪ	uː_____	#	lick	pool
#_____	uː	ɔː_____	#	loop	call

This is a nice simple case. You can see that all of the [l] examples are at the beginning of the word (because they are all preceded by a word boundary). All of the [ɫ] examples, on the other hand, are at the end of the word (they're followed by a word boundary). This is a case of complementary distribution: [l] occurs at the beginning of words and [ɫ] at the end. It's a bit more complicated than that in real life. When there is an *l* in the middle of a word, it can be either [l] or [ɫ], depending on what follows it, and in fact, the rule is that it is [l] when it is in a syllable onset and [ɫ] when it is in a syllable coda. By the way, if you speak with a Scottish or Welsh accent, you might be feeling really confused now because those accents don't have this distinction. In most Scottish accents, all *l*'s are dark or velarised, and in most Welsh accents all *l*'s are clear.

So having established that these two sounds are in complementary distribution, the final question is whether they are phonetically similar. Yes, they are similar. The phonetic realisation of velarisation is that the tongue is extended towards the velum (soft palate). Apart from that, the articulations are identical, with the tongue against the alveolar ridge but air flowing down the sides. That is, they are both alveolar lateral approximants. Therefore, according to the flowchart, these two sounds should be considered allophones of a single phoneme

Having established that they are allophones of a single phoneme, the rule or rules that define which one occurs where need to be specified. This can be done in simple English, as I did here, but linguists use a particular format to define **phonological rules**. These rules have a basic format as follows:

$$X \rightarrow Y / C_1 \underline{\qquad} C_2$$

This says that X is realised as Y when it comes after C_1 and before C_2. C_1 and C_2 together are called the **context**. You might not need to specify both C_1 and C_2. This rule format is used for specifying the allophones of a phoneme, but also for defining other changes that happen to sounds, which you will see in later chapters.

Going back to the simple example of /l/, I said that [l] occurs at the beginning of a word and [ɫ] occurs at the end of a word. The rules to specify that would look like this:

/l/ → [l] / # _____
/l/ → [ɫ]/ _____ #

This is a simple example, which involves just one phoneme and which could be defined by referring only to word boundaries. Often it's necessary to specify a class of sounds in some or all of the positions. For example, you might want to say that all voiceless plosives in English are aspirated word initially. To do that, you can use features:

[– voice, + plosive] → [+ aspirated] / # _____

This says that any sound which has the features [– voice] and [+ plosive] will also have the feature [+ aspirated] when it occurs after a word boundary. This isn't quite enough to give the whole picture. This tells us that these sounds are aspirated at the beginning of a word, but it doesn't tell us that they are not aspirated in other positions. Another rule is needed for that. However, it wouldn't be very elegant to specify all of the different contexts where the sounds are unaspirated (at the ends of words, in the middles of words), so as an abbreviation, linguists simply say 'elsewhere':

[– voice, + plosive] → [– aspirated] / elsewhere

11.8 Transcription

Earlier in the chapter I talked about using slashes and brackets for phonemes and allophones. When you do a transcription, you can choose how detailed and how abstract you want to make it. This means that you can choose to either do a **phonemic** or a **phonetic transcription**. When you want to actually transcribe speech, by definition you need to do a phonetic transcription. However, phonemic transcriptions are often useful. If you look in a dictionary, for example, you will often find a transcription that tells you how to pronounce the word. This isn't a transcription of an actual speech event; it's an abstraction or generalisation of how it is normally pronounced. A phonemic transcription is written with slashes to show that it is not a representation of an actual speech event. It's actually very rare, though, that you'll find a genuine phonemic transcription, in the strictest interpretation of the term *phoneme*. In the next chapter I look at some of the ways that phonemes can't explain everything that happens, and some of these affect how phonemic transcriptions tend to be done. For example, think about a word like *above*. What vowel would you put in the first syllable? If you are representing the way it is pronounce then you'll probably use a schwa, [ə]. What about the second vowel in the word *atom*? Again, you'd probably say that it's a schwa. Now, on one level, that's fine, but schwa is not usually considered to be a phoneme of English. In fact, as you'll see in the next chapter, this could be considered an allophone, but of lots of different vowel phonemes. The problem for phonemic transcription is that you need to make decisions about this which don't necessarily serve a practical purpose. So what is called a phonemic transcription is often not really strictly phonemic, but has a similar level of abstraction as phonemes. The important point about a phonemic transcription is that you don't need to include most kinds of allophonic variation. You don't need to include aspiration because it follows naturally once you know that there is a voiceless plosive phoneme in word-initial position.

Phonetic transcription is different. It, technically at least, represents an actual speech event. In section 2.1, I said that the best way to do a transcription is to record yourself or someone else reading out the passage you want to transcribe. That way you are genuinely transcribing one specific speech event, with all of the idiosyncrasies of that particular occasion. So a phonetic transcription transcribes actual speech rather than an abstract idea of how something should be or is usually pronounced. That means that there would be more detail, and especially detail of allophonic variation. In fact, exactly how much detail you include will depend on why you are doing the transcription and what you are going to use it for. If you are interested in doing a detailed accent study, for example, then you will probably want to include a lot of detail, although often you will only need that detail for particular sounds that you are interested in.

When doing a phonetic transcription, linguists distinguish between **broad** and **narrow** phonetic transcription. Broad phonetic transcription typically includes the main allophones, such as aspiration and velarised *l* in English. Narrow phonetic transcription includes much more detail, such as whether a normally voiced sound is pronounced with less voicing than usual or a normally back vowel is pronounced further forward than usual. In terms of the IPA, the diacritics are often used in narrow phonetic transcription, but much less so in broad phonetic transcription. Other things like stress and syllable boundaries may be included or not. In a broad phonetic transcription, it is usual to include at least primary and often secondary lexical stress. Syllable boundaries are not often included unless the transcription is specifically for studying syllabification, for example, to study how much resyllabification happens across word boundaries. Intonation also is only typically included if that is the particular thing that is being studied.

If you are asked to do a transcription, you will usually be told the level of detail that you need to include. If you are doing a transcription for a study like one of those I talked about in chapter 2, then you will need to make your own decisions about the level of detail you need in order to answer the questions you want to ask.

Additional reading

The phoneme is such a fundamental concept in phonology that it is covered thoroughly in all textbooks. I especially recommend Carr and Montreuil (2013) and Giegerich (1992) for the application to English in particular. McMahon (2002), chapter 3, is a good introduction to the concept, with chapter 7 focusing on the phonemes of English. Ladefoged and Johnson (2015), chapter 2, discusses the distinction between phonetic and phonemic transcription. Knight (2012), chapters 10–13, covers a wide range of types of allophonic variation, and Catford (1988), chapter 10, addresses different sound systems (phoneme inventories) in different languages.

Exercises

1. The following sets of minimal pairs show that English /p/ and /b/ contrast in initial, medial and final positions:

   pit/bit   rapid/rabid   cap/cab

   Find similar sets of minimal pairs for each pair of consonants given:

   (a) /k/ - /g/
   (b) /m/ - /n/
   (c) /l/ - /r/
   (d) /b/ - /v/
   (e) /p/ - /f/
   (f) /s/ - /z/

   Can you think of any problems with finding minimal pairs for (c)?

2. Below is a number of small sets of words from different languages, each using two different phones.

   ■ Establish whether the two sounds are allophones of one phoneme, or whether each sound belongs to a different phoneme.

- Then compare to English – are the sounds in question allophones of one phoneme in English, or do they belong to different phonemes?

(Disclaimer: In most cases, there is a bit of simplification of the data going on, to make the task more manageable. If you happen to speak one of the languages listed here, you might see that.)

(a) Italian [n] and [ŋ]

[n] in		[ŋ] in	
[nero]	'black'	[ʧ iŋkwɛ]	'five'
[rana]	'frog'	[aŋkɛ]	'also'
[ʤɛntɛ]	'people'	[faŋgo]	'mud'
[tinta]	'dye'	[tiŋgo]	'I dye'
[tɛnda]	'tent'	[baŋka]	'bank'

(b) Spanish [d] and [ð]

[d] in		[ð] in	
[dolor]	'pain'	[fiðel]	'faithful'
[drama]	'drama'	[oðio]	'hatred'
[dos]	'two'	[naða]	'nothing'
[durar]	'to last'	[kaða]	'each'

(c) Korean [s] and [ʃ]

[s] in		[ʃ] in	
[son]	'hand'	[ʃinho]	'signal'
[sɛk]	'colour'	[ʃipsam]	'thirteen'
[sosəl]	'novel'	[ʃihap]	'game'
[us]	'upper'	[ʃilsu]	'mistake'

(d) Korean [l] and [r]

[l] in		[r] in	
[tal]	'moon'	[norai]	'song'
[talda]	'sweet'	[keri]	'distance'
[solhua]	'legend'	[saram]	'person'
[sul]	'wine'	[irure]	'reaches'

(e) Setswana [l] and [d]

[l] in		[d] in	
[lefifi]	'darkness'	[dumɛla]	'greetings'
[selɛpɛ]	'axe'	[podi]	'goat'
[loleme]	'tongue'	[kʰudu]	'tortoise'
[lerumɔ]	'spear'	[badisa]	'the herd'
[xobala]	'to read'	[mosadi]	'woman'

12 Problems with phonemes

Quick quiz

1. In the following list of words, what do you notice about the pronunciation of the *s* at the end?

   (a) cats
   (b) dogs
   (c) hubs
   (d) flies
   (e) sips
   (f) nods
   (g) kicks
   (h) baths
   (i) bathes
   (j) hives
   (k) tiffs

2. What are the vowel phonemes in the words *major* and *majority*?
3. How do you know?
4. How would you transcribe the word *hamster*?

In the last chapter I showed how to identify all of the phonemes in a language and then describe all the different ways those phonemes can be realised and in what contexts. That gives quite a lot of information about the sounds of a language, but there are some issues with phonemes and allophones. I have already said that there are factors that affect groups of sounds, like stress and tone, that also need to be explained. It's clear that phonemes can't tell us everything about pronunciation. However, even just looking at individual sounds, the phoneme setup doesn't always work. In this chapter I'm going to look at some of the other problems. The strict interpretation of phonemes says that every sound, or phone, belongs to one (and only one) phoneme. There are two ways in which that can be violated. One is where a sound can belong to more than one phoneme, and the other is where there are sounds that don't belong to a phoneme.

12.1 When phonemes don't tell the whole story

To demonstrate that there is a potential problem here, question 1 in the quiz gives an example from English. English has two sounds, [s] and [z]. Are they separate phonemes? The flowchart first asks if there are any minimal pairs which are different only in those two sounds. Can you think of any minimal pairs for [s] and [z]? Hopefully you managed to come up with something like *sip/zip*, or *sap/zap*. So they must be separate phonemes. Can you think of pairs that have the sounds in different positions, like in the middle or at the end? Well, there are pairs of words like *buses/buzzes* or *bus/buzz*. This all looks very comprehensive. There are examples of pairs of words that only differ in those two sounds, and where the sounds are in a range of different positions. Now think about question 1.

What did you think? Can you hear/feel that they are different? They each have a stem together with a suffix. You should have worked out that some have the voiceless [s] as their suffix, while some have the voiced [z]. If you're still not convinced, try saying them while putting your hand on your Adam's apple to feel the vibration. Which ones have [s]? Did you spot that it's a, e, g, h and k? The others (b, c, d, f, i and j) have the voiced [z]. Can you work out why that is? Have a look at the sounds (remember, sounds, not letters) at the ends of the words. What do you notice about the sounds at the ends of a, e, g, h and k? Look at the transcription of how the stems are pronounced:

(a) [kæt]
(b) [dɒg]
(c) [hʌb]
(d) [flaɪ]
(e) [sɪp]
(f) [nɒd]
(g) [kɪk]
(h) [baθ]
(i) [beɪð]
(j) [haɪv]
(i) [tɪf]

Right, now let's look at the ones that I said have the [s] suffix:

(a) [kæt]
(e) [sɪp]
(g) [kɪk]
(h) [baθ]
(k) [tɪf]

The sounds that they end with are [t], [p], [k], [θ], [f]. What can you say about all of those sounds? If you haven't worked it out yet, think about the difference between [s] and [z]. They differ in their voicing, don't they? So these sounds at the ends of words that take the [s] as their suffix are all voiceless sounds. If you look at the sounds at the end of the other words ([g], [b], [d], [ð], [v]) you should be able to see that they are all voiced sounds, and they are followed by the voiced [z].

There is one word in the list that I didn't include in those lists of end sounds – (d) [flaɪ]. What is different about that one? It doesn't end in a consonant at all, like the others. It ends in a vowel. However, that's actually not important here. Vowels are always voiced, so it belongs with the voiced sounds as it ends with a voiced sound. Can you hear or feel that the -s at the end of *flies* is voiced, that is, it's pronounced [z]?

This looks like a nice example of allophonic variation. A phoneme which is realised as voiced when it follows a voiced sound and voiceless when it follows a voiceless sound. But I said that these two sounds must be separate phonemes, because of all of the minimal pairs.

So what does all of this tell you? [s] and [z] must belong to different phonemes, because there are loads of different minimal pairs, and with the sounds in different positions. Look closer at the final position. Can you think of any English words that have voiceless sounds followed by [z]? There aren't any in the CELEX database (catalog.ldc.upenn.edu/ldc96l14), which has over 30,000 words of English. What about a voiced sound followed by a [s]? Actually, there are lots. For example, *sense, dance, prince, bus, fuss, miss, gas* and so on. Is the [s] in any of these words a suffix? That is, is it a separate morpheme (e.g., either plural or verb ending) No, none of those words has a suffix. This is the crucial point here. The only situation with that particular pattern of behaviour with [s] and [z] is when they represent a suffix. This is a case of allomorphy: the morpheme has different allomorphs depending on where the morpheme appears.

What is happening here? It is clear that [s] and [z] are separate phonemes of English. However, when they represent a suffix, or a separate morpheme, this phonemic distinction is **neutralised**. The idea of neutralisation of phonemic distinctions is one of the ways in which phonemic analysis does not tell the whole story. In some cases sounds that must belong to separate phonemes cannot always occur in all different environments. Sometimes this is because of the morphology, as in the [s]/[z] example here. Other times there are phonetic environments where the distinction between phonemes is neutralised. I'm now going to look at two more examples from English.

12.2   Case study 1: nasals

The example of /s/ and /z/ was a very specific kind of example, where the sound(s) in question perform a particular grammatical role. But there are examples of neutralisation happening in certain phonetic environments. Think about another list of English words:

1. impossible

2. imbalance

3. interminable

4. indecisive

5. incomplete

6. inglorious

7. inaudible

Before you start thinking about the pronunciation of these words, I'd like you to think about the spelling. They are all words that begin with the Latin prefix *in-*, which is a negative prefix. That is, *in-X* means the same as *not X*, so *incomplete* means *not complete*. Now that you know that, what do you notice about the spelling of the prefix? In all but two of them, it's spelled the same way, *in-*, but in the first and second it's spelled *im-*. What do you notice about the words spelled with *im-*? What letters come immediately after the prefix? For the first, it's *p*, and for the last it's *b*. Okay, now think about pronunciation. What can you say about the consonants represented by those two letters in English? First *p*: it's usually pronounced as the voiceless bilabial plosive, [p]. Now *b*: it's usually pronounced as the voiced bilabial plosive, [b].

Just to make sure you're still on track with the whole letter/sound thing from Chapter 1, can you think of any situations where the letter *p* isn't pronounced as a voiceless bilabial plosive? What about words like *photograph* and *ephemeral*? There it's paired with *h* to make the sound [f]. In a word like *psychology* is isn't pronounced at all – we say it's silent. Can you think of any words where *b* isn't pronounced as a voiced bilabial plosive? It is also silent in words like *lamb* and *debt*. That's why I've said that these letters are usually pronounced as those sounds.

So what can you tell me about the pronunciation of *m*? It is (again, usually) pronounced as a bilabial nasal. So you can see that, when a bilabial plosive follows the prefix, there is a bilabial nasal. This is probably not a coincidence, but look at the other words, too. Think about numbers 3 and 4 next. In those words, the prefix is followed by the letters *t* and *d*. These are usually pronounced as a voiceless alveolar plosive and a voiced alveolar plosive respectively. What can you say about the pronunciation of the prefix? The *n* here is normally pronounced as an alveolar nasal. Here the same thing is apparently happening. There is an alveolar nasal when it's followed by an alveolar plosive. So this is looking good. So far the place of articulation (in these examples, bilabial or alveolar) seems to be shared by the plosive and the nasal that comes before it.

What about the next two? If you just look at the spelling, there seems to be a problem. The letters *c* and *g* here are pronounced as a voiceless velar plosive and a voiced velar plosive respectively, but the prefix still has *n*, which I said was pronounced as an alveolar nasal. This is where you need to really try to listen to the pronunciation (or feel the articulation). Try saying the word *incomplete* – first of all, very slowly, with a bit of a break between the *in* and the *complete*. You probably pronounced the first part as [ɪn], with the alveolar nasal. Now try saying it faster and joined together. While you're saying it, concentrate on where exactly your tongue touches the roof of your mouth. You should be able to feel that when you say the word fast and joined up, your tongue touches the roof of your mouth towards the back, at the velum, in fact, and not at the alveolar ridge. So the velar plosives are actually preceded by a velar nasal after all. You might be wondering why this is not reflected in the spelling. The most obvious answer is that English doesn't have a single letter that represents the velar nasal, like the bilabial nasal. In order to make clear that it's [ŋ], it is written as *ng*, like in *sing*. I talked about the history and spelling of [ŋ] in chapter 5.

Now there is just one word left to think about: *inaudible*. What kind of nasal does this have? It's an alveolar nasal. And what does the stem begin with? It begins with a vowel. In the other words, the nasal had the same place of articulation as the consonant that follows. In this case, there isn't a consonant following, so the nasal here is the default – the one that is used when nothing has caused it to change.

Now, if you were doing a phonemic analysis and only looking at the examples here, you might decide that the three nasals [n], [m], and [ŋ], are allophones of a single phoneme. It is clear where each one occurs, and it can be defined in clear phonological terms. But you know from other words of English that these sounds are actually contrastive – they occur in minimal pairs or sets, like *sun, sum* and *sung*, What is happening here is neutralisation of the contrast between these three phonemes in a particular phonological context. In the [s]/[z] example, I said that only happened when the sounds were appearing as specific suffixes. Think about the morphology of the nasal cases. I talked about the prefix and stems in the example words, so it might be tempting to say that this is the same kind of thing, with the *in-* prefix showing the neutralisation behaviour. Indeed, there are a few different prefixes that all show the same behaviour: *con-*, as in *condemn, complete, congregate*; *un-* as in *untidy*, *unplug* and *unkind*. (Notice here that *unplug* doesn't have the *m* in the spelling. I'll come back to the spelling in a minute.) The question is whether the same behaviour occurs when a nasal comes before another consonant when it is not in one of these prefixes.

Think about a few different kinds of examples:

1. send [sɛnd]

2. imp [ɪmp]

3. ink [ɪŋk]

4. under [ʌndə]

5. crumple [kɹʌmpl]

6. trinket [tɹɪŋkɪt]

The first three all have a nasal followed by a plosive at the end of the word. Is the same thing happening as in the examples with the prefix? Yes, it is. The spelling here gives a clue. In both cases where the plosive is a bilabial, we find *m*, not *n*. The spelling doesn't help with the velar plosive examples in 3 and 6, but as I said earlier, there are other reasons for that, and if you listen and feel how you pronounce them, you should be able to tell that the nasals here are both velars, So far, so good – it looks as though the same thing is happening. However, it's not enough to only think about examples that do have these patterns. It's necessary to show that there are no examples where a nasal has a different place of articulation from a following consonant. Are there any words where [n] is followed by [p], [b], [k] or [g]; any words where [m] is followed by [t], [d], [k] or [g]; or any words where is [ŋ] followed by [p], [b], [t] or [d]. Thinking about spelling for a start, there are plenty of examples: *simcard, tomcat, gumdrop, humdrum* (I'm ignoring the [n]/[ŋ] distinction for the moment because, as I said, this isn't reflected in the spelling anyway). What do you notice about these examples? There's definitely a morphological element to these examples. In all of these cases, the words can be viewed as being made up of two separate words: *sim-card, tom-cat, gum-drop, hum-drum*. These, as you should remember from chapter 6, are all **compound words**. If you say them reasonably slowly and carefully, they sound as if they are two separate words. In these cases, it is not necessarily the case that the nasal has to have the same place of articulation as the following plosive. So it looks as though the neutralisation only happens within words. It happens when a word is made up of a prefix and a stem, but not when it is a compound. Now try saying the words very quickly. If you speak quickly and casually enough, it's often the case that the nasal is pronounced with the same place of articulation as the consonant that follows. In fact, it even happens across word boundaries. So when I say *in Brighton*, the *in* may well be pronounced [ɪm]. I come back to exactly what is happening here in chapter 13. For now, I'm going back to some of the issues with spelling that I've touched on.

In some of the words, the bilabial plosive [m] is spelled as *m*, but not quite all. I used one example word, *unplug*, where it was spelled with *n*. Why is this? The simple answer is that for some prefixes the spelling reflects the pronunciation (e.g., *in-* and *con*) but for others it reflects the history or etymology (*un-*). For these cases, there's not really anything more to say. But there are other interesting things going on with the spelling of nasals. In the examples I mentioned the fact that *ng* is not used to represent [ŋ] when it's in a prefix, but it is in words like *sing*. Why? Well there's actually a good historical reason for this. In chapter 5, I explained the history of the [ŋ]. At the point when most of English spelling was standardised, [ŋ] was not a separate phoneme of English. It only occurred as an allophone of the phoneme /n/, appearing before a velar plosive. When a sound is only an allophone, it is not usually represented in the spelling. There is no need for the spelling to reflect pronunciations that are completely predictable from the sounds around them. At this time, /m/ was a different phoneme, so it did get used in the spelling, even when its occurrence was in fact determined by the neutralisation of the contrast. This is why the [ŋ] is not represented as *ng* except in those words where a historical [g] (or [k]) has been lost over time.

One final aspect of the spelling of nasals is important to note. Think about the word *sandwich*. How do you pronounce it? Do you say [sændwɪʤ]? Do you really? Are you sure?! Say it quickly, in a sentence like *Do you fancy a sandwich?* I suggest that you probably don't pronounce the /d/ at all. In fact, alveolar consonants are often dropped in clusters (although, slightly confusingly, /d/ and /t/ were not lost in words like *send* and *sent*, unlike the /b/ in *lamb*). Now I also suggest that you don't say [n]; you say [m]. In fact, you'll sometimes see it written as *samwich,* reflecting this pronunciation. The whole morphology question is important here. I have been talking about a distinction between phonetics and phonology. Phonetics is what is actually said, whereas phonology is what happens in your mind. But that's not the only distinction that is relevant here. There is a distinction between **lexical phonology** and **post-lexical phonology**. Lexical phonology is what happens to the sounds when stems, prefixes, suffixes and so on combine to build words, and post-lexical phonology is what happens when words are combined into phrases and sentences. I talk more about these types of processes in chapter 13. What you need to know for now is that, for the most part, lexical phonology gets reflected in the spelling, but post-lexical phonology doesn't.

This example is important for another reason. There's no bilabial plosive here. It's [w], a labial-velar approximant, and that leads to the final thing I want to say about nasals and neutralisation. I have given lots of examples that all have nasals followed by plosives, but the same neutralisation happens with nasals before other kinds of consonant. The approximant [w] is one example (and it also shows that the labial-ness of the [w] is more important than its velar-ness). The same thing happens with fricatives. If you say the word *informative* quickly and casually, you will find that the nasal is pronounced as [ɱ], the labiodental nasal.

12.3   Case study 2: unstressed vowels

What happens with nasals can be explained as simply saying that nasals, in most situations, have the same place of articulation as a following consonant. It's not difficult to see that this is a case of sounds becoming more like sounds around them. The next case is a bit different. It involves vowels, and in this case it's not about the influence of neighbouring sounds.

The second quiz question at the start of this chapter asked you to think about the words *major* and *majority* and how you would pronounce them. The first one has the stress on the first syllable, and the second one has the stress on the second syllable. How would you transcribe them? You should have said something like ['meɪʤə] and [mə'ʤɒɹiti:]. Ignore the *-ity* bit for now, and just compare the two bits that are spelled the same. The consonants are the same in both, but the vowels are different. In the first syllable the vowel is written *a*, and in the first word it is pronounced [eɪ]. In the second word, however, it is pronounced [ə]. This is the schwa. It appears that the phoneme /eɪ/ is realised as [eɪ] when it is in a stressed syllable, but as [ə] when it is in an unstressed syllable. This suggests that schwa is an allophone of /eɪ/. Now look at the second syllable. Here the vowel is written *o*, realised as [ɒ] in the second word when it is stressed, but as [ə] when it is unstressed. So once again it seems that the phoneme /o/ is realised as [ɒ] when it is stressed, but as [ə] when it is unstressed.

So far, so simple. But the strict phonemic principle doesn't allow a single sound to be an allophone of more than one phoneme. If there is a schwa, how do you know what the underlying vowel is, or which phoneme it belongs to? There are two answers to this. One is that you don't. Technically, if you hear a schwa, you have no way of knowing which phoneme it is realising. The schwa in the first syllable of *majority* is the same as the schwa in the second syllable of *major*, and there is nothing about its phonetic environment to indicate which vowel phoneme it represents. The second answer is that the spelling shows it. This is a bit of a chicken and egg situation. The letter *o* is used because it is the phoneme /o/ that is in that first syllable, regardless of how it is pronounced, so saying that the phoneme can be determined from the letter is a bit of a circular argument. The more interesting side to this is that the spelling does represent more than just someone's guess about which phoneme is represented by a sound. In the case of the vowels of English, linguists believe that the schwa did not really become common until the Middle English period; before that the vowels were all pronounced differently. The spelling in this case represents the historical pronunciation, which has not been updated to reflect the present-day pronunciation. Another side to the same coin is that the spelling of these words are as they are so that the relationship between the two words can be easily seen. If the spelling changed to more accurately reflect the pronunciation, then the spelling might end up as something like *maju* and *mujority*, which don't look as though they are related.

You might be wondering what all this has to do with neutralisation, as I've gone off on a bit of a tangent. The point here is that rather than saying that schwa is an allophone of all of the short vowels in English, it is more accurate to say that the contrast between the short vowel phonemes is neutralised when they occur in unstressed syllables.

12.4 Sounds with no phoneme

The examples I've looked at so far are all cases where it looks as though some sounds seem to belong to more than one phoneme. A second type of problem with phonemes is where there are sounds that don't appear to belong to a phoneme at all. Chapter 13 shows that sounds can be either deleted or inserted. Deleting a sound is not a problem for phonemes, but inserting a sound is. One of the places where sounds are often inserted is between two vowels. In chapter 5, I said that a lot of languages don't like to have two vowels together (not diphthongs, but two vowels in different syllables). This is called hiatus. Some languages avoid it by deleting one of the vowels; some turn one of the vowels into a consonant. Those don't give our phoneme idea any difficulties. Other languages, including (at least some accents of) English, insert a consonant between two vowels. If the vowel before the hiatus is a high front vowel, [j] is inserted, as in *be aware*, [biːjəwɛə]. If the vowel is a high back vowel, a [w] is inserted, as in *two eggs*, [tuːwɛgz]. If it is any other vowel, an [ɹ] is inserted, as in *draw up* [dɹɔɹʌp]. I say more about this in chapter 13. That solves the problem of hiatus, but it is a problem for the idea that every sound is the realisation of an underlying phoneme. Where does that consonant come from? It's not restricted to English either. Some languages don't like to start words with a vowel, and so they insert a glottal stop before a vowel. And it's not restricted to consonants being inserted. Vowels are often inserted to break up clusters of consonants. In some accents of English, for example, *film* is pronounced [fɪləm].

Another type of situation where a sound appears to be pronounced that doesn't have an underlying phoneme happens in words like *hamster*. Note the spelling here – there is no *p*. Quiz question 4 asked about this. How did you think you would transcribe it? With a [p]? Say the word aloud. Can you hear a [p] sound? Not everybody does it, but for a lot of English speakers, the pronunciation is [hæmpstə]. Where does that [p] come from? What's happening here is that when the [m] is pronounced the lips are closed, the velum is lowered, and the vocal chords are vibrating. When the [s] is pronounced, the lips are open, the tongue is at the alveolar ridge, the velum is raised, and the vocal chords are not vibrating. When speakers shift from the [m] to the [s], they don't make all of these changes at the same time, so there is a brief time when the lips are still closed, but the velum is raised and the vocal chords have stopped vibrating, and that makes a voiceless bilabial plosive, or a [p].

12.5 Ambiguity

A final problem with phonemes is that sometimes there are situations where there is clearly a case of sounds being affected by the sounds around them, but it's not possible to work out which is influencing which. Look at the following examples from Norwegian:

[tɑːk]	'roof'	[tɑkː]	'thanks'
[reːkə]	'shrimp'	[rekːə]	'line, row'
[viːn]	'wine'	[vinː]	'wind'

Length is contrastive in Norwegian, both on vowels and consonants. These examples show that it is predictable that if the vowel is long, the consonant is not, and vice versa. The problem is that there is no way of knowing whether the vowel length is determined by the length of the consonant or whether the consonant length is determined by the length of the vowel. Of course, a linguist can just decide that one is basic and write the rules accordingly, but that doesn't truly capture what is happening in the language.

The final example of issues with phonemes is not exactly a problem with the concept *per se*, but just a question of exactly how abstract phonemes should be. Remember the nasal [ŋ]? I said that it must be a separate phoneme from /n/ because there are minimal pairs like *sin* and *sing*. However, I also said that [ŋ] doesn't appear everywhere that /n/ can appear, and I explained that there were historical reasons for that. Situations like that, where the status of a sound has changed over time, do leave some questions. One way of looking at this is to say that [ŋ] is actually not a separate phoneme, but appears as an allophone of /n/ when there is a velar plosive following. This means that the velar plosive in the spelling of words like *sing* is part of the underlying form but is deleted after the realisation of /n/ as [ŋ] has been determined. There are potentially good phonological reasons for suggesting this, including the fact that it is not always deleted. One possible explanation is that the morphology is relevant. If the /g/ is at the end of a morpheme, as in words like *singer*, then the /g/ isn't pronounced, but if it is in the middle then it is, as in words like *finger*. However, that doesn't always work, as words like *longer* show. This is two morphemes, *long+er*, so the /g/ is at the end of a morpheme, but it is still pronounced. On the whole, linguists tend to avoid explanations that involve abstract sounds in a word that are never pronounced.

12.6   What is the problem?

The problems I've looked at in this chapter are problems for the strict traditional definition of phonemes. But how much of problem are they really? Neutralisation isn't really a problem, as long as it is clear that the system of phonemes and their allophones is only a part of the picture. There is no problem with saying that in some situations phonemic contrasts can be lost. The same rule formalism as I introduced in section 11.7.1 can be used to express the neutralisations. For example, the fact that short vowels are realised as schwa in unstressed syllables can be simply stated:

V [– long] → [ə] / [– stress]

There are lots of good reasons for making use of the idea of phonemes. The fact that there are some problems with the strict theoretical interpretation of phonemes doesn't mean that they should be completely abandoned, and, in fact, thinking about pronunciation in these terms often leads to a better understanding of how sounds work by looking more closely at the cases that don't seem to fit the phoneme framework properly.

Additional reading

Katamba (1999), chapter 8, and Lass (1984), chapter 3, give very traditional explanations of the problems caused to phonemic analysis by neutralisation. Davenport and Hannahs (2010), chapter 10, also covers issues arising from suprasegmentals. See the suggested reading at the ends of chapters 7, 8 and 9 for more on suprasegmentals, and at the end of chapter 13 for more on the ways in which phoneme contrasts are neutralised.

Exercises

1. This chapter showed that there is a neutralisation involved in the English plural suffix. Can you explain what happens with the past tense (*-ed*) suffix by looking at the list of words below?

   (a) added
   (b) worked
   (c) loved
   (d) bullied
   (e) sipped
   (f) stuffed
   (g) bathed (past tense of *bathe*)
   (h) earthed

2. German is one of many languages which is considered as inserting a glottal stop to prevent words beginning with a vowel. Look at the words transcribed below and work out exactly where this happens.

['ʔapfl]	'apple'	[ʔais]	'ice'
['ʔumlaut]	'umlaut'	['ʔide:]	'idea'
[ʔoˈʔa:zə]	'oasis'	[teˈʔa:tɐ]	'theatre'
['kaos]	'chaos'	[kaˈʔo:tiʃ]	'chaotic'

3. Transcribe the following words and phrases of English. Pay special attention to the nasal sounds. Which show examples of lexical and which of post-lexical phonology?

   (a) incongruous
   (b) ingratiate
   (c) unbelievable
   (d) inform
   (e) imply
   (f) envied
   (g) encompass
   (h) enthrone
   (i) on point
   (j) on call
   (k) in Thetford

Part VI

Phonological theory

This final part of the book gives a brief introduction to some of the key phonological theories. The first chapter pulls together the various things that happen to sounds in natural speech, explaining the different types of process and why they happen. The second chapter first looks at the kinds of ideas that the theories have to account for and the main differences in approach before summarising the main theories, starting with the early approaches to historical sound change and ending with recent theories such as Optimality Theory and Feature Geometry.

13 Processes

Throughout this book I have shown that using spoken language involves a lot more than just pronouncing a sequence of separate sounds. From chapter 5 onwards, I've looked at all sorts of factors that can affect the way sounds are pronounced. I've shown that sounds can be affected by their position in a syllable, whether the syllable they're in is stressed and which sounds come before and after, for example. At various points I've also hinted at some of the reasons why they happen. In this chapter I want to bring together the various ways in which a sound can be affected and the various reasons why they happen. When I talk about 'processes', I just mean anything that can happen to make a sound (or sequence of sounds) different. For most of this book, I've concentrated on what is called **synchronic** linguistics. That is studying what happens in the language as it is used today. Occasionally, though, I've also mentioned changes that have happened, especially in English, at other points in history and how they have led to the language as it is today. That is known as **diachronic** linguistics. The study of processes can be done either synchronically or diachronically, but I think it makes sense to consider both together. One reason for this is that what happens synchroncially is basically the same as what happens diachronically, and sometimes the easiest examples of a particular process to understand might be synchronic, but sometimes they might be diachronic. The other reason is that the changes that happen diachronically in a language tend to start off as synchronic processes.

Quick quiz

1. Say the sentence 'I am going to live in Brighton.' Start by saying it really slowly and carefully, and then repeat, getting faster each time.

    (a)   What happens to the nasal in *in* as you get faster?
    (b)   What happens to the vowel in *to* as you get faster?
    (c)   What happens to the word *am* as you get faster?

2. Now say the sentence 'I live in Portsmouth,' slowly and quickly.

    (a)   What do you notice about the vowel in the second syllable of *Portsmouth*?
    (b)   How exactly do you pronounce consonants in the middle of *Portsmouth*?

3. Now say 'I live in Eastbourne,' again slowly and then quickly.

    (a)   How many consonants do you pronounce in the middle of Eastbourne?

    (b)   Which consonants do you pronounce?

13.1   Single sounds

There are two main ways that the pronunciation of an individual sound can be affected. The first of these is **assimilation** or **dissimilation**, when a sound becomes either more or less similar to a neighbouring sound. The other is **strengthening** or **weakening**, when a sound becomes either stronger or weaker. These are also known by their Latin names: **fortition** and **lenition**.

13.1.1   Assimilation

Assimilation is very simply when a sound becomes more similar to a neighbouring sound. There are lots of different ways in which assimilation processes are classified according to which particular feature or articulatory parameter is affected, which direction the process happens in and whether the sound that causes the assimilation is next to the other sound.

Place assimilation

When a sound takes on the place of articulation of a neighbouring sound, it is called place assimilation. I've already given an example of this with the nasals in English. Question 1a in the quick quiz is about this. You almost certainly say [ɪmbɹaɪtən], at least as you get faster. The nasal sound at the end of *in* becomes the bilabial [m], becoming more similar to the consonant sound at the beginning of the next word. It isn't only the nasals that do it, though. In English, if you're speaking quite fast, you might well assimilate other consonants. Try saying 'at Gatwick' quite fast. If you really think about where your tongue is, you'll probably find that what you're saying is more like [ækgæʔwɪk]. The consonant at the end of *at* assimilates in place of articulation to the consonant that comes after it.

Manner assimilation

When a sound takes on the manner of articulation of a neighbouring sound, it is called manner assimilation. It is quite hard to find examples that are clearly just cases of manner assimilation, but there are examples of both manner and place assimilation. If you say *good morning* quite fast you may well find that the [d] at the end of *good* becomes [m], assimilating in both place and manner to the sound at the beginning of *morning*.

Voice assimilation

Another very common type of assimilation is voice or voicing assimilation. English has the suffixes -s and -ed which show voice assimilation. When each suffix is added to a stem that ends in a voiced sound, the suffix is voiced, and when it is attached to a stem that ends in a voiceless sound, it is voiceless. So English has the plurals [kæts] (*cats*), but [dɒgz] (*dogs*); and the past tense verbs [wɜːkt] (*worked*), but [lʌvd] (*loved*).

Direction of assimilation

When a sound becomes more similar to a sound that follows it, it is called **anticipatory assimilation**. This is because the sound that comes first antici-pates some feature of the sound that comes after. When a sound assimilates to a sound that came earlier, it is called **perseverative assimilation**. This is because some feature of the earlier sound perseveres into the following sound. These are also know as **regressive assimilation** and **progressive assimilation**, but these terms are confusingly sometimes used in the opposite way, so I prefer to avoid them and use *anticipatory* and *perseverative* (even though *perseverative* is not particularly easy to say!)

Each of these is illustrated by one of the English examples I've talked about. The nasal place assimilation in English is a case of anticipatory assimi-lation because the nasal sound anticipates the place feature of the following word. The voice assimilation in the suffixes is perseverative because the voice feature of the sound at the end of the stem perseveres into the suffix.

Contact and distant assimilation

The final way in which different types of assimilation are distinguished addresses whether the sounds in question are right next to each other. Most cases of assimilation, and all of the ones I've mentioned here, are cases of contact assimilation. Distant assimilation is much more rare. The most com-mon kind of distant assimilation is what is called **vowel harmony**. In some languages, all of the vowels in a word have to share a feature or features. For example, the vowels in a word must all be high or low, front or back, rounded or unrounded. This means that when an affix is added to a stem, the vowels in the affix and the stem must all share the relevant feature. The most famous example of vowel harmony is in Turkish. The situation in Turkish is quite complicated, with different suffixes requiring different features to be shared with their stems. Have a look at the examples in table 13.1.

This table gives the nominative singular, which is just the root, and then the nominative plural, which has a suffix added. You can see that the nomina-tive plural suffix takes one of two forms: /ler/ or /lar/. Can you see which one comes where? Look at the vowels in the stems. In the first four lines, where the suffix is /ler/, the vowels are /i/, /e/, /y/ and /ø/. In the next four lines, where the suffix is /lar/, the vowels are /u/, /o/, /i/ and /a/. What do you notice

Gloss	Nom.sg.	Nom.pl.
'rope'	ip	ipler
'house'	ev	evler
'rose'	gyl	gyller
'eye'	gøz	gøzler
'stamp'	pul	pullar
'arm'	kol	kollar
'girl'	kiz	kizlar
'horse'	at	atlar

TABLE 13.1   TURKISH VOWEL HARMONY

about these sets of vowels? The vowels in the first set are all front vowels. The other set is a bit less obvious – it's not simply the case that they are all back vowels. However, they are all vowels that are not properly front vowels. There are two back vowels: /u/ and /o/. Then there is the central vowel /i/, which is definitely not a front vowel. Finally there is /a/, which is technically a front vowel. However, you may remember from chapter 10 that the low vowels often do not properly distinguish front and back, and /a/ often behaves as if it was a back or central vowel. That's what's happening here. So the nominative plural suffix is /ler/ when the stem vowel is front and /lar/ otherwise.

A brief aside on English vowel harmony . . .

Vowel harmony is not rare in the world's languages. Interestingly, it used to be a part of English, many centuries ago. The English vowel harmony worked in the other direction from Turkish, so that stem vowels changed to be more like the suffix vowels. It is because of the Old English vowel harmony that English has words like *man/men, goose/geese* and *mouse/mice*. Once upon a time, these words would have had an -*es* suffix added, pronounced [ɛz], and if the stem vowel was a back vowel, it would be changed to a front vowel when the suffix was added, in order to obey the vowel harmony. Gradually the vowel in the suffix was lost, and the vowel harmony stopped happening. For most nouns that meant that the suffix is just -*s*, but for a handful of nouns, the vowel change in the plural just stuck, even though the suffix in these words was completely lost. In fact, the two things are connected. Because the vowel change stuck, there was no need for a suffix to show that it was plural.

Any kind of assimilation can be defined as either contact or distant; anticipatory or perseverative; and place, manner or voice (for consonants) or height, backness or rounding (for vowels). The Turkish vowel harmony is distant (because the vowels are not next to each other), perseverative (because

the later sound changes to be more like the earlier sound) and involves backness. The English suffix assimilation is contact, perseverative and involves
voicing. The English nasal assimilation is contact, anticipatory and involves
place of articulation.

Coalescence

Sometimes the process of assimilation goes even further than one sound
becoming more like another. In some cases, the two sounds merge into a
single sound which has some features of each one. This is called **coalescence**.
When two sounds coalesce, the resulting sound might have the place of
one and the manner and voicing of the other, for example. There are a few
instances of this in English. How do you say the word *issue*? Do you pronounce it [ɪsjuː] or [ɪʃuː]? The first pronunciation is not very common these
days, but you do sometimes hear RP speakers say it this way. This is (sort of)
reflected in the spelling. That is, it isn't spelled *ishue*. The reason I said 'sort
of' is that the letter *u* can be pronounced as either [uː] or [juː]. Which one
you say will depend on which consonant comes before it and also what your
accent is. For most SSBE speakers, the words *lunar* and *duty* represent the
different pronunciations. I'll say more about the [j] and where and when it
is pronounced in section 13.2.2. Another example of the same thing comes
in words that end in *-sion*, like *tension* or *permission*. You almost certainly
pronounce them with the same final syllable: [ʃən]. In these cases the spelling gives a bit more of a clue about the original pronunciation. In fact, if
you're familiar with either French or German, you may recognise that these
words are from Latin and also occur in these languages. If you know how
to pronounce them in French or German, you'll know that the 's' and the 'i'
are both pronounced how the spelling suggests. The word *aggression* is used
(written the same) in both French and German. In French it is pronounced /
agʁɛsiːɒ̃/ and in German /agʁɛsiːõːn/.

What has happened here is that the two sounds [s] and [j] have merged
into a single sound. It's not quite as simple as just combining their features,
though. Think about the features of each. The [s] is a voiceless alveolar
fricative. The [j] is a voiced palatal approximant. The resulting sound is a
voiceless post-alveolar (or palato-alveolar) fricative. So what has happened
here is that the first sound has just changed its place of articulation a little
bit, taking on some of the palatal quality of the [j]. The voicing and manner
of articulation have stayed the same.

13.1.2 Dissimilation

Dissimilation is, as it sounds, when two sounds become more unlike each
other. This is much more rare than assimilation. There are not really any
obvious examples of dissimilation that seem to happen in English today, but

there are examples that have happened over time. For example, the word *military* comes from the Latin *militaris*. This is a stem *milit-* with the suffix *-aris*. But in most words that use this suffix, it is *-alis*. In words, like *milit-*, which have a /l/ in the stem, the /l/ in the suffix is changed to /r/, to avoid having two laterals too close together. This is an example of dissimilation.

There is an example in another language that is synchronic. In fact, it happens in a whole family of languages, and it's even got a special name: Dahl's Law. The examples in table 13.2 are from Kikuria, a Tanzanian language (from Odden 1994).

These are all words with a prefix, which is either [oko] or [ogo] (and one case of [ugu], but don't worry about the vowels). Look at the consonant in the prefix of each word. In the first two lines, all of the words have the voiceless velar plosive, [k]. In the next two lines, the words all have the voiced velar plosive, [g]. Now look at the first consonant in the stem in each of the words. What do you notice about the voicing of these consonants? If you look at the consonant at the start of the stem in the top two lines, the consonants are [g], [r], [r] and [b]. In the bottom two lines the consonants are [t], [k], [s] and [k]. The first set are all voiced and the second set are all voiceless. So the words that have the voiceless sound [k] in the prefix all have a voiced sound at the start of their stem. The words that have the voiced sound [g] all have a voiceless sound at the start of their stem. This is known as voicing dissimilation, and it happens in the Northeast Bantu languages.

oko-gaamba	'to say'	oko-reenda	'to guard'
oko-raara	'to sleep'	oko-bara	'to count'
ogo-tema	'to hit'	ogo-sooka	'to respect'
ogo-koɲoonta	'to split'	ugu-kuura	'to cry'

TABLE 13.2   EXAMPLE WORDS FROM KIKURIA

13.1.3   Weakening

The idea of weakening is connected to the idea of sonority. You'll remember sonority – it's relevant to the classification of consonants and to the structure of syllables. When I talked about syllables, I said that every syllable has a peak of sonority, usually a vowel, and that this sound is usually the loudest. It might surprise you a bit when I now tell you that these sonorant sounds are actually classified as **weak** sounds. Weakness in sounds relates to how easy they are to pronounce, or how much effort is used in producing them. The sonority hierarchy, reproduced below, therefore not only defines which sounds are more or less sonorous, but also which are weaker or stronger. The most sonorous sounds are the weakest, and the least sonorous sounds are the strongest. Vowels are therefore the weakest sounds – they require the least effort to produce and involve the smallest degree of closure in the mouth. Plosives are the strongest sounds as they require the most effort and involve the greatest closure. Voiced sounds are weaker than voiceless sounds, and glottal sounds are weaker than sounds produced with a closure in the mouth. Vowels are the weakest sounds, but there are also differences between the vowels. The more central a vowel is, the weaker it is. That means that schwa, as the absolute central vowel, is the weakest sound there is. When you think about what you have to do to produce a schwa sound – pretty much nothing except open your mouth a little bit and let some air vibrate through your vocal chords – it's easy to see why this is considered a weak sound.

> Vowel > Glide > Approximant > Nasal > Voiced Fricative > Voiceless Fricative > Voiced Affricate > Voiceless Affricate > Voiced Plosive > Voiceless Plosive

It should be fairly obvious that a weakening process involves making a sound weaker. It can be viewed as a shift along the sonority scale from less to more sonorous. Any process that involves a sound becoming (more) voiced, that changes a plosive to an affricate or a fricative, or changes the place of articulation to glottal, for example, is a weakening process. There are lots of examples in English – different ones in different accents. Many varieties of British English, even RP, use the glottal stop ([ʔ]) in some places where there is a *t* in the spelling. For proper Cockney speakers this will happen a lot. They will say [bʌʔə] instead of [bʌtə], for example. But in words like *Portsmouth*, even a conservative RP speaker will usually use a glottal stop: [pɔːʔsməθ]. Did you think that you said *Portsmouth* with a glottal stop when you answered question 2 in the quick quiz? In a word like *butter,* you might also use a glottal stop rather than a [t], but that will depend a lot more on your accent. The reason there are often weakened sounds in words like *butter* is that the position, in between two vowels, is a weak position, so consonant sounds in that position will often be weakened there. If you have an American accent, you may also weaken the [t] sound when it is between two vowels, but you probably won't use a glottal stop. American accents tend to weaken the [t] to the voiced tap/flap [ɾ]. As a voiced sound, this is clearly weaker than the voiceless [t], but it is also weaker in its manner of articulation. Even though a tap/flap sound does involve a complete closure, it is only a very brief one compared to a plosive. The American weakening doesn't only happen with [t] either. It also happens with [d], and this means that some pairs of words that are pronounced differently in British English accents sound the same in American accents. The words *litre* and *leader* will sound different in an English accent: [liːtə] (or [liːʔə]) versus [liːdə]. If you speak with an American accent, on the other hand, they will both be pronounced [liːɾə]. If you're American, you'll also spell *litre* differently, as *liter* – and actually, you probably won't even use litres, because it's all gallons, pints and fluid ounces – but that's a whole other story!

What is also a little bit confusing is that the term *weak* is used to refer to both the sounds and the positions where they are found. There are different kinds of weak positions. The ends of words, as compared to the beginnings, are considered weak, and so weak sounds tend to occur there. The middles of words, and in particular the position in between vowels, are considered weak. Unstressed syllables, as compared to stressed syllables, are also considered weak.

There are often cases of processes that could be categorised as different types. One example is the weakening that is seen in American. This is widely defined as a weak position and a place where weaker sounds are likely to occur. However, a voiceless sound becoming voiced when it is between vowels also looks like a case of voicing assimilation. There is one voiceless sound with voiced sounds on either side – it's not very surprising that it takes on the voicing. That doesn't mean that the position between vowels is not a weak position. The fact that some British English accents have glottal stops in that position shows that there is a case for weakening processes happening here, as the glottal stop cannot in any way be said to be more similar to the surrounding vowels than the original /t/. The voiced /d/ in American accents also becomes a tap/flap, so it can't be simply voicing assimilation. What this shows is simply that in some cases, at least, there may be more than one explanation for the processes that happen.

One final word on weakening processes. I said earlier that schwa is the ultimate result of weakening, but that's not strictly true. Following through with the idea of making as little effort as possible, then the logical end point is to not pronounce a sound at all. When that happens – and believe me it does, quite a lot – it's called deletion, and I look at that in section 13.2.2.

13.1.4 Strengthening

Not surprisingly, strengthening is the opposite of weakening. Just as with assimilation and dissimilation, one of them is much more common than the other. In this case, weakening processes are more common than strengthening processes. Strengthening processes involve sounds becoming stronger or less sonorous, and requiring more effort to produce. Once again, there are strong positions where these processes tend to happen, such as at the beginnings of words and in stressed syllables. I said that voiced sounds are weaker than voiceless sounds. Another aspect related to voicing is aspiration. Aspiration, and voicing are separate features, and it is quite possible for them to be completely independent of each other. In terms of the strong/weak measure, aspirated sounds are stronger than unaspirated sounds. English plosives can be either voiced and unaspirated, voiceless and unaspirated, or voiceless and aspirated, and this is the order of strength, with voiced being the weakest. Aspirated plosives in English occur in very specific positions. Can you remember where they occur? It's at the beginning of words and at the beginning of stressed syllables. These are strong positions, so that's why the stronger sounds are found there.

Strengthenings are not as common as weakenings, but they are not rare. One of the most widely found processes that is technically a strengthening process is what we call **final consonant devoicing**. This is something that happens in lots of languages, including German, Dutch, Spanish and Finnish. Final consonant devoicing is when an obstruent consonant becomes voiceless when it occurs at the end of a word (or a syllable). In German, for example, the words *Rad* (meaning 'wheel') and *Rat* (meaning 'council') are both pronounced [ʁat]. When they are plural and have suffixes added, though, the pronunciations of the roots are different, reflecting the spelling: [ʁɛdə] and [ʁɛtə]. What is happening here is that, when the suffix is added, the consonant at the end of the root becomes the onset of the final syllable rather than the coda of the first. When the sound is in an onset, the underlying voiced consonant /d/ can be pronounced as voiced. When there is no suffix, however, the consonant is at the end of the word or, more accurately, in a coda, and it then has to be devoiced.

What is odd about final consonant devoicing is that even though according to the sonority hierarchy, and therefore the notion of strong and weak sounds, this should be viewed as a case of strengthening, the position of word or syllable final is actually a relatively weak position. The sounds at the ends of words should become weaker rather than stronger. Because of this apparent paradox, some linguists have taken to trying to come up with different possible accounts. One suggestion is that it should be viewed as a case of assimilation to the following silence. This might, at first, appear to be a rather odd suggestion, but I'll follow the logic through. I said that assimilations happen when the various articulators don't quite all move in exact synchronicity. A voiceless sound may become voiced after a voiced sound, because the vocal chords don't stop vibrating at the same time as the primary articulation begins. In the case of final consonant devoicing, at least when it occurs at the end of a sentence, the vocal chords are going to stop vibrating for the end of the sentence (i.e. the silence), and so, if they stop vibrating a bit early, then a sound that is voiceless, or at least, a bit less voiced results.

That is the logic, and it does make perfect sense . . . but only if the end of the word is actually followed by silence. In fact, devoicing processes happen in many languages, and not only when a word is sentence final, so a better explanation is needed for this.

13.2   Groups of sounds

So far in this chapter, I have concentrated on what happens to individual sounds. I'm now going to switch attention to what happens to groups of sounds, that is, syllables, morphemes and words. First of all I have a look at when sounds are either inserted or deleted. Then I have a look at what happens when morphemes are combined into words and when words are combined to make sentences.

13.2.1   Insertion

Sounds get inserted for a range of reasons, usually to make pronunciation easier. If there are a lot of consonants together, then vowels may be inserted to break up the sequence of consonants. On the other hand, if there are even just two vowels next to each other, a consonant may be inserted to separate them. Languages often have specific combinations of sounds that are not allowed, and so inserting a sound may be a good way to avoid those combinations. In chapter 5, I said that some languages only allow syllables with a single consonant in the onset. Sometimes it might not necessarily be clear that this is a requirement in the language. Maybe that language just happens to have words that all start with a single consonant. That doesn't necessarily mean that words starting with a pair of consonants are not allowed, does it? Well, this idea can be tested by looking at what happens when words from other languages, with different syllable structures, are borrowed or adopted. Japanese is a language that is claimed to have a CV(N) syllable structure. All syllables have to have an onset, but it can only have one consonant, and no syllable can have a coda, except for a single /n/. Japanese has borrowed a lot of English words. What happens when one of these borrowed English words does not conform to the Japanese syllable structure? Here are some example words:

fesutibaru	'festival'
zippu koodo	'zip code'
sutoraiku	'strike'
disuku	'disk'

The word *festival* in English has the syllable structure CVC.CV.CVC. This violates Japanese syllable structure twice, with two codas. (If you want to argue that the *st* should both be in the onset, this is still a violation of Japanese syllable structure, but I'd advise you to go back to section 5.5 if you do believe this to be the case!) So how does the Japanese version deal with this? It simply inserts vowels wherever there are two consonants next to each other (as with *s* and *t*) and also adds a vowel at the end, so that there is no coda at the end of the word. If you look at the words here (and indeed, if you look at Japanese words generally), they always end with a vowel or /n/. So if an English word is borrowed that ends in another consonant, a vowel will always be added. The third of these words is possibly the most striking (sorry, couldn't resist!). The English word *strike* begins with not two, but three consonants. A three-consonant onset is way out of bounds for Japanese, so there are two vowels added in between those three consonants, as well as the obligatory vowel at the end. The fact that these changes happen – and they happen consistently and predictably – gives us proof that there really are rules about the syllable structure of Japanese.

English, as I showed in chapter 5, is very tolerant of sticking lots of consonants together in both onsets and codas, so it doesn't often need to insert vowels in order to deal with problems like the Japanese examples. However, one thing that really doesn't often occur in English is having two vowels next to each other. I'm not talking about diphthongs here. They are technically single vowels that have shifting quality. Crucially, they occur in a single syllable. I am talking about when there are two vowels in two different syllables, but there are no consonants in between, either in the coda of the first syllable or the onset of the second. When that happens, a consonant will often be inserted between the vowels. I explain more about this in section 13.2.4.

13.2.2   Deletion

Just as sounds can be inserted, they can also be deleted. Sometimes sounds are deleted for the same reason they are added – to make words more easily pronounceable and/or to conform to syllable structure rules. When young children are learning to speak, they often start out with an idea of syllable structure that is very similar to that of Japanese. This means that, when they try to say a word like *spoon*, they may struggle with the /sp/ cluster at the beginning. That is why you will often hear children calling a *spoon* a [pu:n]. They delete one of the consonants.

There are many different accents of English that delete particular sounds. Cockney and other traditional London and Southern accents do what is called **h-dropping**. For some speakers, there are simply no /h/ sounds pronounced at all. In parts of East Anglia, there is an accent feature known as **yod-dropping**. The yod here is the /j/. It isn't dropped completely, like the /h/ in Cockney. You will still find a /j/ in words like *yellow* /jɛləʊ/. In these accents, the yod is 'dropped' in words like *suit*, *new* and *funeral*. Yod dropping is an interesting accent feature because different English speakers vary enormously in exactly where they pronounce a yod and where they don't. It depends on their accent and also what consonant comes before the /uː/ sound.

There is a question about whether some of these examples should really be viewed as deletion processes. It is certainly possible to argue that, synchronically, Cockney speakers don't really go around deleting /h/; they just don't have it there in the first place. One argument against this view is that the *h* is still there in the spelling, and for the most part, Cockney speakers would definitely write the words *house*, *hotel* and *him* with an *h*. This is not necessarily an argument that there is an underlying sound in their mental phonological representations, however. A more convincing argument comes from the evidence of hypercorrection. This is where people try to 'correct' their own speech, but in doing so they go too far. You may have heard examples of people trying very hard to put the /h/ in the right place but ending up adding an /h/ when there shouldn't be one. A classic example of this is one that has caught on across large portions of the population, namely the word for the letter *h* itself. How do you say it? Do you say /eɪtʃ/ or /heɪtʃ/? The spelling of the name, as you'll find in dictionaries, is *aitch*, so on that basis, the 'correct' pronunciation is /eɪtʃ/. However, linguists are descriptive, not prescriptive, so they are happy to accept variation and change. If the population generally starts to pronounce the name /heɪtʃ/, then that will become the accepted and therefore the correct pronunciation. The situation with this one is interesting.

A brief aside on aitch and haitch . . .

A student of mine did a project where she asked people how they pronounced this word and also lots of questions about what they thought other people did and their views on it. She found that there was a wide range of views, even within families. One family where she interviewed the mother, the father and one son showed the sometimes misguided views people have. The father and son both said that they used /eɪtʃ/ but that other members of their family (the other son was identified) said /heɪtʃ/. The mother, on the other hand, said that she didn't know anyone who said /heɪtʃ/!

13.2.3   Morpheme boundaries

I have talked about a lot of different types of processes, and in describing examples of them, I've talked about various places where these processes occur. In several of these examples, the processes happen when morphemes are combined to make words. That can mean putting roots together in compounds or adding affixes to stems. (If you can't remember what these are, go back and look at chapter 6.) A lot of processes happen at morpheme boundaries. When different morphemes are combined, this forces sounds to be close together and that proximity can make the processes happen. The processes I've discussed that involve adjacent sounds affecting each other, such as (contact) assimilation, for example, often happen at morpheme boundaries. Even distant assimilation tends to happen in the context of morphemes being combined. The vowel harmony processes I described, for example, happen when an affix is added to a stem.

Another thing that tends to happen when morphemes combine is some-thing called **resyllabification**. Chapter 5 said that English, like most languages, tends to favour consonants in onsets rather than codas. This means that, when morphemes are put together, any consonants that are at the end of the first morpheme will often shift to the onset of the second morpheme – assuming that they follow the rules for English onsets. The compound word *comb-over*, for example, is made up of two roots, *comb* and *over*. Their syllable structures when they occur on their own are shown in figure 13.1. When they are com-bined into a single, hyphenated word, though, the [m] becomes the onset of the second syllable, so it has the syllabic structure shown in figure 13.2.

13.2.4   Word boundaries

What happens at morpheme boundaries can also happen at word bounda-ries. This depends on how fast and casual the speech is. When speaking in a very fast and casual way, more of the processes happen across the word

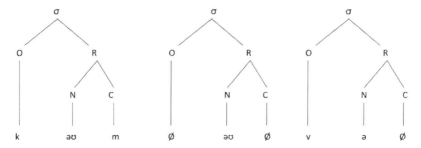

FIGURE 13.1   SYLLABLE STRUCTURE OF *COMB-OVER* AS SEPARATE WORDS

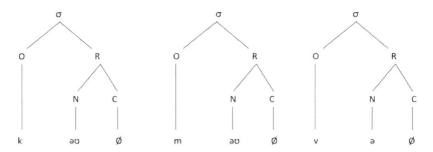

FIGURE 13.2   SYLLABLE STRUCTURE OF *COMB-OVER* WHEN JOINED AS A COMPOUND

boundaries. I have already talked about the fact that consonants are added, or inserted, between vowels at word boundaries. There are special names for processes that happen at word boundaries. There are two terms, which come from the languages they were first described in. The first is **liaison**. This is a French term, and it was first used to refer to a specific thing that happens in French. French words often have consonants at the end in their spelling that are not pronounced. A word like *grand*, for example, which is the masculine form of *big*, is pronounced [gʁɑ̃]. The feminine version, written *grande* is pronounced [gʁɑ̃d]. When the masculine form comes before a word that begins with a vowel, as in *grand esprit* ('big spirit'), the /d/ is pronounced: [gʁɑ̃dɛspʁiː].

The other word comes from Sanskrit and was initially used to refer to the processes that happen in that language. That word is **sandhi**, and it's from the Sanskrit word meaning 'joining'. Sandhi is divided into internal and external sandhi. Internal sandhi happens within words across morpheme boundaries, and external sandhi happens across word boundaries. The term is now used to refer to all of the processes that happen in these positions, including deletion and insertion of sounds and assimilation.

Quick quiz

How do you think you pronounce the following?

1. here and there
2. India and China
3. Thai and Cambodian
4. Sue and Bill

English tries to avoid hiatus. This mostly happens by inserting a consonant in between two vowels. What did you answer for the quick quiz examples? The first two illustrate two very different but closely related processes that happen in English. What do you think happens in between *here* and *and*? I expect you pronounce it [hɪeˌɹənðɛə], with the *r* pronounced. If you have a non-rhotic accent, then the *r* in *here* will not be pronounced if it is at the end of a sentence or before a word that begins with a consonant. In number 2, most speakers with non-rhotic accents will insert an *r* here as well, even though there is no *r* in the spelling, and people with rhotic accents won't pronounce an *r* at the end of *India*. The first example is called **linking r,** and the second is called **intrusive r**. Can you see why? In the first one there is an underlying /ɹ/ which is normally deleted, but which is kept in order to link the two words when the following word begins with a vowel. In the second one, the /ɹ/ is inserted for the same reason, but it is an intruder; it doesn't come from an underlying phoneme that is normally deleted. In the third and fourth examples in the quiz, there is a similar thing happening, but it's not an /ɹ/ that 'intrudes'. What is inserted instead? In the third it is the glide /j/, whereas in the fourth it is the other glide /w/. Can you see why? A glide is inserted when the vowel before the word boundary is a high vowel. If it is a high front vowel, the palatal glide /j/ is inserted, and if it is a high back vowel, the labial-velar /w/ is inserted.

The other processes that happen at morpheme boundaries can also happen at word boundaries, like resyllabification and assimilation. I have already mentioned examples of nasal assimilation that happen in phrases like 'in Brighton', where the pronunciation might be [ɪmbɹaɪtn̩].

Additional reading

For a range of different discussions of the processes covered here, see Spencer (1996), chapter 2; Roach (2000), chapter 14; Katamba (1999), chapter 5; and Lass (1984), chapter 8. Knight (2012) has three chapters, 15–17, which address different kinds of processes in detail. Kennedy (2017) also has a few chapters, 2–4, which are relevant. Clark and Yallop (2006), chapter 3, gives a nice perspective on how the technicalities of articulation lead to some kinds of processes.

Exercises

1. The following transcriptions are of English words or phrases which have undergone some processes. First work out what they say, and then identify what processes have happened where.

   (a) [ɪŋˈgɹæʔɪˌtʃuːd]

   (b) [ˌɒkɹəɹəmpʰˈteɪˌtəʊ kʌɹiː]

   (c) [ˈsæ̃mˌwɪʤ]

2. In the passage below, work out where you would expect to find the following for SSBE speakers:

   (a) velarised (dark) *l*

   (b) aspirated voiceless plosives

   (c) intrusive *r*

   (d) linking *r*

   (e) glide insertion

This, then, was the explanation of the stealthy expeditions at night and the light at the window. Was it possible that this stolidly respectable person was of the same blood as one of the most notorious criminals in the country?

Yes, sir, my name was Falla, and he is my younger brother. We humoured him too much when he was a lad, and gave him his own way in everything, until he came to think that the world was made for his pleasure, and that he could do what he liked in it. Then, as he grew older, he met wicked companions, and the devil entered into him, until he broke my mother's heart and dragged our name in the dirt. From crime to crime he sank lower and lower, until it is only the mercy of God which has snatched him from the scaffold; but to me, sir, he was always the little curly-headed boy that I had nursed and played with, as an elder sister would. (Adapted from *The Hound of the Baskervilles* by Sir Arthur Conan Doyle)

14 Theoretical approaches

This chapter discusses some of the key questions that phonological theories have to address and then introduces some of the major theoretical approaches.

14.1 Levels of representation

The earlier chapters of this book have addressed various different levels of representation. This section is going to briefly look at the different theoretical questions raised by those different levels.

14.1.1 Segments

The starting point for the book was individual sounds. Chapter 1 looked at the relationship between sounds and spelling, and specifically the relationships in an alphabetic language like English. These sounds are absolutely fundamental to phonetics and phonology, and they are the basis for the description and transcription of spoken language. There is plenty of evidence that these sound segments are important in the mental representation of language for the native speaker, and not just for linguists analysing language. Psycholinguists have done experiments that show that speakers have awareness of these segments. It might be tempting to think that this comes down to learning to read and write, when children are taught to recognise sound segments, but this awareness develops in children even before they start learning to read and write and is also present in speakers of languages which have non-alphabetic writing systems.

This fundamental role of the segment is assumed in most of the major phonological theories. The key questions the theories need to address are these:

1. How many different sounds are there:

    (a) in a language?

    (b) in an utterance?

2. What kinds of variation in their realisation are there?

3. How do neighbouring sounds affect each other?

4. How can sounds combine

   (a) in a specific language?

   (b) in all languages?

5. How do sounds group together into classes?

The different theories focus on different questions and take different approaches to them.

14.1.2   Features

A lot of the answers to the questions about segments involve talking about the features they have. In chapters 3 and 4, the articulatory descriptions involved the separate parameters of description, which were then referred to in chapter 10 as potential phonological features. In that chapter features were also used to define classes of sounds which shared certain features. Features were also used to describe the ways in which sounds can vary in their realisation. For most of the major theories, features play an important part, and in some they are considered to be at least as fundamental as segments. Crucially, some theories associate features only, or primarily, with individual segments, whereas others treat them as more free, associating them with levels from the segment upwards.

14.1.3   Suprasegmentals

Chapters 5, 7, 8 and 9 showed that some of the things that happen in speech require reference to units above the level of the segment. Syllables merit a mention in most theories, although their status varies. In some theories syllables are central, but for most they are referred to only as required, for example, to explain the different behaviour of sounds in onsets or codas. The realisation that describing and defining segments alone was not enough came mainly from the study of languages with linguistic tone, even though it quickly became clear that even languages like English need reference to intonation and stress in order to fully describe the phonological behaviour and variation across accents.

14.2   What versus why

14.2.1   Processes and constraints

In explaining the kinds of processes that happen in languages, I've talked in previous chapters about the reasons why they happen. Assimilation processes happen because it is easier to pronounce sounds next to each other if they are more similar. It is also possible to think about it in a more technical and/ or detailed way. If you think about the exact articulation of a sound, you can identify various different actions that have to happen together – what the tongue is doing, what the lips are doing, what the glottis is doing and what the velum is doing. In chapter 12, I explained how the pronunciation of the sounds /ms/ in a word like *hamster* sometimes result in a perceived /p/ sound because the movements of the different articulators don't happen at the same time.

These processes tend to happen, whatever language you are speaking. I said that assimilation processes are very common. That's because whatever sounds you are using in whatever language, it's very normal for your articulators to not quite move all at the same time, which means that some of the articulation from one sound seeps into a neighbouring sound. Sometimes they don't just happen accidentally. They always happen in a particular language. When this is the case, linguists talk about a language having a particular **constraint**. Think again about the nasal sounds in English. Nasals, as I said in the previous chapter, tend to assimilate to a consonant that comes after them. That is, they become more similar. Specifically, they assimilate in their place of articulation. As I said, this can happen within morphemes, between morphemes within a word and also between words. So an /n/ will be pronounced as [m] when it is followed by a /p/ or a /b/. Across word boundaries, such as when saying 'in Brighton', this assimilation is optional and depends on how quickly or casually you are speaking. However, when it happens within a single syllable, when the /n/ and the other consonant are both in the coda, it is absolutely required that it happens. This is what is called a constraint. This constraint can be explained without actually saying anything about processes. The constraint says that, in English, a nasal consonant must be **homorganic** with a following consonant within the same syllable. The word *homorganic* means literally 'with a single organ' and so it means that the sounds must be produced with the same articulators, hence at the same place of articulation. There is a clear difference between the constraint and the process that happens to make sure the constraint is obeyed. This particular constraint in English doesn't actually say that the nasal must take on the place of articulation of the consonant that follows it. The constraint would be fulfilled just as well if a process of assimilation made the following consonant take on the place of articulation of the nasal.

As another example, consider syllable structure, processes. I said that a consonant is often inserted when there would otherwise be two vowels next to each other. In English, either a /ɹ/ or a glide (/j/ or /w/) is inserted in between words which end and begin with vowels. The relevant constraint here is that there should not be two adjacent vowels. There is a special term for when there are two vowels next to each other. It is called **hiatus**. The main reason there's a special word for it is that it's something that most languages tend to try to avoid. So avoiding (or not allowing) hiatus is not only a constraint in English; it's a constraint in a lot of languages. However, the way in which hiatus is avoided varies. **Hiatus resolution** is the term for any of the ways in which languages manage to avoid hiatus. There are a number of possibilities. One simple way to avoid having two vowels next to each other is to delete one of them. Another way is to insert a consonant between them. That's what English does. Very often when a consonant is inserted, it is the kind of consonant that is most like the vowel(s), that is, a glide. Another way that languages avoid hiatus is by turning one of the vowels into a consonant, again usually a glide.

Phonological theories differ in the weight they place on either rules or constraints. Both are important for a full picture of the phonology of a language. It's important to know which constraints apply in that language, but it's also important to know which of the many possible strategies that particular language uses in order to avoid violating the constraint.

14.2.2   Constraints and universals

Constraints and the processes that arise because of them are specific to individual languages. However, some constraints are more common than others, and some really do seem to apply in all or virtually all languages. Even when constraints aren't rigidly obeyed in all languages, there are some very clear tendencies. These are called **universals**. I have talked at various points about things that languages tend to like or not to like. For example, in chapter 5, I said that on the whole, languages tend to prefer syllables that have onsets rather than codas. This is a universal, even though it is definitely not the case that there are always onsets and never codas. It is a universal because **typological** studies of languages and their syllable structure show that languages with no codas are much more common than languages with no onsets. In fact, there are no known languages with no onsets. Also, even in languages that have both onsets and codas, there are more onsets than codas. Another thing that makes a constraint a universal is if it is often seen in children's language. For example, consonant clusters, either in onset or coda, are not very popular in the world's languages. This is also seen in the speech of children who are learning a language that does have clusters. A child learning English may well pronounce *spoon* as /puːn/, for example.

It is important to remember here that the term *universal* doesn't mean that it always happens. A universal, in typological terms, is a statement of a tendency. Typologists study large numbers of languages to work out what tendencies there are at all levels of linguistic representation. In terms of phonology, there are certain types of sound that are very common (plosives, fricatives, alveolars) and sounds that are very rare (clicks, pharyngeals, dental fricatives). The other main type of phonological universal relates to syllable structure, as I've already said. And there are different types of universal. Some say that languages will tend to have X or Y, but others say, for example, 'If a language has X, it will always also have Y.' For example, if a language has affricates, it will always also have plosives.

The relation between universals and constraints is the kind of thing that linguists like to argue about. There are different theories that try to explain those tendencies I just talked about and how it is that some languages nevertheless manage to have things that are generally not 'popular'. It's interesting to think about. If click sounds are so rare in the world's languages, that must be because they are not 'good' or 'ideal' in some universal linguistic sense. And yet there are still languages that have them. How is that? If languages tend to change in directions that keep and increase the universally 'good' things, how are there still click sounds and consonant clusters at all? There are lots of different kinds of answers to that. One kind of answer looks at languages as systems that are not just isolated communication systems, but part of a culture and a society. People will hang on to aspects of a language that set it apart from other languages as a part of their social identity. Another type of answer is that there are lots of universals or tendencies, but a lot of them are in conflict. This means that in order to maximise one particular universal, you might have to minimise another. There's a really clear example of that in what I said about processes. Speakers tend to use ways of speaking that are easiest for them. Of course, that makes perfect sense. I'm going to make life easier for myself if I can, so I use assimilation and weakening processes because they make speech easier. However, I would be completely wasting my time and effort if what I said could not be understood, or I had to always repeat it. That means that there is a limit to how much I can be lazy or economical in my speech. I need to maximise the perceptual distinctions so that anyone listening can actually understand what I'm saying. Speech is always a tension between these two things. Less effort is ideal for the speaker, but more effort is ideal for the listener. The balance is very much in favour of the speaker, because the speaker is in control, but the needs of the listener put a brake on the tendencies for certain types of process.

14.3 Phonological theories

In this final section I give a brief introduction to the major phonologial theories. There are many textbooks that cover these theories in much greater depth, but this chapter gives a flavour of the key theories and the different approaches they take.

14.3.1   Neogrammarians and sound change

At the end of the nineteenth century, linguistic interest centred on phonological change and specifically the ways in which languages had divereged from their common ancestor languages. The Neogrammarians, a group of young linguists working in Germany, proposed the theory of exceptionless sound change, which held that sound changes take place in a language in very strict rule-governed ways. Their goal was to explain how languages like English and German ended up with words that were pronounced differently, even though they originally came from the same word in the ancestor language, Germanic. They also wanted to provide ways of working out what the original forms of words were in ancestor languages that there is no evidence for. This was all part of the big European enterprise of reconstructing Proto-Indo-European, the ancestor language of most European and many Indic languages. Their work was important because it really started the idea that linguistics should be approached in a principled scientific way, and they started the move towards looking at the sounds of language in this principled way.

14.3.2   Phonemes

Chapter 11 introduced the idea of the phoneme as a phonological representation of the variations in phonetic realisations. It showed that a lot can be said about the phonology of a language by working out how many and which sounds a language uses to distinguish different word meanings and the ways in which those sounds are pronounced in different contexts. This term dates back to the end of the nineteenth century and the Polish linguist Jan Baudouin de Courtenay. It was developed during the early twentieth century by the British linguist Daniel Jones and members of the American structuralist school including Edward Sapir (also known for the Sapir-Whorf hypothesis) and Leanard Bloomfield. Bloomfield (1933) is one of the key works in the devleopment of linguisics as a discipline, and his explanation of the idea of the phoneme is one of the earliest. The idea was further developed throughout the first half of the twentieth century with Bloch (1941), Pike (1947) and Hockett (1955) all refining the definition and status of phonemes.

There are two aspects of the phoneme idea that are important. The first is the basic idea that speech can be divided into individual segments. The second is how those segments are different because of the context they occur in. It is generally accepted that there is real psychological reality to the sound segment. Evidence comes from speech errors where individual sounds are swapped (e.g. spoonerisms like 'par cark' instead of 'car park') and from processes where individual sounds are deleted or inserted. The fact that people who speak languages that are written with non-alphabetic writing systems also make the same kinds of errors shows that this is not just influenced by the representation of sounds as individual letters.

The second part of the phonemic theory (known as the **phonemic principle**) is a bit more controversial now. Although a lot of changes that happen to sounds can be explained in terms of phonemes and allophones, many cannot. This was discussed in chapters 1 and 12. The phonemic principle doesn't have anything to say about stress and tone, for example, and it doesn't deal well with cases of neutralisation and free or random variation. Interestingly, when Bloomfield explained the idea of the phoneme, he contrasted the situation in English, where pronunciations of the word *man* with different pitch were still the same word, with the situation in Chinese, where pronunciations of the word with different pitch were not the same word. In spite of his recognition of this difference, he goes on to ignore the question of how tone should be accounted for and the fact that it is not accounted for in phonemic analysis.

It is fair to say that despite the issues that have been identified with phonemes and the phonemic principle, the idea is still crucially important in all of the main phonological theories.

14.3.3 Distinctive feature theory

I mentioned the American structuralist school earlier, but this was not just an American thing. The early twentieth century saw the emergence of structuralist linguistics in Europe as well. The big change from the Neogrammarian approach was in looking at languages as complex systems, viewed as a snapshot in time. The emphasis moved from historical (diachronic) studies of how languages changed to describing the ways in which languages made use of the resources available to them. In terms of phonology, two of the big names were Nikolai Trubetskoy and Roman Jakobson. Trubetskoy (1939) was one of the people who contributed to the development of the idea of the phoneme, but he also developed the idea of defining those phonemes in terms of the features that make them up. Jakobson and colleagues developed the theory of **distinctive features** (Jakobson, 2002). He recognised that the sound systems of different languages made use of the distinctions between sounds in different ways. English, for example, distinguishes between voiced and voiceless plosives, but other languages distinguish between aspirated and unaspirated plosives. Jakobson proposed that the sounds of each language should be defined in terms of just those features required to distinguish them from all of the other sounds of that language. So, according to his theory, a language that does not use voicing to distinguish sounds does not need the feature [± voice].

In chapter 10, I talked a bit about different sets of features. I said that some linguists use features that are quite different from the phonetic features discussed earlier in the book. Distinctive feature theory is where a lot of those features originally came from. In particular, the theory used features to divide up the different places of articulation in different ways. Rather than talking about 'bilabial', 'alveolar' and so on, there are features that refer to which part of the tongue is used, whether the sound is produced in the front or back of the mouth and so on. Similarly, the different manners of articulation are divided up according to whether they have a complete closure in the mouth, whether they involve a 'strident' sound and so on.

Distinctive feature theory addressed the individual sounds of language, but didn't have anything to say about combinations of sounds or how they can influence each other. It was really in the second half of the twentieth century that those aspects started to be looked at.

14.3.4   Generative Phonology

Noam Chomsky is one of the biggest names in linguistics, and he is best known for his work on syntax. He came up with the theory of Generative Grammar, which aimed to explain how sentences are generated from the underlying forms in our minds. He also extended the theory to phonology, and the theory of Generative Phonology (GP) influenced work on phonology for decades. The theory of GP built on the work of the distinctive feature theorists, assuming a similar set of features. The key work of Chomsky and Halle (1968) has been used as the basis of many accounts of English.

Generative Grammar assumed that a set of phrase structure rules and transformational rules combines words from a lexicon into grammatical sentences. The lexicon provides information about the phonology of the words and then the surface forms, or actual pronunciations, are determined by a set of phonological rules.

Probably the most influential aspect of this theory is the development of the phonological rules and the formal notation to define them. Chapter 11 introduced this formalism, which defines the relationship between an underlying form (the phoneme) and the surface form (the allophones, or actual phones that are pronounced). This was the main emphasis of the theory in the early stages. Later, during the 1960s and 1970s, GP switched focus to the representations themselves and the relationship between phonology and other components of the grammar, such as the lexicon, morphology and syntax. Subsequent work in the GP framework focused on the nature of the segment as well as syllables, tone, stress and intonation, as described in Katamba (1999).

14.3.5   Autosegmental Phonology

Although GP was developed later to include the non-segmental aspects of phonology, newer theories began to put these non-segmental aspects right at the centre of attention. The theory of Autosegmental Phonology (AP) was developed specifically to address the behaviour found in the tone languages of Africa, but it has proved to have more to offer in other areas as well.

The theory was first proposed by John Goldsmith (Goldsmith, 1979). It proposes that there are many different tiers, which are connected by associa-tion lines. At the simplest level, phonemic segments are associated with the various features, such as voice, place and manner features. In AP, however, the features aren't necessarily associated with a single segment. This means that it is possible to account for processes like assimilation by associating features with neighbouring segments. It also means that a single segment can be associated with more than one value for a feature as well, so it is easier to represent diphthongs and affricates. The many different levels make it possible to explain relations between all different phonological units, from features up to syllables.

As I said, the original motivation for the theory was the tone found in African languages. In some of these languages, tone is spread and shifted across words and even between words, as in the example in chapter 8. For example, tones can shift from one word to another, as in the example from Gikuyu.

14.3.6   Optimality Theory

In the second section of this chapter, I talked about the difference between rules and constraints. Constraints were originally proposed as part of Generative Phonology to prevent the application of some rules. They were believed to be inviolable, but a realisation in later years that most constraints were not inviolable led to a revision of the idea and the the development of Optimality Theory (OT), which places constraints right at its heart. OT does not attempt to define the ways in which surface forms are derived from underlying forms. What it does do is explain why, for a particular language, one surface form is chosen ahead of other possible ones.

The basic idea behind OT is that there are a host of constraints which are universal. There are two types of constraint, known as faithfulness constraints and markedness constraints. Faithfulness constraints state that the surface form should, ideally, be the same as the underlying form. Markedness constraints state other requirements for surface forms, such as a voiced consonant should not be next to a voiceless consonant. These constraints come into conflict with each other. For example, if one of the faithfulness constraints says that a consonant on the surface should have the same voicing as the underlying form, and one of the markedness constraints is the one that says that two consonants next to each other should have the same voicing, then they could come into conflict if a suffix that begins with a voiced consonant is added to a stem that ends in a voiceless consonant. The markedness constraint says that those two consonants should not be next to each other, but the faithfulness constraint says that the voicing of a consonant should not change. OT explains how these conflicts are resolved by giving rankings. So, if the language does change the voicing, OT says that the markedness constraint is ranked higher than the faitfulness constraint. The language will tolerate the faithfulness constraint being violated in order to avoid the markedness constraint being violated.

14.3.7   Feature Geometry

The final theory I'm going to mention here is one which is related to the theories of AP and OT. AP had different tiers for different levels, such as segments and features. Within these, though, there are lots of different tiers. Segments can be arranged on separate tiers for consonants and vowels, for example. Features can also be viewed as being on separate tiers. Feature Geometry organises the features into a tree-like structure, with place, manner and voice features all connected to a consonant-feature node. The nodes within this feature tree are all on different tiers, so they can be associated separately with segments on the segment tiers. One thing that makes Feature Geometry especially useful is that it can explain connections between the features of consonants and vowels. In chapter 4, I said that the consonant /w/ is very similar to the vowel /u/, and the consonant /j/ is very similar to the vowel /i/. In Feature Geometry these links can be made explicit because the articulatory features for vowels, linked to a V-Place node, are also linked to the C-Place node, which dominates the consonant place features.

14.3.8   Summary

What I've tried to do here is give a flavour of the kinds of theories that try to explain the way sounds work in languages. There are many different versions of these theories – and many more that I haven't mentioned at all.

The important thing to take from this is that the different theories generally focus on different aspects of phonology. Some try to explain how the different sounds are actually pronounced, and others try to explain why different options are chosen by any particular language. The development of the different theories, as in any field, has been led by research that both tested the theories against the data that was already there and sought out new data to test the theories against. Although the early theories were mostly developed and tested against European languages, more recent work has examined languages from across the world and from very different language families. That has led to the development of theories that can account for things like linguistic tone.

I hope that this book has given you a clear idea of all of the fascinating aspects of language that phonetics and phonology looks at, and maybe even inspired you to look at phonology in more depth. The additional reading section in this chapter has some pointers for where you can find more detail about these aspects and other theories. You will also find a lot of studies on a huge range of different languages. If you are really just interested in English, though, there is still plenty of scope for studying the variety of pronunciations found in the accents of English right across the world.

Additional reading

There are many books which cover the theories covered here as well as other theories in depth. For Generative Phonology, Katamba (1999) is an excellent source, which also gives some detail about Distinctive Features and Phonemes. Spencer (1996) also covers these earlier theories in detail. For the more recent theories, I recommend Carr and Montreuil (2013), which has good chapters on Autosegmental Phonology, Feature Geometry and Optimality Theory. Kennedy (2017) provides a good practical introduction to a range of theories and has a particularly helpful chapter on how to apply the newer theories. The Neogrammarian Hypothesis is covered in Millar (2015), chapter 8.

Answers to exercises

Chapter 1

1. I can think of 18, including French loan words with and without accents:

   (a) *ay* tray

   (b) *ey* grey

   (c) *a – e* make

   (d) *ea* break

   (e) *ai* rain

   (f) *aigh* straight

   (g) *eigh* eight

   (h) *ae* sundae (or bae)

   (i) *a* acyclic

   (j) *ei* vein

   (k) *aig* campaign

   (l) *eig* reign

   (m) *e* canape

   (n) *ee* toupee

   (o) *ée* fiancée

   (p) *é* café

   (q) *ait* café au lait

   (r) *et* ballet

Examples (k) and (l) are words that came into English from Norman French. Example (j) is an example of a Latin word, and example (i) is a borrowing from Greek. Examples (m)–(r) are all more recent borrowings from French which may or may not lose their accents. Examples (a)–(h) are not because of borrowings; they come from the Old English words *trig, græg, macian, brechan, regnian, streaht* and *ehta*. The spellings in Old English reflect the different pronunciations at the time. Nobody knows why *sundae* is not spelled the same as *Sunday* – probably just to distinguish the two words!

2. (a) /əʊ/ s<u>o</u>

   (b) /ɒ/ c<u>o</u>t

   (c) /ʌ/ s<u>o</u>n

   (d) /ɪ/ w<u>o</u>men

   (e) /ə/ less<u>o</u>n

   (f) /u:/ l<u>o</u>se

   (g) /ʊ/ w<u>o</u>man

   (h) /wʌ/ <u>o</u>ne

3. My name is quite simple, pronounced [lɪn], but it could be spelled *llokn*, using the *ll* from *bill*, the *o* from *women* and the *kn* from *knee*.

4. The spellings for some sounds are only possible in certain positions in a word. Bernard Shaw's *gh*, for example, only ever represents the sound [f] at the end of a word, so it's not really possible to have it represent the [f] at the beginning of *fish*. The *o* in *women* is just a unique weird exception, and *ti* is only pronounced [ʃ] when it's part of *tion* in words that come from Latin.

5. (a)   The items that are different from standard writing are as follows:

c	see	plsd	pleased
u	you	r	are
18r	later	cumin	coming
wud	would	th@	that
eva	ever	def	definitely
uvva	other	gd	good
im	I'm	gonna	going to

(b)   There are some examples of rebus writing (*c, u, 8, r,*), abbreviations (*plsd, def, gd*) and dialect or phonetic spellings (*eva, uvva, cumin, gonna*). There are also no upper-case letters and missing punctuation in *im*.

(c)   The rebus writing is influenced by pronunciation in the sense that it uses different characters that are pronounced the same. The dialect or phonetic spellings are more explicit attempts to represent the pronunciation more accurately. Note that *eva* and *gonna* don't represent a specifically different accent from standard spelling, but *uvva* represents an accent that has [v] instead of [ð] (*th*), and in *cumin* there is the *u*, which is just a more accurate representation of the standard pronunciation, and *n* instead of *ng*, which indicates a different accent.

Chapter 2

1. I would expect that you thought that you pronounce the word on its own more clearly and especially that the vowel sound will be more of a classic *a* sound. In the sentence, the word *sat* is likely to be unstressed, so the word will probably be pronounced as shorter, with a shorter vowel, more like the vowel sound in the first syllable of *above*, for example. In the final example, when you read a whole passage, the shortening is likely to be even more noticeable. When we say a word on its own, we usually pronounce it carefully, slowly and more as we would expect from the spelling. When we say it in a sentence, it is more naturally pronounced,

and certain words, in particular, are less stressed and so shorter and reduced in other ways. However, if you are just asked to read a sentence aloud, you will probably still pronounce it more slowly and carefully than if you are just speaking naturally. Reading a whole passage will get to a more natural pronunciation because you are concentrating on reading the whole passage and not on the pronunciation of individual words. It still isn't completely natural, of course, and if you say the word in a normal conversation, it might well lose its vowel completely.

2. (a) *rubbing* should be *running*. The change is a change of the consonant [n] to [b].

   (b) *Will come* should be Welcome. There are two things happening here. The vowel is different: ([ɪ] becomes [ɛ]), and one word has become two. This second thing is very difficult to spot in natural speech, though, because there are no pauses between words in speech.

   (c) *filo* should be *feel low*. Again there is a mistake over the word boundary – this time two words have been interpreted as one. Here, we would also expect there to be two *l* sounds, but when we pronounce two words together like this, the two identical consonants often get merged into one.

   (d) *Police* should be *Please*. Here there has been a vowel added between the *p* and *l*, and the final consonant has been changed from [z] to [s].

3. Depending on the language the person speaks as their native language, you will find different sounds that are problematic. For speakers of many Asian languages, the sounds [r] and [l] are difficult because the sounds both occur in their language, but they are not contrastive. Speakers of many languages have difficulty with the *th* sounds in English because they are not sounds that are found in a lot of languages. Vowel sounds also often prove difficult because they can be quite subtly different, and it isn't always easy to explain the differences between the vowels of different languages – unless you learn about phonetics, of course!

Chapter 3

1. (a) [ʃ] is post-alveolar; the others are all alveolar.

   (b) [f] is labiodental; the others are all bilabial.

   (c) [ɢ] is uvular; the others are all velar.

2. For all the words except *kind*, the place of articulation is the same for all the consonants. The words should be as follows:

   (a) [kaɪnd] (velar, alveolar, alveolar)

   (b) [sɛnt] (alveolar, alveolar, alveolar)

   (c) [pɑːm] (bilabial, bilabial)

   (d) [əlaɪn] (alveolar, alveolar)

   (e) [leɪziː] (alveolar, alveolar)

3. In the first sentence all the consonants are fricatives; in the second they are all approximants; and in the third they are all plosives.

4. (a) *big* [b]   (c) *leg* [l]

   (b) *frog* [f]   (d) *sit* [s]

5. (a) *improbable* (English only has three bilabial consonants: [m], [b] and [p].)

   (b) *spit* (English has lots of voiceless plosives, fricatives and affricates.)

   (c) *mining* (English only has three nasal consonants: [m], [n] and [ŋ].)

   (d) *tense* (English has the alveolar consonants: [t], [d], [s], [z], [n], [l] and [ɹ].)

6. (a) dental ([ð])   (d) alveolar ([s])

   (b) post-alveolar ([ʃ])   (e) alveolar ([n])

   (c) palatal ([j]   (f) labiodental ([f])

7. (a) voicing: voiceless/voiced

   (b) place: alveolar/post-alveolar

   (c) place: bilabial/velar

   (d) manner: fricative/plosive

   (e) voicing: voiceless/voiced

   (f) place: labiodental/alveolar

   (g) manner: plosive/nasal

   (h) place: labiodental/dental

   (i) voicing: voiceless/voiced

   (j) manner: approximant/lateral approximant

Chapter 4

1. *suit* and *meat* contain high vowels.

2. *wad*, *lard* and *lad* contain low vowels.

3. *fed*, *cat* and *kit* contain front vowels. Technically, [ɪ] is a near-front vowel, but it is considered a front vowel for most purposes.

4. *coop*, *cop* and *good* contain back vowels. Technically, [ʊ] is a near-back vowel, but it is considered a back vowel for most purposes.

5. *who* and *put* contain rounded vowels.

6. (a) [ɔ] is a rounded vowel; the others are all unrounded.

   (b) [a] is the odd one out. It is low, whereas the others are either high or high-mid. It is also lax, whereas the others are tense.

   (c) [ɯ] is back; the others are all front.

7. (a) *spooky*, [uː] and [iː].

   (b) *cartoon*, [ɑː] and [uː].

   (c) *coupon*, [uː] and [ɒ].

8. The numbered sounds match up to the lettered words as follows:

1	o	11	h
2	n	12	g
3	a	13	i
4	d	14	k
5	f	15	m
6	r	16	p
7	j	17	s
8	b	18	c
9	e	19	l
10	q	20	t

9. (a) [θiːf]   (e) [ʃɪp]

   (b) [ʤʌʤ]   (f) [hɛd]

   (c) [bɑːθ]   (g) [saɪn]

   (d) [bʊk]   (h) [kɔːk]

Chapter 5

1. (a) Words with a zero onset: *act, edge, ice, ox*

   (b) Words with one C in the onset: *bald, chain, dog, faith, home, lend, world, use*

   (c) Words with two Cs in the onset: *blame, crisp, drip, dwarf, flaw, grasp, skin, snow, twin*

   (d) Words with three Cs in the onset: *screw, split, spring, squat, stretch*

2. (a) The syllable structure for [ɹiːzn] is as follows:

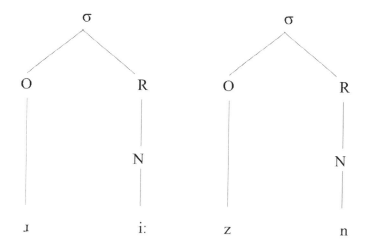

   (b) The transcription for *computer* is [kəmpjuːtə]. The syllable structure is as follows:

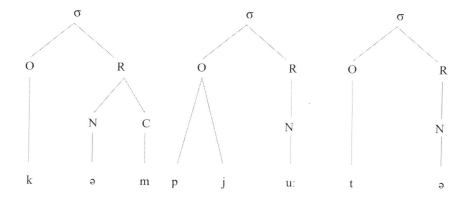

(c) The transcription for *carbuncle* is [kɑːbʌŋkl]. The syllable structure is as follows:

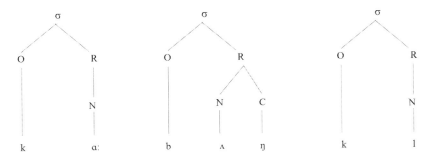

3. (a) The toddler does not have any consonant clusters. All the onsets (and the codas, for that matter) are single consonants.

(b) Where there are words which have consonant clusters in their onset in normal adult speech, the toddler deletes one or more of the consonants. Which consonant is deleted varies, but there are rules. For a start, there are no [r] sounds at all, so they are always deleted. There are now several different consonant pairs in the onsets. Where there is a plosive followed by a sonorant, the sonorant is deleted (e.g. [pet]). Where there is an [s] followed by another consonant, the [s] is deleted if the other consonant is anything other than an alveolar consonant (e.g. [pun]), but the other consonant is deleted if it is an alveolar (e.g. [se]).

Chapter 6

1. (a) dis+content+ed; *content* is the root; *dis-* is a derivational prefix; *-ed* is an inflectional suffix. There is a slight complication here in that the past tense suffix is added to the verb *content*. Once it has that suffix, the verb form can become an adjective. Then the prefix is added to the adjective.

(b) un+wari+ly; *wary* is the root; *un-* is a derivational prefix; *-ly* is a derivational suffix. Note that the *y* is changed to an *i* in the spelling of the root, but this doesn't reflect a change in pronunciation.

(c) kind+ness+es; *kind* is the root; *-ness* is a derivational suffix; *-es* is an inflectional suffix.

(d) un+happi+er; *happy* is the root; *un-* is a derivational prefix; *-er* is an inflectional suffix.

2. (a) Nouns: *-s* (plural); *-en* (plural – but only for *ox/oxen*, although *children* and *brethren* are similar); *-'s* (possessive – technically a clitic rather than a suffix); there are some borrowed nouns that have singular and plural suffixes, such as *cactus/cacti* from Latin and *antenna/antennae* from Greek.

   (b) Verbs: *-s* (third person singular); *-ed* (past tense/past participle); *-ing* (present progressive); *-en* (past participle – irregular verbs).

3. I'm not going to list them all! There are easily a hundred, but it's difficult to say exactly how many. That's because there are some suffixes which are used in English but come from other languages, and not everyone would accept that they are genuinely English (e.g. *xeno-* is a prefix in the word *xenophobia*, but most people would probably agree that they wouldn't use it to form new words). There are also some possible prefixes which could be considered compounds (e.g. *up* in a word like *upshift*).

4. (a) *-ness* attaches to adjectives and turns them into nouns. For example, the adjective *happy* becomes the noun *happiness*.

   (b) *un-* attaches to adjectives and verbs and changes their meaning, to be the negative. For example, the adjective *happy* becomes the adjective *unhappy*, with the opposite meaning, and the verb *tie* becomes the verb *untie*.

   (c) *-age* attaches to verbs and turns them into nouns. For example, the verb *block* becomes the noun *blockage*.

   (d) *pseudo-* attaches to nouns and changes their meaning to mean 'fake'. For example, a *pseudo-city* is not a real city. This is a marginal example of a derivational prefix. In words from Greek, like *pseudonym* (literally 'fake name') and *pseudopodia* (literally 'fake foot'), it is clearly a prefix. When it is used productively in English, however, it usually appears as a separate word, for example *pseudo Georgian facade*.

Chapter 7

1. Transcribe the following words, marking primary stress:

   (a)   i.   diplomat: [ˈdɪpləmæt]
         ii.   diplomacy: [dɪˈpləʊməsiː]
        iii.   diplomatic: [dɪpləˈmætɪk]

(b) i. billow: [ˈbɪləʊ]

   ii. below: [bɪˈləʊ]

(c) i. strategy: [ˈstrætədʒiː]

   ii. strategic: [strəˈtiːdʒɪk]

(d) i. notorious: [nəˈtɔːɹɪəs]

   ii. notoriety: [nəʊtəˈɹaɪətiː]

2. (a) delinquent (n): [dɪ.lɪŋ.kwənt]. Ignore the last syllable; the one before it, [lɪŋ] , is heavy, so it takes the stress: [dɪ.ˈlɪŋ.kwənt].

(b) equity: [ɛ.kwɪ.tiː]. Ignore the last syllable; the one before it, [kwɪ] , is light, so the stress goes on the syllable before: [ˈɛ.kwɪ.tiː].

(c) furnish: [fɜː.nɪʃ]. Ignore the final consonant; the final syllable is now [nɪ] , which is light, so the stress is on the one before: [ˈfɜː.nɪʃ].

(d) arrive: [ə.ɹaɪv]. Ignore the last consonant; the final syllable is now [ɹaɪ] , which is still heavy, so it takes the stress: [ə.ˈɹaɪv].

(e) demure: [dɪ.mjʊə]. This is an adjective that follows verb rules because there is no derivational suffix and no consonant at the end; the last syllable, [mjʊə] , is heavy, so it takes the stress: [dɪ.ˈmjʊə].

(f) picturesque: [pɪk.ʧə.ɹɛsk]. This is an adjective with an auto-stressed suffix, so the stress goes on the suffix: [pɪk.ʧə.ˈɹɛsk].

(g) proverbial: [pɹə.vɜː.bɪ.jəl]. This is an adjective with -al suffix, so it follows the noun rule: remove the last syllable (suffix); the previous syllable, [bɪ], is light, so the stress goes on the previous syllable: [pɹə.ˈvɜː.bɪ.jəl].

(h) compact (v): [kəm.pækt]. Remove the last consonant; the final syllable now is [pæk], which is heavy, so it takes the stress: [kəm.ˈpækt].

(i) advantageously: this is a complicated one! Morphologically, it is *advantage+ous+ly*. The root is a noun, which follows the noun rule when it is on its own: [əd.vɑːn.tɪʤ]. Ignore the last syllable; the one before it is heavy, so it takes the stress: [əd.ˈvɑːn.tɪʤ] . The -ous suffix is stress-shifting, so it attracts the stress to the syllable before it: [æd.vɑːn.ˈteɪ.ʤəs] . The -ly suffix is stress-neutral, so it doesn't affect where the stress goes: [æd.vɑːn.ˈteɪ.ʤəs.liː]. Note that there are some syllables here that have secondary stress, but I've just marked primary stress for the purposes of this exercise.

3. (a)   is a basic trochaic sentence. (b) is from Shakespeare's *Richard III* – an
example of iambic pentameter – so the feet are W S, rather than
S W. (c) is trochaic metre, from William Blake's *London, Songs of
Experience.*

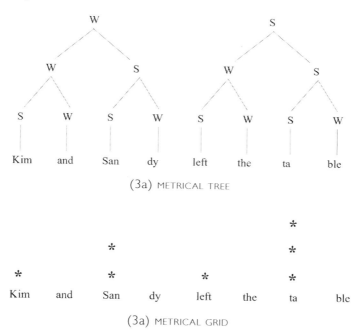

(3a) METRICAL TREE

(3a) METRICAL GRID

4. This limerick has a pattern of five lines. The first two lines each have eight
syllables, the next two have five and the final line has eight syllables again.
The syllables are grouped into iambic feet (weak syllable first), but they
don't pair up neatly. The pattern for the eight syllable lines is W S W W S
W W S, and for the five syllable lines it is W S W W S. In poetry the W
W S pattern is called an anapest, and it is generally assumed that the three
syllables in a limerick that form this pattern are trisyllable feet. However,
as I said in this chapter, linguists tend to prefer strictly binary feet, in
which case the foot structure is (W S) W (W S) W (W S) for the first,
second and fifth lines and (W S) W (W S) for the third and fourth. The
first, second and fifth lines should all rhyme, and the third and fourth
lines should rhyme. This is called an AABBA pattern.

Note that it is possible to have extra syllables in the lines, but they will
always be weak syllables, and if there are any extra syllables in one line,
there must be the same in the matching lines (i.e. 1, 2 and 5, or 3 and 4).

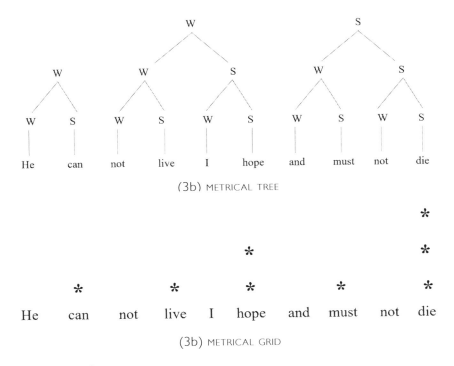

(3b) METRICAL TREE

(3b) METRICAL GRID

Chapter 8

1. This is how I would transcibe these sentences. There are possible variations, but the key thing is to get the differences between the two in terms
   of intonation groups and the different tones in *children* and *football.*

   (a) [‖ðə ʧíldɹən hūː làɪkt fɔ̃tbɔ̀ːl ‖pléɪd āʊtsâɪd‖]

   (b) [‖ðə ʧíldɹən ‖hūː làɪkt fótbɔ̀ːl ‖pléɪd āʊtsâɪd‖]

2. (a) As a statement: [kìm lắɪks īːtīŋ kèɪk]
       As a question: [kím làɪks ìːtìŋ kḗɪk]

   (b) As a statement: [sɛ̀ndīː ìnsístìd ōn ìt]
       As a question: [sɛ́ndīː īnsìstīd ɒ̆n ít]

3. As a simple example, think about the song 'Happy Birthday to You.' If you
   just say those words in a natural way, there will most likely be higher pitch
   on the first syllable of *birthday.* If you sing the normal tune, that syllable is
   higher, but the highest note is sung on *to.* In English, though, it's not usually a
   problem for understanding because the pitch doesn't indicate the core seman-
   tic meaning of words or sentences. There are other factors at play as well. For
   one thing, context usually makes possible ambiguities unproblematic. For

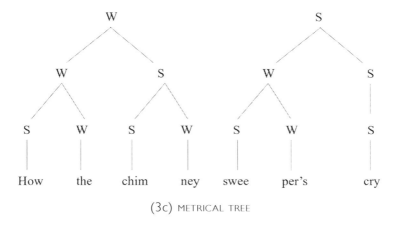

(3c) METRICAL TREE

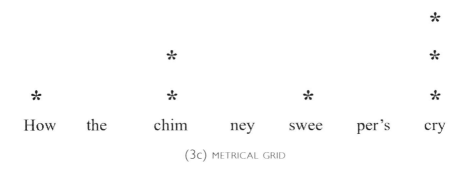

(3c) METRICAL GRID

another, a lot of songs have lyrics that don't make a lot of sense anyway, so there are rarely specific problems caused by intonation mismatches.

Chapter 9

1. (a)   short vowel [ɪ]

   (b)   long vowel [iː]

   (c)   diphthong (long) [aɪ]

   (d)   long vowel [uː]

   (e)   short vowel [ʊ]

   (f)   long vowel [ɜː]

   (g)   diphthong (long) [əʊ]

2. The short vowel [ɪ] is the shortest, [æ] next, then [iː], with [aɪ] the longest. For each one, it will be shortest before [t], then before [n] and longest before [d]. If you look at table 9.1, though, you can see that it's quite complex. According to that table, the full ranking as follows:

(a) bit   (g) ban

(b) bin   (h) bean

(c) bat   (i) bad

(d) beat   (j) pine

(e) bid   (k) bead

(f) bite   (l) bide

3. (a) The [ʊ] in *would*.

   (b) The [ɑː] in *calm*.

   (c) Yes, in that [ʊ] is a short vowel, and [ɑː] is a long vowel. Bearing in mind the durations from table 9.1, the short vowel is still shorter than the long vowel when the former is before a voiced obstruent and the latter before a nasal. Another factor here is stress, with *calm* being the most stressed word, and so likely to be pronounced longer than if it were unstressed.

   (d) Again, the following sounds can, at least partially, explain this. The [iː] in *be* is followed by a voiceless obstruent, [k]. The [iː] in *she* is followed by a voiced consonant, [w]. Stress is also a factor here, as *she* is likely to be more stressed than *be*.

4. *eighteen* and *rattrap* are the only words likely to have geminate consonants. The other words all have single [t] sounds (regardless of their spelling), with the exception of *pizza*, which has [ts]: [piːtsə] .

Chapter 10

1. (a) [g] has the features [velar], [plosive], [+ voice], [− sonorant], [+ consonant]. There are other possible features. For example, it is [− aspirated], it is [− anterior] and [− coronal] according to traditional distinctive features. It belongs to the classes: plosives, voiced plosives, velar sounds, velar plosives, voiced velar plosives, obstruents, voiced obstruents, consonants.

(b) [ʧ] has the features [post-alveolar], [– voice], [plosive], [fricative] (or [affricate]), [– sonorant], [+ consonant]. According to traditional distinctive feature theory, it has the features [+ strident], [+ coronal], [– anterior]. It is in the natural classes: affricates, obstruents, voiceless sounds, voiceless obstruents, post-alveolar sounds, voiceless affricates, post-alveolar affricates, consonants.

(c) [w] has the features [labial], [velar], [approximant], [+ voice], [+ sonorant], [+ consonant]. In some theories, the [velar] feature is replaced with the vowel feature [+ back], and (because it is very vowel-like) it can have other vowel features, [+ high], [+ round], [– low]. It belongs to the classes: approximants, labials, sonorants, voiced sounds, glides, consonants.

(d) [i:] has the features [+ high], [– low], [+ front], [– back], [– rounded], [+ tense], [+ long], [– consonant]. It belongs to the classes: vowels, voiced sounds, high vowels, front vowels, high front vowels, unrounded vowels, unrounded front vowels, unrounded high vowels, tense vowels, long vowels.

(e) [l] has the features: [alveolar], [lateral], [approximant], [+ voice], [+ consonant], [+ sonorant], [– nasal]. It belongs to the classes: approximants, laterals, alveolar sounds, voiced sounds, voiced alveolar sounds, voiced laterals, lateral approximants, alveolar approximants, consonants.

2. (a)   The first set are [– consonant], [+ front], [– back]. The second set are [– consonant], [– front], [+ back]. They differ in their front and back features.

(b)   The first set are [– consonant], [+ high], [– low]. The second set are [– consonant], [– high], [– low]. They differ in the high feature.

(c)   The first set are [– consonant], [– round]. The second set are [– consonant], [+ round]. They differ in the round feature.

(d)   The first set are [– consonant], [+ tense], [– low]. The second set are [– consonant], [– tense]. They differ in the tense feature.

(e)   The first set are [+ consonant], [plosive]. The second set are [+ consonant], [fricative]. They differ in their manner features.

(f)   The first set are [+ consonant], [– sonorant]. The second set are [+ consonant], [+ sonorant]. They differ in the sonorant feature.

(g)   The first set are [+ consonant], [– sonorant], [– voice]. The second set are [+ consonant], [– sonorant], [+ voice]. They differ in their voice feature.

(h)   The first set are [+ consonant], [+ sonorant], [+ voice], [– nasal]. The second set are [+ consonant], [+ sonorant], [+ voice], [+ nasal]. They differ in their nasal feature.

(i)   The first set are [+ consonant]. The second set are [– consonant].

(j)   The first set are [+ consonant], [alveolar]. The second set are [+ consonant], [velar]. They differ in their place feature.

In one sense, all the sets could be considered natural classes because they can be defined as sharing at least one feature. However, some of these would not be considered 'natural'. For example, the first set in (h), the non-nasals, would not generally be considered natural. Note that I did not contrast the alveolar sounds in (j) with a set of 'non-alveolar' sounds, but with a set of velar sounds. These two sets are both natural classes. Another problem with the idea of natural classes is that in most of the cases here it is very unlikely that in any particular language the sets here would be the complete set of, for example, fricatives or nasals.

3. (a)   The first set are voiced plosives ([+ consonant], [plosive], [+ voice]); the second set are voiced fricatives. To change the first set to the second set, the [plosive] feature changes to [fricative].

(b)   The first set are voiceless fricatives ([+ consonant], [fricative], [– voice]); the second set are voiced fricatives. To change the first set to the second set, the [– voice] becomes [+ voice].

(c)   The first set are unaspirated voiceless plosives ([+ consonant], [plosive], [– voice], [– aspirated]); the second set are aspirated voiceless plosives. To change the first set to the second set, the [– aspirated] becomes [+ aspirated].

(d)   The first set are high vowels ([– consonant], [+ high], [– low]); the second set are high-mid vowels. To change the first set to the second set, the [+ high] becomes [– high].

(e)   The first set are tense mid vowels ([– consonant], [– high], [– low], [+ tense]); the second set are lax mid vowels. To change the first set to the second set, the [+ tense] becomes [– tense].

(f)   The first set are velar plosives ([+ consonant], [velar], [plosive]); the second set are post-alveolar affricates. To change the first set to the second set, the [velar] becomes [post-alveolar] and the [plosive] becomes [affricate] (or the feature [fricative] is added).

Note that with all of these I have not included every possible feature. If I had been complete, I would have had to include [± lateral], [± nasal],

[± aspirated] and so on and even [± high], [± low] for all sounds, not just vowels. It is normal in phonology to only specify the features that are really needed, and which features are needed, will depend on the language in question.

Chapter 11

1. (a)   cot – got; bicker – bigger; dock – dog

   (b)   map – nap; rummy – runny; sum – sun

   (c)   lip – rip; belly – berry; ???

   (d)   bat – vat; gibbon – given; dub – dove

   (e)   pit – fit; ripping – riffing; top – toff

   (f)   sap – zap; fusses – fuzzes; fuss – fuzz

   The problem with (c) only arises if you have a non-rhotic accent. In that case, there will be no minimal pairs with the sounds at the end of a word, because in a non-rhotic accent, /ɹ/ never comes at the end of a word.

2. In all of the examples, I assume that the two sounds are phonetically similar and there are no minimal pairs/free variation.

   (a)   Italian:

[n]		[ŋ]	
#_____	e	i_____	k
a_____	a	a_____	k
ɛ_____	t	a_____	g
i_____	t	i_____	g
ɛ_____	d	a_____	k

   Both sounds can be preceded by a vowel. Only [n] can be followed by a vowel. Both can be followed by a consonant. However, the consonants that follow are different. [n] is followed by [alveolar] consonants, and [ŋ] is followed by [velar] consonants. [n] never comes before a velar consonant, and [ŋ] never comes before either a vowel or an alveolar consonant. They are therefore in complementary distribution. They must be allophones of a single phoneme. The rules as follow:

   /n/ → [ŋ] / _____ [velar]

   /n/ → [n] / elsewhere

In English, the two sounds are separate phonemes, as there are minimal pairs, such as *sin* and *sing*. However, it is a bit more complicated than that, as shown in chapter 12.

(b) Spanish:

	[d]		[ð]	
#	___o	i	___e	
#	___r	o	___i	
#	___o	a	___a	
#	___u	a	___a	

[d] always comes at the beginning of a word. [ð] always comes between two vowels. Therefore, they are in complementary distribution. They must be allophones of a single phoneme. With the data here it is not possible to work out an 'elsewhere'.

/d/ → [d] / # _____

/d/ → [ð] / V _____ V

In English they are separate phonemes because there are minimal pairs, such as *den* and *then*.

(c) Korean:

	[s]		[ʃ]	
#	___o	#	___i	
#	___ɛ	#	___i	
#	___o	#	___i	
o	___ə	#	___i	
u	___#			

Both sounds can come at the beginning of a word, and both can come before a vowel. Only [s] comes after a vowel. Crucially, [ʃ] always comes in exactly the same context: at the beginning of a word and before the sound [i]. [s] never appears in that context, so they are in complementary distribution and are allophones of a single phoneme.

/s/ → [ʃ] / # _____ [i]

/s/ → [s] / elsewhere

In English they are separate phonemes because there are minimal pairs, such as *sip* and *ship*.

(d) Korean:

[l]	[r]
a_____#	o_____a
a_____d	e_____i
o_____h	a_____a
u_____#	i_____u
	u_____e

Both sounds can be preceded by vowels. [l] can be followed by a consonant or a word boundary (it can be word-final). [r], on the other
hand, can only occur between two vowels. [l] never occurs between
two vowels, so they are in complementary distribution. They are
allophones of a single phoneme.

/l/ → [r] / V _____ V

/l/ → [l] / elsewhere

In English they are separate phonemes because there are minimal
pairs, such as *lip* and *rip*.

(e) Setswana:

[l]	[d]
#_____e	#_____u
e_____ɛ	o_____i
#_____o	u_____u
o_____e	a_____i
#_____e	a_____i
a_____a	
ɛ_____a	

Both sounds can occur at the beginning of a word. Both can occur
after a vowel, and both always occur before a vowel. However, if you
look at the types of vowel that follow them, you can see that [l] is
followed by a mix of high-mid, low-mid and low vowels, but [d] is
always followed by high vowels. They are, therefore, in complementary distribution and are allophones of a single phoneme.

/l/ → [d] / _____ V [+ high]

/l/ → [l] / elsewhere

In English they are separate phonemes because there are minimal
pairs, such as *lip* and *dip*.

Chapter 12

1. (a) added [ˈædɪd]   (e) sipped [sɪpt]

   (b) worked [wɜːkt]   (f) stuffed [stʌft]

   (c) loved [lʌvd]   (g) bathed [beɪðd]

   (d) bullied [ˈbʊliːd]   (h) earthed [ɜːθt]

   In (b), (e), (f) and (g), the suffix is /t/. In (c), (d) and (g) it is /d/. In (a) it is /ɪd/ . It is a very similar thing to what happens with the plural suffix. Where the suffix is /t/, the last sound in the stem is voiceless. Where the suffix is /d/, the last sound is voiced (including the vowel in (d)). Where the suffix is /ɪd/, the last sound is an alveolar plosive. Because the suffix is an alveolar plosive, a vowel is inserted when there would otherwise be two alveolar plosives together. In the other cases, there is a neutralisation of the voicing contrast between /t/ and /d/.

2. The glottal stop is inserted where a word would otherwise begin with a vowel. It is also inserted at the beginning of syllables within words, but not always. It only happens at the beginning of a stressed syllable, so it is inserted in [kaˈʔoːtɪʃ], but not in [ˈkaos]

3. (a) [ɪŋˈkɒŋgɹuːwəs]   (g) [ɪŋˈkʌmpəs]

   (b) [ɪŋˈgreɪʃiːjeɪt]   (h) [ɪn̪ˈθɹəʊn]

   (c) [ʌmbəliːvəbl̩]   (i) [ɒm pɔɪnt]

   (d) [ɪɱˈfɔːm]   (j) [ɒŋ kɔːl]

   (e) [ɪmˈplaɪ]   (k) [ɪn̪ ˈθɛtfəd]

   (f) [ˈɛɱviːd]

   (i), (j) and (k) must be post-lexical because they are separate words. (d), (f) and (h) would normally also be considered post-lexical because they result in allophones, rather than phonemes, of English.

Chapter 13

1. (a) This is *ingratitude*. The nasal has assimilated to the following /g/ (contact, anticipatory place assimilation). The alveolar /t/ has been glottalised – a weakening process. The /t/ and /j/ have coalesced into the affricate /ʧ/.

(b) This says *okra and potato curry*. There is an intrusive *r* (insertion, hiatus resolution) between *okra* and *and*. The *and* has lost its final consonant (deletion); its vowel has been reduced to schwa (weakening); and the nasal has assimilated to the following /p/ (contact, anticipatory place assimilation). The first vowel in *potato* has been deleted. The /p/ has become aspirated (strengthening).

(c) This is *sandwich*. The first vowel has become nasalised (contact, anticipatory manner assimilation). The /d/ has been dropped (deletion), and the nasal has assimilated (contact, anticipatory place assimilation). Arguably, the final consonant has become voiced, from an underlying /tʃ/ (weakening).

2. This, then, was the explanation of the stealthy expeditions at night and the light at the window. Was it possible that this stolidly respectable person was of the same blood as one of the most notorious criminals in the country?

Yes, sir, my name was Falla, and he is my younger brother. We humoured him too much when he was a lad, and gave him his own way in everything, until he came to think that the world was made for his pleasure, and that he could do what he liked in it. Then, as he grew older, he met wicked companions, and the devil entered into him, until he broke my mother's heart and dragged our name in the dirt. From crime to crime he sank lower and lower, until it is only the mercy of God which has snatched him from the scaffold; but to me, sir, he was always the little curly-headed boy that I had nursed and played with, as an elder sister would.

In the passage, I have marked all cases of dark *l* in bold and all aspiration with underlining. Intrusive *r* only occurs between *Falla* and *and*. Linking *r* occurs between *pleasure* and *and*, between *lower* and *and* and between *lower* and *until*. Glide insertions happen between *stealthy* and *expeditions*, between *he* and *is*, between *way* and *in*, between *grew* and *older* and between *mercy* and *of*. All of these will be /j/, except after *grew*, which will be /w/. These are all of the possible places where these insertions will occur. They may not happen in more careful speech.

Appendix A

Phonetic alphabets

Throughout this book I have used the IPA, and this is the most important and widely used phonetic alphabet. However, as I said in chapter 1, sometimes you might need an alphabet that is computer readable. What that means is that you might need to use only characters that are part of a much more limited set of characters which are more easily recognised by computer programs. If you need to write computer programs to process phonetic representations, for example, to translate them into another representation like spelling, you might find that using plain ASCII is less prone to errors.

There are several different ASCII representations, developed by different people to use for different purposes. The most widely recognised is the SAMPA (Speech Assessment Methods Phonetic Alphabet) set, developed as part of the Speech Assessment Methods project. Because of the limitations of ASCII characters, this set makes use of numbers and punctuation marks as well as upper- and lower-case letters. Another thing that makes the SAMPA alphabet different from the IPA is that it was not intended to be used for comparing different languages, so there are different sets for different languages. The website https://www.phon.ucl.ac.uk/home/sampa/ gives sets for 25 different languages. These are mostly European languages, but sets for non-European languages are being added, including Arabic, Cantonese and Thai.

Tables A.1 and A.2 give the SAMPA characters for the English consonants and vowels, added to the tables of IPA representations given in chapter 3 and chapter 4.

IPA	SAMPA	Example
p	p	as in *pie*
b	b	as in *buy*
t	t	as in *tie*
d	d	as in *die*
k	k	as in *kite*
g	g	as in *guy*
tʃ	tS	as in *chide*
ʤ	dZ	as in *jive*
f	f	as in *fine*
v	v	as in *vine*
θ	T	as in *thigh*
ð	D	as in *thy*
s	s	as in *sigh*
z	z	as in *Zion*
ʃ	S	as in *shy*
ʒ	Z	as in *measure*
h	h	as in *high*
m	m	as in *my*
n	n	as in *nigh*
ŋ	N	as in *sing*
l	l	as in *lie*
ɹ	r	as in *rye*
j	j	as in *yikes*
w	w	as in *wine*

TABLE A.1   THE CONSONANTS OF STANDARD SOUTHERN BRITISH ENGLISH

SSBE (IPA)	SSBE (SAMPA)	GA (IPA)	GA (SAMPA)	Example
Short vowels				
iː	iː	iː	iː	*beat*
ɪ	I	ɪ	I	*bit*
ɛ	E	ɛ	E	*bet*
æ	{	æ	{	*bat*
ʌ	V	ʌ	V	*but*
ɑː	A:	ɑ	A	*Bart*
ɒ	Q	ɑ	A	*pot*
ɔː	O:	ɔː	O:	*bought*
ʊ	U	ʊ	U	*put*
uː	uː	uː	uː	*boot*
ɜː	3:	ɝ	3r	*bird*
ə	@	ə	@	*again*
Diphthongs				
eɪ	eI	eɪ	eI	*bait*
əʊ	@U	oʊ	oU	*boat*
aɪ	aI	aɪ	aI	*bite*
aʊ	aU	aʊ	aU	*bout*
ɔɪ	OI	ɔɪ	OI	*boy*
Centring Diphthongs				
ɪə	I@	iɹ	ir	*beer*
eə	e@	ɛɹ	er	*bear*
ɔə	O@	oɹ	or	*boar*
ʊə	U@	uɹ	ur	*boor*
Triphthongs				
aɪə	aI@	aiɹ	air	*buyer*
aʊə	aU@	auɹ	aur	*bower*

TABLE A.2 THE VOWELS OF SSBE AND GA

Appendix B

Praat

There is a range of software packages which can help in recording and analysing spoken language. Any software which allows you to record sound, edit it and save it in different formats can be used for speech as well as for music, for example. What I'm going to tell you about here, though, is one very specialist software package called **Praat**.

What you need to think about in terms of collecting the data is that, whether you want to use software to analyse it or just listen very carefully yourself, you'll need good-quality audio, with as little background noise as possible. With the ability to record on just about everyone's phone these days, it is tempting to just use your phone, but if you want to do serious analysis, you really do need to invest in (or borrow!) a decent microphone. Similarly, if you're going to do your analysis by ear, you'll need decent speakers or headphones.

'*Praat*' is the Dutch word for 'talk' (it's from the same root as *prattle*!) and it was developed in the Netherlands by Paul Boersma and David Weenink. It's freely available – just search for it by name, and you can download the software to your computer. There are also a lot of text and video tutorials and other documentation to help you work out how to use it. I should give a warning here that it was developed a long time ago, when user interfaces were not like they are today. It's not difficult to use once you get used to it, but you will need to follow the instructions. Praat will accept sound files in any of several different formats: WAV, AIFF/AIFC, NeXT/Sun (.au), NIST, FLAC and MP3. If you want to analyse a recording that is in a different format, you will need to convert it to one of these first, but there are plenty of programs that will do this for you, and most computers and laptops nowadays have audio programs built in that will do it.

If you want to analyse your own pronunciation, you can do it easily from within Praat. When you open the program, you will get two windows: Praat Objects and Praat Picture. To record, use the Praat Objects window. From the New menu at the top, choose either 'Record mono sound' or 'Record stereo sound'. For speech, I usually use the mono recording. That opens a new window: SoundRecorder. (From this window you can change your mind if you want to do a stereo rather than a mono recording.) Simply click 'Record', speak into your microphone and click 'Stop' when you've finished. You can then click 'Play' to hear back what you've recorded. Now you'll need to give the recording a name in the 'Name' box and then click 'Save to list', or 'Save to list and close' if you don't want to do any more recording right now. Now your recording should appear in the list of 'Objects' in your 'Praat Objects' window.

If you want to analyse a recording that you already have on your computer, you will need to put that into the 'Objects' list. You do that by choosing 'Read from file' from the 'Open' menu at the top of the 'Praat Objects' window. If your recording is quite long then you'll need to choose 'Open long sound file'. You can do all of these things with keyboard control sequences as well. To open the recording window, press Ctrl R; to open a sound file, press Ctrl O; and to open a long sound file, press Ctrl L.

Now you have a list of objects that you can analyse. Once you've got at least one file in your list, you have a selection of buttons on the right side of the 'Praat Objects' window. To look at the spectrogram of your file, click 'View & Edit'. This will open a new window with the waveform at the top and the spectrogram underneath. Below this are two bars: 'Visible part' and 'Total duration'. If your file is quite short, then these will be the same; that is, the whole file/recording will be visible. You can click on either of these bars, and it will play the sound, with a cursor line moving along to show you which part of the spectrogram/waveform is which part of the recording.

There are lots of things that you can do with this, and I'm just going to tell you about the things that I've talked about in the book. If there are other things you want to do, look at the help files that come with Praat, or find tutorials and advice on the Web.

One fun thing you can do is use the cursor and mouse to select a small portion of the spectrogram. When you do this, another bar appears below the spectrogram, with the timings of the selected part and the parts either side of it. If you click on the selected part, it will play just that bit. This is useful for pinpointing which sounds are where. It can also be quite amusing to hear very small parts of speech isolated and repeated!

For linguistic analysis, Praat has numerous things that you can choose to show on the spectrogram. If you choose 'Show pitch' from the 'Pitch' button at the top of the window, a series of blue lines will appear on the spectrogram, showing the pitch for each of the vowel parts. Pitch isn't marked on the consonants because it isn't reliably measurable on them. This gives you an overall picture of how the pitch rises and falls during the utterance. The spectrogram from chapter 3 is shown with pitch marked in figure B.1. When you view this in Praat, the pitch is marked in blue. (Note that I revised the image in chapter 3 to include lines with the words and transcription. These tiers can be added using Praat. It's not trivial, but there are tutorials to show you how to do it if you want to.)

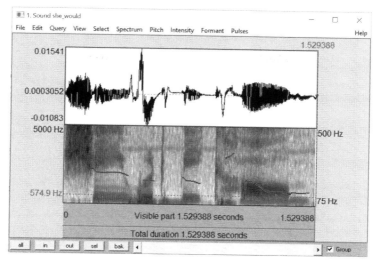

FIGURE B.1   PRAAT SOUND EDITOR WINDOW WITH PITCH MARKED

If you want to analyse your vowel sounds, choose 'Show formants' from the 'Formant' menu at the top. This will then give you a load of lines on the spectrogram. It's probably best to get rid of the pitch lines to make it easier to see what's happening. The spectrogram from chapter 4 is shown with formants marked in figure B.2. When you view this in Praat, the formants are marked in red. With the formants, you should see that there are bits where there are dots all over the place. These are the consonants, where there are no neat lines. Where the dots join together to make clearer lines are the vowels.

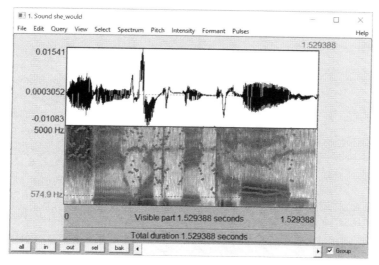

FIGURE B.2   PRAAT SOUND EDITOR WINDOW WITH VOWEL FORMANTS MARKED

The four formants mentioned above are labelled F1, F2, F3 and F4, from the bottom of the spectrogram up. The really important ones for identifying vowels are F1 and F2.

Formant F1 is the one nearest the bottom. It indicates how high or low a vowel is. If F1 has a relatively high value, then it is a relatively low vowel. The actual range for the vowel chart I've been talking about above is around 235 Hz for a high vowel to 850 Hz for a low vowel. Even though individual people have very different pitches – women and children typically have much higher pitched voices than men, for instance – that does not affect the F1 values, which will fall within that range for all speakers.

Formant F2 is the next one up on the spectrogram. It indicates how front or back a vowel is. The higher the F2 formant frequency, the further forward the vowel is. The range of F2 values is bigger for high vowels (i.e. those with a low F1 frequency) and for these the range is around 595 Hz for a back vowel to 2400 Hz for a front vowel. For low vowels the range is from 940 Hz for a back vowel to 1620 Hz for a front vowel.

B.1   Mapping formants to the cardinal vowel space

What this means is that you can draw a graph, with the x-axis representing the F2 value and the y-axis representing the F1 value. These axes need to be reversed in order to plot the vowels according to their F1 and F2 frequencies in a way that matches the vowel chart as seen on the IPA chart. Figure B.3 shows the vowel chart with the F1 and F2 frequencies marked on the axes. You can use this chart to plot the actual frequencies of vowels, rather than just listening or feeling how high or back a vowel is. The central point on the chart – remember the mighty schwa? – has frequencies of around 1500 Hz x 500 Hz.

There are some other complications. I've talked about the height and backness of vowels being measured by the F1 and F2 formants, but what about lip rounding? One of the things I said in chapter 4 was that back vowels (at least, non-low back vowels) tend to be rounded, and front vowels tend to be unrounded. Although this isn't always the case, it does hint at a relationship between rounding and backness, and it is no coincidence that the F2 formant is the one affected by lip rounding as well as backness. Basically, a rounded vowel will have a lower F2 value than an equivalent unrounded vowel, so if there are two vowels that are identical except for their lip rounding, it will appear on the chart as though the rounded one is further back than the unrounded one.

So far in this section I've only talked about monophthongs. What about diphthongs? These can be mapped onto the vowel space as well, but (at least) two points need to be measured. That makes it a bit trickier. With a monophthong, you can choose a point to measure that is right in the middle,

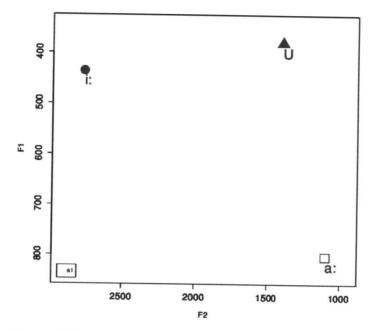

FIGURE B.3   CHART SHOWING THE POSITION OF THE THREE VOWELS

so you know it's not being influenced too much by the sounds either side of it. For a diphthong you need to measure the start and finish, but you can't go too close to the sounds surrounding the vowel. The standard way of doing this is to measure points in the whole duration of the vowel that are one fifth of the distance from the start and the end. Once you've measured these two points, you can plot them on the chart as an arrow going from the start point to the end point.

In order to get the measurements, highlight sections of the spectrogram where they are and ask Praat for the formant measurements. It's best to try to highlight a section that has consistent straight lines. The easiest way to do this is to highlight the whole section that you think is the vowel you're interested in and choose 'Zoom to selction' from the 'View' menu. This then stretches the vowel part to the whole window. Now select the central part that has nice straight horizontal lines. The 'Formant' menu has several options. If you choose 'Formant listing' it will give you a list of all of the measurements for each of the four formants. For the vowel analysis that I talked about in chapter 4, only the F1 and F2 values are relevant, and you'll need the average values across the pronunciation of that vowel. For these, select 'Show first formant' and 'Show second formant'.

When I did this for the three vowels in the words *she, would* and *calm,* it gave the results in table B.1.

Vowel	Word	F1	F2
[iː]	she	436	2766
[ʊ]	would	380	1398
[ɑː]	calm	803	1098

TABLE B.1   F1 AND F2 FORMAT VALUES FOR THE THREE VOWELS

You can see here that the high front vowel, [iː], in *she* and the high back vowel, [ʊ], in *would* have relatively low F1 values compared to the low back vowel, [ɑː], in *calm*. The two back vowels, [ʊ] and [ɑː], both have lower F2 values than [iː]. This is what is expected. Another piece of software which is useful here is the Normalisation package, which can be accessed on the Web. You can enter the numbers from Praat in a simple text file with columns for the speaker (in case there are different speakers you want to analyse), the vowel, the context (e.g. the word it's in) and the formant values. For this, you need to also measure the F3 values because this gives a reference point to account for the fact that different speakers have different fundamental frequencies. You can upload this file, and the website will give you a nice chart, plotting the vowels on the vowel space. Figure B.3 shows the results for the three vowels above. This kind of chart can also be generated by spreadsheet software. You just need to enter the measurements with appropriate column labels and then use the graph drawing options to change the direction of the axes.

So that is how you can use Praat to analyse vowel frequencies and NORM to plot them on a chart. As I said, there is a lot more that Praat will let you do, but for this book, vowel plotting is the most important.

Appendix C

Classroom exercises

Getting to grips with the IPA and transcription can be tricky, and it's helpful to have different ways to practise thinking about pronunciation in this way. Two activities that I do in my classes, once I've covered the consonants and vowels, might help here. The first is IPA bingo. There are game cards and sound cards available from Cascadilla Press, and they can be downloaded for free from their website. I adapt them slightly because I prefer to use the term *plosive* where they use *stop*, for example. Each student has a game card (or they can have one between two). I then read out the articulatory description on the caller cards, and the students work out what the symbol is and cross it off their game card, if it's there. I usually start by letting them have their IPA chart in front of them, but then get them to play without the chart as they get more familiar with the IPA.

The other game I play is IPA hangman. I ask two students to work out a transcription for a word, check it with me, then draw the lines for each sound as in letter hangman. (I specify that diphthongs and affricates each have a single line as they count as single sounds.) Then the other students take it in turn to suggest a sound, but they have to give the articulatory description. So a student might say 'A voiced bilabial plosive,' and the students who chose the word have to work out the IPA symbol and write it on the board, on the appropriate line if it is in the word or at the side if it isn't. The other students then have to guess the word before the stick man is hanged!

In the early stages I also get students to write their name in IPA on the board. If they don't know one another's names at this point, it's a good exercise for getting them to think about transcription as well as introducing them to one another (and me).

Bibliography

Ashby, Michael and Maidment, John. *Introducing Phonetic Science*. Cambridge University Press, Cambridge, 2011.

Bauer, Laurie. *Word Formation in English*. Cambridge University Press, Cambridge, 1984.

Bloch, Bernard. Phonemic overlapping. *American Speech*, 16:278–84, 1941.

Bloomfield, Leonard. *Language*. Holt, New York, 1933.

Carr, Philip. *English Phonetics and Phonology*. Blackwell, Oxford, 1999.

Carr, Philip and Montreuil, Jean-Pierre. *Phonology*. Palgrave Macmillan, Basingstoke, 2013.

Catford, J. C. *A Practical Introduction to Phonetics*. Clarendon, Oxford, 1988.

Chomsky, Noam and Halle, Morris. *The Sound Pattern of English*. MIT Press, Cambridge, Mass., 1968.

Churma, D. G., 'Jets fans, Raider Rooters, and the interaction of morphosyntactic processes'. In J. F. Richardson, M. Marks and A. Chukerman (eds), *Papers from the Parasession on the Interplay of Phonology, Morphology, and Syntax*. University of Chicago Press, Chicago, 1983.

Clark, John and Yallop, Colin. *An Introduction to Phonetics and Phonology*. Wiley-Blackwell, Hoboken, N.J., 2006.

Coleman, John. *Introducing Speech and Language Processing*. Cambridge University Press, Cambridge, 2005.

Collins, Beverley S. and Mees, Inger M. *Practical Phonetics and Phonology: A Resource Book for Students*. Routledge, Oxford, 2013.

Coulmas, Florian. *Writing Systems: An Introduction to Their Linguistic Analysis*. Cambridge University Press, Cambridge, 2002.

Crystal, David. *Texting: The gr8 db8*. Oxford University Press, Oxford, 2009.

Daniels, Peter D. and Bright, William, eds. *The World's Writing Systems*. Oxford University Press, New York, 1996.

Davenport, Mike and Hannahs, S. J. *Introducing Phonetics and Phonology*. Arnold, London, 2010.

Giegerich, Heinz J. *English Phonology*. Cambridge University Press, Cambridge, 1992.

Gimson, A. C. *Gimson's Pronunciation of English*. Arnold, London, 2001.

Goldsmith, John. *Autosegmental Phonology*. Garland Press, New York, 1979.

Goldsmith, John, ed. *Handbook of Phonological Theory*. Blackwell, Oxford, 1996.

Gussenhoven, Carlos and Jacobs, Haike. *Understanding Phonology*. Hodder Arnold, London, 2005.

Hockett, Charles. *Manual of Phonology*. Indiana University Press, Bloomington, Ind., 1955.

Jakobson, Roman. *Selected Writings: Phonological Studies*. Mouton de Gruyter, New York, 2002.

Katamba, Francis. *An Introduction to Phonology*. Longman, London, 1999.

Katz, William F. *Phonetics for Dummies*. Wiley, New York, 2013.

Kennedy, Robert. *Phonology: A Coursebook*. Cambridge University Press, Cambridge, 2017.

Kenstowicz, Michael. *Phonology in Generative Grammar*. Blackwell, Oxford, 1994.

Knight, Rachel-Anne. *Phonetics: A Coursebook*. Cambridge University Press, Cambridge, 2012.

Ladefoged, Peter. *Vowels and Consonants*. Blackwell, Oxford, 2001.

Ladefoged, Peter and Johnson, Keith. *A Course in Phonetics*. Cengage Learning, 2015.

Lass, Roger. *Phonology: An Introduction to Basic Concepts*. Cambridge University Press, Cambridge, 1984.

Lieber, Rochelle. *Introducing Morphology*. Cambridge University Press, Cambridge, 2015.

Matthews, Peter. *Morphology*. Cambridge University Press, Cambridge, 1983.

McMahon, April. *An Introduction to English Phonology*. Edinburgh University Press, Edinburgh, 2002.

Millar, Robert McColl. *Trask's Historical Linguistics*. Routledge, Oxford, 2015.

Odden, David. 'Adjacency Parameters in Phonology'. *Language*, 70 (1994): 289–330.

Ogden, Richard. *An Introduction to English Phonetics*. Edinburgh University Press, Edinburgh, 2009.

O'Grady, Gerard. *Key Concepts in Phonetics and Phonology*. Palgrave Macmillan, Basingstoke, 2013.

Pike, Kenneth. *Phonemics: A technique for Reducing Language to Writing*. University of Michigan Publications in Linguistics 3, Ann Arbor, Mich., 1947.

Roach, Peter. *English Phonetics and Phonology: A Practical Course*. Cambridge University Press, Cambridge, 2000.

Roca, Iggy and Johnson, Wyn. *A Course in Phonology*. Blackwell, Oxford, 1999.

Ryalls, Jack and Behrens, Susan. *Introduction to Speech Science*. Pearson, Cambridge, 1999.

Sampson, Geoffrey. *Writing Systems: A Linguistic Introduction*. Equinox, Sheffield, 2015.

Spencer, Andrew. *Phonology: Theory and Description*. Blackwell, Oxford and Cambridge, Mass., 1996. ISBN 978-0-631-19233-6.

Tench, Paul. *Transcribing the Sounds of English*. Cambridge University Press, Cambridge, 2011.

Trubetskoy, Nikolai. *Grundzüge der Phonologie*. University of California Press, Berkeley, 1939. English translation *Priciples of Phonology* by C. Baltaxe, 1969.

Wells, J. C. *Accents of English (three volumes)*. Cambridge University Press, Cambridge, 1982.

Wells, J. C. *Sounds Interesting: Observations on English and General Phonetics*. Cambridge University Press, Cambridge, 2014.

Wells, J. C. *Sounds Fascinating: Further Observations on English Phonetics and Phonology*. Cambridge University Press, Cambridge, 2016.

Wiik, Kalevi. *Finnish and English Vowels. A Comparison with Special Reference to the Learning Problems Met by Native Speakers of Finnish Learning English*. PhD thesis, Annales Universitatis Turkuensis, Series B, 94, 1965.

Zsiga, Elizabeth C. *The Sounds of Language: An Introduction*. Wiley-Blackwell, N.J., 2013.

Index

Printed in Great Britain
by Amazon